A NEW ACCOUNT OF THE EAST-INDIES

1688-1873

A NEW ACCOUNT OF THE EAST-INDIES

BEING THE OBSERVATIONS AND REMARKS OF

CAPT. ALEXANDER HAMILTON

FROM THE YEAR 1688-1723

TRADING AND TRAVELLING, BY SEA AND LAND, TO MOST OF THE COUNTRIES AND ISLANDS OF COMMERCE AND NAVIGATION, BETWEEN THE CAPE OF GOOD-HOPE AND THE ISLAND OF JAPAN

THE SECOND EDITION
IN TWO VOLUMES

VOLUME-I

GYAN

Published by

GYAN

Gyan Publishing House
5, Ansari Road
Darvaganj, New Delhi-110002
Phone: 011-47034999, 9811692060
E-mail: books@gyanbooks.com

Distribution Network

gyanbooks.com
India, USA, Canada, UK, Australia, France

ISBN : 978-81-212-3817-5 (Set)
ISBN : 978-81-212-4740-5 (PB)
First Published, London, 1739

2nd Impression 2020

Printed at: Gyan Press, Delhi.

A New Account of the East-Indies Vol. I
Author: Capt. Alexander Hamilton

A NEW ACCOUNT OF THE EAST-INDIES:

BEING THE

OBSERVATIONS and REMARKS

OF

Capt. *ALEXANDER HAMILTON*,

Who resided in those Parts

From the Year 1688, to 1723.

Trading and Travelling by Sea and Land, to most of the Countries and Islands of COMMERCE and NAVIGATION, between the Cape of *Good-Hope*, and the Island of *Japan*.

The SECOND EDITION.

VOLUME I.

LONDON:

Printed for A. BETTESWORTH and C. HITCH, at the *Red-Lion* in *Pater-noster-row*. 1739.

To his Grace

JAMES

Duke of Hamilton, Chatlerault *and* Brandon, *Marquis of* Clydſdale, *Earl of* Arran, Lanerk *and* Cambridge, *Lord* Avon, Polmount, Machanſchyer, *and* Innerdale, *and Baron of* Dutton, *Knight of the moſt noble Order of the* Thiſtle.

My Lord,

I Have known ſome Scriblers, or Authors, dedicate their Works to great Men who they hardly knew any more of than their illuſtrious

Names; but my Ambition or Preſumption has a juſter Plea in claiming your Grace's Patronage, ſince you have been pleaſed to honour me with ſeveral Inſtances of your Favour; therefore, I humbly preſume to lay theſe curſory Obſervations that I made in my Travels to the *Eaſt Indies*, at your Grace's Feet; and if they find Acceptance, I ſhall not much mind the Cenſure of Criticks, or Satyriſts: For I am perſwaded, that the very Name of ſo illuſtrious a Patron will be ſufficient to protect and defend me.

If I had thought, while I was in *India*, of making my Obſervations or Remarks publick, and, to have had the Honour of of preſenting them to ſo noble a Patron, I had certainly been more careful and curious in my Collections, and of keeping Memorandums to have made this Work more complete: But it muſt now appear, to ſome Diſadvantage, (for want of thoſe Ornaments) in its native ſimple Dreſs, as it came poſting through a weak and treacherous Memory with little Elegancy.

I have ſeen the elaborate Works of ſeveral ingenious Pens, who had travelled thro' many Countries, in Maps, that I have travelled to by Sea and Land; they may have many Advantages to recommend their Works that I want; yet, few (if any) ever had the living

ving Acquaintances that I have had, to inform or inſtruct them in many Particulars relating to the ancient, or preſent State of their Countries, whoſe vernacular Languages can beſt illuſtrate their Hiſtories, ſome of which I underſtood.

All that have travelled in thoſe Countries before me, have omitted ſome Things worthy of Obſervation, and have remarked ſome Things impertinent enough; and, as I take the Liberty to cenſure them, I expect the ſame Treatment from thoſe that may travel after me, and for the very ſame Fault.

Thoſe Five, or Six and thirty Years that I ſpent in the *Eaſt Indies*, ſtrolling from Place to to Place, gave me Opportunities to know ſome topographical, hiſtorical, and theogonal Parts of this Work, from the Natives, of their reſpective Countries, who may be preſumed to be better acquainted with their own Traditions and Cuſtoms, than Strangers, who are often at a Loſs for want of Language.

I will not apologize (as many do) for my Weakneſs or Unfitneſs for this Undertaking, for I aſſure your Grace, if I had not thought my ſelf pretty well qualified for it, I had never ſet about it.

And, as my Travels have been moſt along the Sea-coaſts, I have deſcribed the Harbours, Rivers, and Dangers on them, pretty punctually. I hope thoſe Remarks may be uſeful to ſome of my Fraternity, who may have Occaſion to go into thoſe Seas; and tho' they may get better Pilots than I, yet they cannot be the worſe of my Remarks.

I will not trouble your Grace with Encomiums, either on your ſelf, or your illuſtrious Anceſtors, for your Names and Characters are ſo well known all over *Europe*, and in ſome Parts farther off, by diſtinguiſhing Marks, that it would be but Preſumption in me to offer to add any Thing to them; but pleaſe to accept of my beſt Wiſhes for the Welfare of your Grace, and your illuſtrious Family and Kin-

Kindred; and that the Almighty may protect and direct you in a virtuous Life, and make you a peculiar Favourite in the Court of Heaven, ſhall always be the ſincere Prayer of,

My LORD,

Your Grace's moſt devoted,

and moſt affectionate

humble Servant,

ALEX. HAMILTON.

THE PREFACE.

A Book without a Preface, now a Days, is as unfashionable as a Lady to pretend to be drest A-la-mode *without a Hoop, or a nice Beau without a Snuff-box: Therefore I am resolved to be in the Fashion at any Rate, if I do appear a little akward in my Performance, and I will make no other Apology, but the Thread-bare one, (that many Scribblers have done before me) that it was at the Request, and by the Perswasions of some particular Friends and Acquaintances, that I commit these* Observations *and* Remarks *to Writing.*

I know, ſuch a Miſcellany as this muſt be, will hardly find Favour with every Body, however, if it pleaſe my Friends, I ſhall not be very ſolicitous about what others may ſay of it, or me; and, if there are any notable Errors, or Miſtakes in the Work, (which is more than I know of, if there is) yet take all the Piece together, without Vanity, I preſume, you will find it more particular, correct and extenſive, than any of this Kind, at leaſt, of any that ever I ſaw; and, if any Things are mentioned or advanced, that may ſeem dubious or fabulous, the beſt Way that I know, how to cure your Scruples or Doubts, is, to take a Trip to thoſe Countries from whence they come, and inform your ſelves better than I have done; and when ye return to Britain, *and convict, or convince me of my Miſtakes, I will readily acknowledge them, and beg Pardon.*

But I'll neither do the one nor the other, if I am arraign'd before the Tribunal of Map-travellers, or who have only

only the Sanction of other Mens Journals, or Memoirs to qualify them Judges; and, altho' some amuse the World with large and florid Descriptions of Countries that they never saw, and of Customs they never saw used, yet, since their Stock of Knowledge is all on Tick, the want of being Eye and Ear-witnesses very much depreciates their Accounts; besides, common Experience teacheth us, that Time alters Religions, Customs, Commerce, Oeconomy, &c. *in all Countries; therefore, as these Observations are the most modern, consequently they are the nearer related to the Times we live in.*

I knew a reverend Gentleman, in anno 1690. *who came to* Bombay *in* India, *Chaplain of the Ship* Benjamin, *the Ship was sent on a Voyage to* Atcheen, *and the Streights of* Mallacca, *while the Chaplain stay'd at* Bombay *and* Surat, *employed in his ministerial Duties, and, in making his ingenious Observations and Remarks, which he published when he returned to* England,

land, *for which he received a great deal of Applauſe, and many Encomiums from ſome of his Reverend Brethren, and a particular Compliment from the Governors of the Church ; yet I know, that his greateſt Travels were in Maps, and the Knowledge he had of the Countries, any Way remote from the aforementioned Places, was the Accounts he gathered from common Report ; and, perhaps, thoſe Reports came ſucceſſively to him by Second or Third Hands ; for, to my certain Knowledge, there were none then at* Surat *or* Bombay *that could furniſh him with any tolerable Accounts of ſome Countries that he deſcribes, particularly of the Growth and Nature of Tea, and ſhews its Buſh very prettily among his Cuts ; which Accounts are not eaſily procured, even in* China, *much leſs at* Bombay.

The Taſte of thoſe Times reliſhed all he preſented with a very good Guſto, and the reverend Traveller received almoſt as ample Rewards and Praiſes for

for his personal Travels to Surat *by Sea, and over the rest of* India *by Maps, as Sir* Farncis Drake *had for his Tour round the World; so, that if this Age has retained any Relish for personal Travels, and new Observations of* India, *these have as good a Right to claim a favourable Reception as any that ever came to* Britain *before them.*

The reverend Traveller, nor any that had made Trips to India *before him, could not well be acquainted with many Occurrences that have come within the Reach of my Observations; and I can perceive several Things worth noticing, they have neglected or leapt over, either for want of Curiosity, Language, or some other Impediments, so that if any of them are found in this, I presume they will not be unacceptable.*

But, after all, I am not so vain, or so ill acquainted with the World, to think, that I shall go Scot-free, without Censure, tho' my Observations had been much nicer, and this Work much more per-

perfect than it is, since so great a Man as Bishop Burnet *has been so severely lasht by one that could know no more of his Affairs or Negotiations, than he knows of mine, or of many Countries that I have been in.*

And many a hard Lash, and scurrilous Name the right reverend Father has gotten for writing so favourably of himself, and his own Conduct in his Management of various important Affairs, among Politicians, and Statesmen; yet I am obliged to follow his Example in some particular Cases, where I had Occasion to act on the Stage of the Eastern World, tho' I am not ignorant of the great Odds that the Bishop had of me, both in Education and Capacity; yet when I consider, that the Sun is placed in a much higher Orb than the Moon, and his Splendor much brighter, and his Influences much more beneficent, nevertheless she has some very useful Qualities, that gains her some Admirers as well as he, tho' not so numerous.

I also follow the right reverend Father in giving some People Characters, whom I praise or censure according to my own Experience, or Acquaintance with their Candor or Malversation in the Course of their Affairs with my self or others, or by good Information of their Conduct and Abilities, which Maxim I am not afraid to follow through all my Observations, if I should be called before the arbitrary Tribunal of Criticks or Censurers.

My Task in compiling this had been much lighter, and my Performance perhaps had been better, if Gazetts, and other useful publick Papers were used in those Countries where I travelled, or if I could have read their different Histories in their various vernacular Languages, then the general Accounts of their Laws, Religions, Politicks, &c. *material Observations, had been much fuller and exacter than now they are, but such Helps could not be had. Indeed, as to their Laws, their Kings or Princes being all arbitrary, the Law is lodged in their Breasts, who make and repeal when they please; but, for the Ease of the Populace, they have national Customs and Courts to manage distributive Justice, and that runs in a pretty even Chanel, when it is not interrupted by the Prince's Order, or stopt by Bribes, to those Governors or Judges who have the Distribution of them; and this is not more in Use among the black* Indians *than among the white.*

Their Religions are a Complex of Mysteries, Church-policy, and Superstition, and they are all safely locked up in their Temples, as being too holy to be exposed to the Vulgar, and they seldom appear abroad, but in a Language generally unknown to the Populace; and the Priests are both Authors and Interpreters of the sacred Dreams, and, in most Parts, the Priests have the Keeping of the Keys of their Histories too; and when they come abroad, it may easily be observed, that a Levite *had been trimming or tampering with them,*

them, for they are generally groſly bedaub'd with Hyperboles and Fables and a little God often brought in to father their Inventions, Affirmations, or Notions.

So that what Knowledge I have acquired or gathered, is from the much Converſe I had with the Natives of the reſpective Countries I travelled in, or from thoſe that were familiarly acquainted with the Religions, Laws, and Cuſtoms of their Neighbours.

One great Misfortune that attends us European *Travellers in* India, *is, the Want of Knowledge of their Languages, and they being ſo numerous, that one intire Century would be too ſhort a Time to learn them all: I could not find one in Ten thouſand that could ſpeak intelligible* Engliſh, *tho', along the Sea-coaſts, the* Portugueze *have left a Veſtige of their Language, tho' much corrupted, yet it is the Language that moſt* Europeans *learn firſt, to qualify them for a general Converſe with one another, as well as with the different Inhabitants of* India.

And we Britains, *who either go voluntarily, or are ſent to* Neptune's *Schools in our Youth, to learn Politeneſs and Eloquence, very rarely mee with* Apollo's *bright Sons or Diſciples to inſtruct us in the Knowledge of Languages, or of the State of all Nations, but of that one we are born in, and that but imperfectly too. That may be one Reaſon, among many, why we appear ſo ſimple and aukward in dreſſing up the Obſervations we make of foreign Countries, that we travel in; but I dare ſay, no Body will, or can be ſo ill-natured as to be offended, when he ſees a Plowman take out his Miſtris to dance a Minuet* a-la-mode, *becauſe his Performances are not exactly ſquared with a Dancing-maſter's Rules and Figures, which Reflection makes me hope, that this my Virgin Eſſay will be civilly treated by the unprejudiced Lovers of Travels.*

And

And now, to animadvert a little on the Subjects of my Travels. The geographical, cosmographical or topographical Parts of my Observations have, most of their Places, been settled by others, tho', I think, some of them are a little out of their true Positions, and some I have corrected in the annext Maps, according to my own Observations; and those Maps will shew the Places and their Names in a much easier and clearer Light than if I had mark'd them down in Margines; and, since most of the Continents and Islands ly pretty near the Æquator, the Errors in Longitude are not very great, if at all material.

The theogonal and moral Parts may, without Doubt, deserve some serious Thoughts or Attention, because every Body is, or ought to be concerned in those Speculations, since they shew some Parts of their Religions and Customs, and, comparing them with the inestimable Blessings that we enjoy by revealed Religion and rational Laws, may afford

afford us no small Satisfaction, when rightly considered, and that their wild Notions of a Deity, overclouded with Superstition and Folly, deserve our Pity and Charity; and that our Duty towards God and our Neighbour is, by the Holy Scriptures, *set before us in the brightest Light, while theirs is to be groped out by the dark Glimmerings of very fallible Reason; yet, for all these Disadvantages, I have known many of them practise very much Holiness in their Lives by the Help of Morality, so that some Animadversions on our Advantages, compared with their Disadvantages, may be, in some Measure, both useful and delightful to all thinking Men, except the* Atheist, *whose Numbers, I hope, are very few among us, and I never met with one in* India.

What relates to Navigation, in describing the Seas, and Dangers lying in them, and the Sea-coasts, with the Dangers and Harbours on them, is purely calculated for the Use of my Fraternity,

ternity, who may have Occasion to navigate in those Seas, or on those Coasts, but to others, who have no Call that Way, they are almost useless.

The Commerce on the Continent and the Islands, with the Account of their Productions, Fertility or Sterility, are merely designed for the Assistance of Strangers, Merchants or Seamen, who may hereafter attempt a Trade with the Inhabitants of them: And I am perswaded, that there are several Places, both on the Continent and among the Islands, that ly now neglected by Europeans, *that might produce a good advantageous Trade, if Factories were settled, and Commerce cultivated with the Inhabitants, and would yield much better Profits than many of the old Factories do at present, some of which, I know, carry on but a very faint Trade for their respective Companies, that can hardly defray their little Charges: But indolent People are generally wedded to their old Customs, or their crazy Habitations, without considering what*

Chan

Changes Time makes, in Bodies politick as well as natural, which Diſtemper is a Lethargy in Trade, and in all other Branches of Induſtry, which I can point out in Particulars, if Need were.

Now, as our dear Friends and Allies have engroſſed all the Moluccos *or Spice Iſlands, I can give but a ſuperficial hiſtorical Account of them; and, as they were acquired by bloody and barbarous Induſtry, they keep and govern them with arbitrary Violence. A poor* Britain *dares not approach them, leſt they meet with the Fate that ſome of our Country-men met with there formerly: And even an* Engliſh *Seaman cannot be employed in that Company's Service, for fear of making Obſervations in Navigation, and Remarks on Trade, that may (ſome Time or other, but God knows when) prove detrimental to their Commerce. What I could learn of thoſe Iſlands were ſome curſory Accounts from ſome of my Fraternity, when a Bottle or two had opened their Breaſts.*

Yet

Yet I could have enlarged these Observations, and made my Book look much bigger than it is; but, as I hate Prolixity myself, I treat my Reader with what Brevity I can, in every Part, except it be where the Subject cannot bear too narrow a Contraction in its Illustration.

I understand but little of the Use of the Pencil, for which Reason I do not exhibit many Cuts or Figures that might deserve a Place in the Book, and those that are placed, are not taken by Rule, or from any certain Position, but according to the Ideas of them that my Memory presents to me, yet I am in Hopes, that they will please some, and offend none; and I give them a Place here, because I have not seen them inserted in the Books of former Authors, nor in the Memoirs of Travellers.

But, before I end this Preface or Prologue, I will tell my Reader, who perhaps is unacquainted with me, who I am, and who I am not. First then, I am one who went very young to travel, not for Want, for there ever was, and is enough of that in my own Country; but having a rambling Mind, and a Fortune too narrow to allow me to travel like a Gentleman, I applied myſelf to the Study of nautical Affairs at Neptune's *School, and, in Proceſs of Time, I came to be a Maſter of Arts in that Univerſity. My younger Days I ſpent in viſiting moſt of the maritim Kingdoms of* Europe, *and ſome Parts of* Barbary. *Then my Curioſity led me to* Jamaica, *and then to the* Eaſt-indies, *where I ſpent between five and ſix and thirty Years, ſtill learning my Trade, and how to get Money, and, meeting with ſome Encouragement, I ſet up for myſelf, and took ſome Apprentices, and, according to my Abilities, I taught them, and gave them Encouragement. Now, one would think, that in ſo long a Time in* India, *I might have made a great Deal of Money as well as Obſervations and Remarks; but* Fortunatus *will not lodge in every Houſe there. with honeſt and induſtrious Men more than*

than in Europe; *yet, after many Struglings with adverse Fortune, and heavy Oppressions, I have brought back a Charm that can keep out the* meager Devil (Poverty) *from entring into my House, and so I have got holy* Agur's *Wish in* Prov. xxx. 8. *and I have learned a pretty good Lesson from St.* Paul *in his Epistle to the* Philippians, *Chap.* iv. *Ver.* 11. *which I am resolved to follow as long as I live.*

And now I'll tell you who I am not. I assure you I am no mercenary Scribler, for, altho' I was proferred a good round Sum for a Copy of these following Observations, I refused it, and have made a Present of them to a particular Friend, and, if he thinks them worth the printing, he may print them for his own Benefit and Advantage; and, if he has good Luck in putting them off, perhaps I may make some Additions, Appendixes or Supplements to those Observations already made.

Moreover, I left England *before King* William *came into it as King, which I look on as a ſingular Providence, conſidering the Revolutions and Wars that ſoon followed King* James's *Abdication, for being then young and thoughtleſs, and having but little Experience of the Affairs of a politick World, a fair Tale plauſibly told, with a little ſmooth Perſwaſion, might have drawn me into a wrong Way of thinking, or might have led me away (by taking Part with a wrong Faction) to an untimely End, or, at leaſt, have given me Time enough to make Obſervations on the Miſeries of a penurious Life, as I ſee many now in* Holland *do at this Time, who are plentifully fed with the Bread of Affliction, and their Heat quenched with the Waters of Sorrow, and the Tears of Repentance.*

Now, as theſe Obſervations have been moſtly from the Store-houſe of my Memory, and are the Amuſements or Lucubrations of the Nights of two long Winters, I have even let my Thoughts take their Places, as they came out of my my little Magazine, without ſtudying to put them in Rank and File; according to nice Rules and Forms. So in the ſame Order I leave them to my Reader, with the old Proverb to accompany them, that the Proof of the Pudding is in eating it; *ſo, according to your Taſte or Appetite, you may either condemn or commend.*

THE CONTENTS OF THE Chapters of the First VOLUME.

CHAP

CHAP. XII.

CHAP. XIII.

CHAP XIV.

CHAP. XV.

CHAP. XVI.

CHAP. XVII.

CHAP. XVIII.

CHAP. XIX.

CHAP. XX.

CHAP.

CHAP. XXI.

CHAP. XXII.

CHAP. XXIII.

CHAP. XXIV.

CHAP. XXV

CHAP. XXVI.

CHAP. XXVII.

CHAP. XXVIII.

CHAP. XXIX.

THE Publiſher, Proprietor of this Book, in order to obtain and preſerve the Privileges granted by the *Statute* 19. *Annæ*, *Parl.* 8. intituled, *Act for the Encouragement of Learning*, &c. has duly entred this Book in the Regiſter of Stationers-hall, *London.*

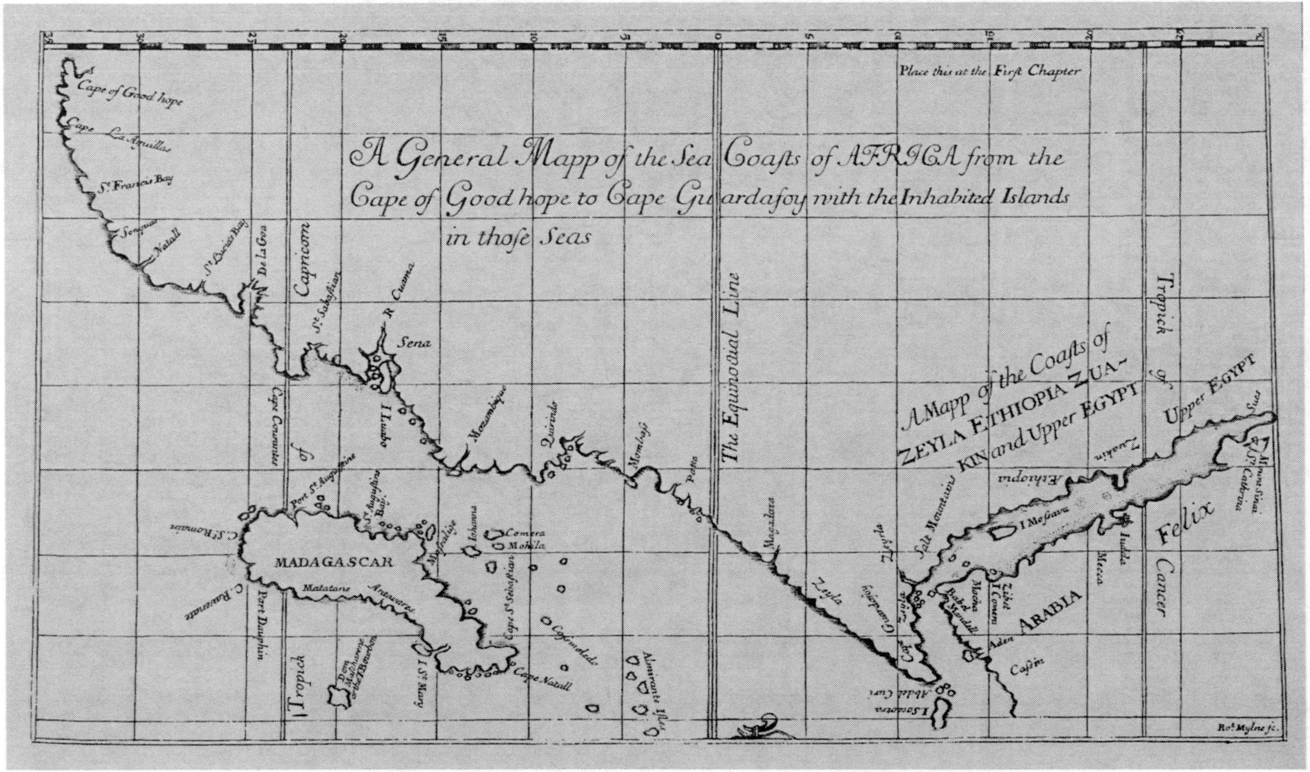
A General Mapp of the Sea Coasts of AFRICA from the Cape of Good hope to Cape Guardafoy with the Inhabited Islands in those Seas
Place this at the First Chapter
A Mapp of the Coasts of ZEYLA ETHIOPIA ZUA-KIN and Upper EGYPT
Upper EGYPT
Tropick of Cancer
Tropick of Capricorn
The Equinoctial Line
Cape of Good hope
Cape La Aquillas
St. Francis Bay
Natall
St. Lucia's Bay
De La Goa
St. Sabastian
R Cuama
Sena
I Luabo
Cape Courantes
Mozambique
Quirindo
Mombasa
Patta
Magadoxa
Zeyla
Cape Guardafoy
Salt Mountains
Ethiopia
Suakin
Suez
Mount Sinai
St. Cathrina
I Messaua
Iudda
Mecca
Felix
ARABIA
Zibet
I Comeri
Mocha
Bab el Mandell
Aden
Cassin
Abdal Curi
I Socotora
MADAGASCAR
Port St. Augustine
St. Augustine Bay
Massalage
Iohanna
Comera
Mohila
Cape St. Sebastian
Cosmoledo
Almirante Isles
Cape Natall
I St. Mary
Antavarres
Matatane
Port Dauphin
C. Ramanatt
C. St. Romaine
Dom Mascarene or the I Bourbon
Tropick
Robt. Mylne sc.

A NEW

ACCOUNT
OF THE

East Indies.

CHAP. I.

Giveth a traditional Account of the first settling of Europeans *at the Cape of* Good Hope, *with some historical Remarks on the maritim Countries between the said Cape and Cape* Guardafoy, *with the inhabited Islands of that Coast.*

THE first *Europeans* that settled at *Cabo de bona Esperanza*, or, in *English*, the Cape of *Good Hope*, were the *English*, in Queen *Elizabeth*'s Time; but the Natives were so unsociable and indocile, that they thought fit to leave it. A few Years after they had left it, the *English East-india* Company considering what Importance a Port would be of to their Shipping, both in their outward and homeward bound Passages to and from *India*, were resolved to make another Trial for a Settlement there, and, in order to accomplish their Design, obtained a Reprieve for three condemned Malefactors, to be carried thither in order to learn the Language, to serve for Interpreters, and to inspect, as far as they could, into the Manners and Customs of the native *Hottentots*, and of the Product and Commerce of the Country.

AFTER they had been there three Years, without being able to learn any of their Language, or to teach any of the Natives a Word of *English*, a Ship was ordered, in her Passage from *India*, to call there, to know what was become of these three Persons, and arriving there, found them all alive, but very tired with their Manner of living, in so much that they fell on their Knees, and, with Tears in their Eyes, beseeched the Captain of the Ship to carry them back to *England*, to receive the Punishment due to their Crimes, rather than be left among the very Dregs of human Nature, who had neither Religion nor Laws, except what every Master of a Family prescribed, and allowed those under his Authority to observe and obey.

SOME Years after the Experiment was made on the aforesaid Criminals, an *English* Ship coming there for Water and Provisions, in in their Way homeward to *England*, the Captain had the Curioſity to detain a Youth that came on board his Ship, and, being ready to ſail, carried him to *England*, where he ſtaid ſome Years, clothed well after the *English* Faſhion, and kept at School to learn to ſpeak and read *Engliſh*; and, when the *Eaſt-india* Company thought him well enough qualified to ſerve for an Interpreter, they ſent him back to his own Country, very well clothed. Aſſoon as he appeared aſhore among his Friends and Relations, he pulled off his *Engliſh* Apparel, and put on his Country Habit, which is a Sheep's Skin about his Shoulders. The Sheeps Guts ſerve both Sexes for Bracelets, and the Tallow, mixt with Soot, is their *Pomatum*, with which they bedaub their woolly Heads, Faces and the reſt of their Bodies. And when they come on board of our Shipping to traffick their Fowls, Roots and Herbs, with our Needles, Scizers, Knives, *&c.* Toys, they go firſt to the Cook-room, and look out for ſome Greaſe to anoint their naſty Carcaſes, and ſcrape the Bottoms of the Kettles for Soot, to beautify their Skins.

NOTWITHSTANDING that they are ſo brutal and indocile, they know the Value of Liberty, and will by no Means be Slaves, at leaſt to any *Europe* Nations; and, in their Diſpoſitions, are not cruel, tho' revengeful. They are not ſuperſtitious, for what Adoration they pay, is to the Sun, and that but ſeldom. The Country is mountainous. The

Hills are ſtored with Deer and Sheep, black Cattle, Lions, Tigers, and other voracious Animals. The Vallies produce good Wheat and Legumen, Grapes in Abundance, and many other excellent Fruits, Oſtriches, and good Fowl both wild and tame: And the Sea and Rivers good Store of Fiſhes, beſides the Manatee, or Sea-cow.

THE *Engliſh* deſpairing of ſettling a Colony there, left it, and ſettled at St. *Helena*, a very high mountainous Iſland, lying between the Coaſt of *Guinea* and *America*, about 620 Leagues North-weſt half Weſt from the Cape of *Good Hope*; and the *Dutch Eaſt-india* Company ſettled a Colony at Cape *bona Eſperanza*, by the Aſſiſtance of ſome *French* Refugees, who have penetrated near 300 *Engliſh* Miles into the Land, and manure the Ground to very good Purpoſe, it yielding them Wines and Wheat in Abundance. The *Dutch* Company has a ſtrong Fort, and a Town on the South Side of a Bay, that ſerves for a good Road for Shipping in all Winds, except thoſe that blow between the North and Weſt. The *Engliſh* call'd generally there, in their Way to and from *India*, in former Times, for Refreſhments; but of late the white *Hottentots* will not permit the poor *Britons* to carry on board their Ships any Cattle, Sheep or Fowls with Life in them, for the Support or Relief of their dear Friends and Allies, notwithſtanding the conſcientious Prices we would willingly beſtow for their Edibles.

The

The black *Hottentots* would ſhew the *Engliſh* much more Humanity, if the white did not reſtrain them ; and ſo I leave them, and proceed to the Eaſtward.

FROM Cape *Bona Eſperanza* to *Natal*, is a dangerous Sea-coaſt, and little frequented, whether by the Unſociableneſs of the *Hottentots* the Inhabitants, or that the Country produces nothing worth the Merchants adventuring thither for, I know not ; but to *Natal* I have known ſome *Engliſh* Veſſels go from *India*, for Elephants Teeth, and did make pretty good Voyages ; but they were Two Years and an Half in performing a Voyage. The Country is fertil, but unwholſom. The Woods are thick ſet with ſeveral Sorts of Trees, and ſtored with Elephants, Lions, Leopards, Bears, Wolves, Deer and Foxes ; the Rivers with Fiſh, Manatees and Crocodiles. Here lived, *in Anno* 1718. a penitent Pirate, who ſequeſtred himſelf from his abominable Community, and retired out of Harm's Way.

THERE is no Commerce on the Coaſt between *Natal* and *Delagoa*, I believe, for the ſame Reaſon that I gave for the Unfrequentedneſs of the Coaſt between the Cape of *Good-hope* and *Natal*; and I believe, the firſt communicative Commerce, either to *Natal* or *Delagoa*, with the *Engliſh*, came by Accident ; for about the Year 1683. an *Engliſh* Ship, called the *Johanna*, was loſt ſomewhere about *Delagoa*. The Natives, who were reputed great Barbarians, ſhew'd the ſhipwrack'd Men much more Civility and Humanity than ſome Nations that I know, who pretend much Religion and Politeneſs, for they accommodated their Gueſts with whatever they wanted of the Product of their Country, at very eaſy Rates, and aſſiſted what they could, to ſave Part of the damaged Cargo, receiving very moderate Rewards for their Labour and Pains. Their Language was by Signs; and for a few Glaſs-beads, Knives, Scizers, Needles, Thread and ſmall Looking-glaſſes, which they are very fond of, they hired themſelves to carry many portable Things (that were ſaved from the Shipwrack) to a neighbouring Country, and procured others, who alſo ſerved them for Guides towards the Cape of *Good-hope*, and provided Eatables for their Maſters, all the while they were under their Conduct; and having carried them about 200 Miles on their Way, by Land, they provided new Guides and Porters for them, for ſome of the aforeſaid Trifles, who conducted them, and provided for them, as the others had done, for 7 or 800 Miles farther, which they travelled in 40 Days, and ſo delivered their Charge to others, who conducted and provided for them, till they arrived at the Cape; and ſome of the *Engliſh* falling ſick on the Way, they carried the Sick in Hammocks, till they either recovered or died, and out of 80 Men there were but 3 or 4 died; but how long they journeyed before they arrived at the Cape, I have forgotten. This Account I had from one of the Travellers, ſers. He told me, that the natural Fertility of thoſe Countries he travelled thro', made the Inhabitants lazy, indolent, indocile and ſimple. Their Rivers are abundantly ſtored with good Fiſh and Water-fowl, beſides Manatees, or Sea-cows and Crocodiles; their Woods with large Trees, wild Cattle and Deer, Elephants, Rhinoceroſes, Lions, Tigers, Wolves and Foxes for Game; alſo many Sorts of winged Fowl and Birds, beſides Oſtriches. They have ſome Notions of a Deity, whom they worſhip with Dancing and Feaſting, for they are generally very much inclined to Mirth, an Inſtance whereof I'll venture to relate, on the Account I had from a Maſter of a Ship, who went thither to trade *in Anno* 1718. *viz.* When they had got their Ship ſecured in a River, the Natives aſſembled in good Numbers to traffick, near the Place where the Ship lay: An arch *Indian* Youth, who was a very good Drummer, carried his Drum aſhore, and in a Thicket pretty near the Aſſembly, beat his Drum very briskly, on which the Young of both Sexes fell a skipping, and a little after the Adult and Old followed their Example, ſo that none ſtood idle Spectators; but the Old beginning to tire, ſome went to the Drummer, and preſented him with Eggs, Fowl and Fruits, and intreated him to leave off, which aſſoon as he did, they all ſat down again on the Ground, well heated.

I ſaw ſeveral Rhinoceroſes Horns brought thence to *Bombay*, much longer than ever I ſaw in *India* or *China*, and one was three Horns growing from one Root; the longeſt was about 18 Inches, the ſecond about 12. and the third about 8. but ſmaller, in Proportion, than what is in *India*, and much ſharper about the Point. The Maſter of the forenamed Ship brought alſo a black Fowl, as big in the Body as a large Duck. It had a long, ſtraight, thick, but pointed Bill, and hollow Eyes, its Legs about 12 or 14 Inches long, but thick and ſtrong; it was very voracious after Fleſh or Fiſh, and was an excellentFrog and Rat-catcher. Aſſoon as he caught any living Game, he toſſed it up about two Yards high, and caught it on the Point of his Bill, and ſo repeted his Toſſings till the Animal died, and then greedily devoured it.

BETWEEN *Delagoa* and *Moſambique* is a dangerous Sea-coaſt, it formerly was known by the Names of *Suffola* and *Cuama*, but now by the *Portugueze*, who know that Country beſt, it is called *Sena*. It finds Dominions for many different Princes, for they are contented with ſmall Territories. The Inhabitants are all *Negroes*, and almoſt all Barbarians, except a few that the *Portugueze* have converted to Popery; and they, by their Converſion, are generally leſs humane to *European* Strangers than the Barbarians.

Sena abounds in Elephants Teeth and low Gold, of 18 or 19 *Carects* Fineneſs; but the People having Plenty of all Things convenient for them, are very ſupine. They have large ſtrong Bodies and Limbs, and are very

ry

ry bold in War. They'll have Commerce with none but the *Portugueze*, who keep a few Priests along the Sea-coasts, that over-aw the silly Natives, and get their Teeth and Gold for Trifles, and send what they get to *Mosambique*.

I have heard a *Portugueze* say, who went from *Mosambique* thither, that, carrying some small Glass-beads of divers Colours for Traffick, the Natives made a Hole in some clay Ground, which would hold as many Beads as they wanted, and taking the Beads out of the Hole, filled it up with Gold-dust. He also told me, that for some coarse chequer'd Cloth, called *Cambaya Lungies*, made of Cotton-yarn, the Natives would bring Elephants Teeth, and measure the Length of a Tooth by the Cloth, and bartered the Tooth for so much Cloth as it measured: But the *Portugueze* Relations are hardly to be credited, for if Gold and Teeth were so easily purchased, how can they be so miserably poor, as they are, every where in their Colonies, all over *India*?

I rather believe, that this was the *Ophir* or *Tarshish* of the *Jews*, whither *Solomon* sent his Ships out of the *Red Sea*, than *Sumatra*, where they could not possibly go and return in three Years along the Sea-coasts, which might easily be effected to *Sena*.

Mosambique is an Island belonging to the Crown of *Portugal*, it is well fortified both by Art and Nature, but is very unwholsom, in so much, that when any *Reynol*, or *Euro-*

pean

pean Portugueze in the King of *Portugal's* Service in *India*, commits any capital Crime, instead of puniſhing him according to their national or martial Laws, they are baniſhed to *Moſambique*, for as many Years as the Vice-roy of *Goa* and his Council ſhall order, and very few ever return from their Exile, for 5 or 6 Years is a long Life there. It alſo ſerves for a refreſhing Place for the *Portugueze* Ships, that are bound from *Europe* to *India*, where they generally ſtay about 30 Days to recruit their Soldiers and Sea-men, (not with freſh Numbers, but freſh Victuals and Whores) who, by their Inactivity and Lazineſs at Sea, contract the Scurvy and Dropſy, which the acid Fruits and nouriſhing Roots ſoon diſpel. Their Ships are generally at Sea the whole Month of *Auguſt*, between *Moſambique* and *Goa*.

THE Inhabitants of *Moſambique*, as well as thoſe on the Continent, are all *Negroes*, of a large Size, handſom, and very well limb'd, and make good Slaves. The King's Ships, as well as private Traders, bring good Store of them to *India*, both Sexes being in high Eſteem with the *Indian Portugueze*, both having Services, proper to their Sex, allotted them. Aſſoon as the Boys can ſpeak a little *Portugueze*, they are baptized, and ſo become very zealous Catholicks, fit to execute any baſe Deſign their ghoſtly Fathers ſhall think fit to put them on; and after Baptiſm, they have a little Crucifix, or a Saint of Braſs or Ivory, hung about their Necks, which they are as fond

fond of, as a Monkey is of a young Kitten to play with.

And ſome that have the good Fortune to be young and docile, and fall into the Hands of a zealous ſuperſtitious Maſter, are brought up to Letters, and in the End come to be Prieſts. I have known many Coal-black Prieſts about *Goa*.

The Country of *Quiloa* lies between *Moſambique* and *Mombaſs*, its Sea-coaſt is dangerous, which admits of no Trade but in Boats. The Diſtance between *Moſambique* and *Mombaſs* is about 225 Leagues.

Mombaſs is alſo an Iſland that lies near the Continent, ſlightly fortified by Art, but very well by Nature; it belonged to the *Portugueze* for near 200 Years, but *in Anno* 1698. the *Muskat Arabs* took it with very little Trouble, and put about 20 *Portugueze* to the Sword, that were there to defend it, and the Conquerors found a Booty of about 200 Tuns of Teeth, which was worth in *India*, about 125000 *L. Sterl.* The Elephants of this Country are very large, and ſo are the Men, who are all Barbarians, except thoſe who were near Neighbours to the *Portugueze*, who, for Conveniency, were baptized, and became good Catholicks; and ſince the *Arabians* are become their Neighbours, they are turned very zealous Muſſulmen, which Religion pleaſes their Stupidity better, being better adapted to their Humours, and dear Cuſtom of Polygamy and Concubinage.

Patta is now in the Hands of the *Muskat*

Arabs,

Arabs, and affords good Store of Teeth and Slaves for *Muskat*. Formerly the *Engliſh*, *Portugueze*, and *Moors* from *India*, had a ſmall, but advantagious Trade thither, which the *Arabs* envied them of, and ſent a Colony about the Year 1692. and ſettled there, prohibiting Commerce with all other Nations. The inland Countries are inhabited by Barbarians, but on the Sea-coaſts of *Magadoxa*, *Zeyla* and *Yeman* to Cape *Guardafoy*, which ſtretches about 330 Leagues North Eaſt-ward. The Religion, by Law eſtabliſhed, is *Mahometan*, yet every Country retains ſome Fragments of their ancient Cuſtoms and Ceremonies, with the Traditions of their Fathers. The *Arabians* from *Mocha*, and other Parts of *Arabia* the *Happy*, who reckon themſelves *Mahomet*'s beſt Diſciples. and who have travelled much to teach and confirm them in their Religion and Philology, declare them to be the greateſt Schiſmaticks and obdurate Hereticks that profeſs the *Mahometan* Religion.

Magadoxa, or, as the *Portugueze* call it, *Magadocia*, is a pretty large City, about 2 or 3 Miles from the Sea, from whence it has a very fine Aſpect, being adorn'd with many high Steeples and Moſques. There are ſeveral Reaſons why Merchants do not frequent it on account of Traffick; one is, that a Reef of Rocks lies all along the Shore, about a Mile more or leſs from the ſandy Strand, between which and the Rocks it is pretty ſmooth, and two or three Fathoms Water; but there is no River to ſecure Veſſels when a ſtrong Sea

Sea Wind bloweth. The ſecond Impediment is, that Violence and Robberies are ſo much practiſed and countenanced, that common Faith is not to be relied on: And I'll give a very tragical Inſtance of their Barbarity, *viz. In Anno* 1700. the *Engliſh* new *Eaſt-india* Company ſent out a Ship called the *Albemarle*, commanded by Captain *William Beawes*. Being bound for *Surat*, he had the Miſfortune to meet the Eaſterly Monſoons or Trade-winds, ſooner than he expected. In the Chanel between *Madagaſcar* and the Coaſt of *Ethiopia*, thoſe Eaſterly Monſoons always bring ſtrong Currents with them from the Eaſtward, which check'd him over to the Coaſt of *Magadoxa*, but that being a dangerous Shore, he ſtood over to the Iſland of *Johanna*, and was forced to harbour his Ship on the South-weſt Side of that Iſland, till the Eaſterly Monſoons were blown over, and in the Month of *March* he ventured to put to Sea, which was too ſoon, becauſe the Currents ſtill ran ſtrong to the Weſtward, and he ſtanding over to the *Ethiopian* Coaſt, fell in again with *Magadoxa*; which, by the handſom Figure it made from the Sea, made him believe it to be ſome Place of Commerce, and being curious to know if it was ſo or no, ſent his Yole aſhore, with his Purſer and four Seamen, to bring Information, and gave them ſtrict Orders to be on their Guard, and only one Perſon to go aſhore at a Time. When the Boat got over the Rocks, they anchored cloſe to the Beech, and the Natives came from

from the Town, driving Store of Cattle and Sheep before them for Sale. The Purſer, being young,. and unexperienced, forgot his Orders, and went aſhore himſelf with three of his Crew, leaving one only to ſtay in the Boat, and thoſe that went aſhore, were ſo ſilly, as to leave their Fire-arms in the Boat, and by the feigned Civilities that the Natives ſhew'd them, they heedleſly mingled themſelves with the Natives, who, finding ſo unexpected an Opportunity, hurl'd them away to the Town; and the Boat-keeper, neither hearing nor ſeeing what was done to his Comrades, ſuffered ſome Natives to come into the Boat, who ſeized him alſo, and haled the Boat a good Way up on the Land.

THOSE on board the Ship, ſaw, by their Proſpectives, what was acted aſhore, and ſent their other Boats, well mann'd, to try if they could ranſom the Captives, but in four Days fruitleſs Endeavours, they could never bring the Natives to a Parley, and ſo the Ship was obliged to leave them to repent of their Folly; but it never came to our Knowledge in *India*, what became of them, or what their Fate was.

YET on the Coaſts of *Zeyla* and *Yeman*, which both terminate at Cape *Guardafoy*, the Natives will bring off Sheep, Goats, Hens, Fiſh and Fruits to ſell to Shipping that ſometimes ly becalm'd on their Sea, near the Shore. The People are tall, meagre and large bon'd, very ſwarthy, but not quite black in their Complexions; they are treacherous, cruel, and

and avaricious in their Temper; their Habit is a Pair of Breeches to their Ancles, or a Piece of coarſe Cloth about their Loyns, and a Gown open before, and without Sleeves, called a *Camlin*; it is made of Camels Hair, or of their Sheeps Wooll, that is fully as hard and coarſe as Hogs Hair. On their Heads they wear a Turbant of coarſe Calico, and then they are equipped. Their Sheep are all white, with jet black Heads, and ſmall Ears, their Bodies large, and their Fleſh delicate, their Tails as broad as their Buttocks, and about 6 or 8 Inches long; ſo they are in the Shape of a Pillow wanting Corners, and from the lower End of that Bundle, comes a ſmall Tail about 6 Inches long, almoſt like a Pig's.

And now having travelled along the Shore of the Continent, from the Cape of *Good-hope* to Cape *Guardafoy*, I'll ſurvey the Iſlands that lie in the *Ethiopian* Sea; but as they afford nothing for Commerce, but Slaves and Proviſions, they are little minded by Merchants: So beginning with the Weſtmoſt, I'll bring them in Order to the Eaſtward.

CHAP. II.

Giving a ſhort Deſcription of the Iſlands in the Ethiopian *Seas, with ſome remarkable Paſſages hiſtorical and accidental.*

MADAGASCAR, or, as the *Portugueze* chriſtned it, St. *Laurence*, is one of the largeſt Iſlands in the known World, and affords moſt Part of the Requiſites of human Life: It produces very large Cattle, whoſe Fleſh is excellent, eſpecially their large Humps that grow between their Neck and Shoulders. They have alſo Goats and Deer plenty enough, and when the *Portugueze* firſt ſailed along the Coaſts of this Iſland, they left a Brood of Hogs, that has mightily increaſed. They alſo chriſtned many Rivers and Capelands that are not now frequented, but only known by their Names, and ſerve for Neſts to Pirates. The *French* made a Settlement on the Eaſt Side of it, and called it *Port Dauphin*; but finding that the Commerce there would not bear the Expence of the Colony, they left it again.

THE *Engliſh* formerly drove a Trade for Slaves on the Weſt Side of the Iſland, particularly at St. *Auguſtine*'s Bay, and at new and old *Meſſalige*, but now they are afraid of the Pirates, tho' ſome venture their Necks in going to trade with them. There have been ſeveral Squadrons of *Britiſh* Men of War ſent to cruize on the Pirates, but have had very ill Succeſs in finding them out; but one

Scots

Scots Ship commanded by one *Millar*, did the Publick more Service in destroying them, than all the chargeable Squadrons that have been sent in Quest of them; for, with a Cargo of strong Ale and Brandy, which he carried to sell them, *in Anno* 1704. he killed above 500 of them by carousing, tho' they took his Ship and Cargo as a Present from him, and his Men entred, most of them, into the Society of the Pirates.

It was reported in *India*, that Commodore *Littleton* had some of that Gang on board the *Anglesey* at *Madagascar*, but, for some valuable Reasons, he let them go again; and because they found Difficulty in cleaning the Bottoms of their large Ships, he generously assisted them with large Blocks and Tackle-falls for careening them. Whether those Reports were true or false, I will not undertake to determine, but I saw a Pirate at *Bengal*, in the *French* Company's Service, that affirmed it.

Madagascar is invironed with Islands and dangerous Sholes, both of Rocks and Sand. St. *Mary*'s, on the East Side, is the Place where the Pirates first chose for their *Asylum*, having a good Harbour to secure them from the Weather, tho' in going in there are some Difficulties, but hearing that Squadrons of *English* Ships were come in Quest of them, they removed to the main Island for more Security, and there they have made themselves free Denizons by Marriage: And I am of Opinion, that it will be no easy Matter to dispossess them. *In Anno* 1722. Mr. *Matthews* went in Queſt of them, but found they had deſerted the Iſland of St. *Mary*'s, leaving behind them ſome Marks of their Robberies, for in ſome Places they found Pepper a Foot thick, lying on the Ground in the open Air. The Commodore aforeſaid went with his Squadron over to the main Iſland, but the Pirates had carried their Ships into Rivers or Creeks, out of Danger of the Men of War, and to offer to burn them with their Boats, would have been impracticable, ſince they could have eaſily diſtreſſed the Boats Crews out of the Woods. The Commodore had ſome Diſcourſe with ſome of them, but they ſtood on their Guard, ready to defend themſelves, if any Violence had been offered them.

I have heard it reported by ſome who had frequented *Madagaſcar* for Trade, that the Natives that live far from the Sea, are of a tawny Complexion, and have long Hair on their Heads, whereas thoſe that are born near the Sea, are very black, and their Hair like Lamb-wooll. What Religion they profeſs, I know not, and the Pirates are but ſcurvy School-maſters to teach them Morals.

THERE are many Iſlands and Sholes lying to the Eaſtward of *Madagaſcar*. St. *Apolloni* is uninhabited; *Domaſcarenhas* is inhabited by the *French*, but formerly by the *Engliſh*, and was called by them, *The* Engliſh *Foreſt*. *Maritius* was formerly inhabited by the *Dutch*, but *in Anno* 1703. they had Orders to leave it, and repair to *Batavia*, and the *Dutch* Com-

Company ſent Shipping for their Tranſportation. *Diego Rais*, which is the next Iſland to *Maritius*, was made a *French* Settlement, but finding it barren, they left it in 3 Years, all the reſt were always uninhabited, as well to the Eaſtward as the Northward, and but 3 or 4 to the Weſtward, who ly in the Chanel between *Quiloa* and *Madagaſcar*.

Comora is the Weſtmoſt of the inhabited Iſlands, and affords nothing but a ſcrimp Maintenance for a Parcel of poor miſerable Creatures. *Johanna* is within Sight of *Comora*, and is a plentiful Iſland in Cattle, Goats, Fowls and Fiſh, with good Lemons and Oranges, ſo that moſt Part of the *Engliſh* Shipping bound to *Mocha*, *Perſia* and *Surat*, uſually call'd there for Refreſhments, till the Pirates began to frequent it. There are two memorable Accidents fell out at that Iſland, to the *Engliſh Eaſt-india* Company's Shipping. One was in the Year 1690 or 91. to Captain *Burton* in the *Herbert*, a Ship of 800 Tons, mounted 56 Guns. He was attacked by three *French* Ships, each gunn'd and mann'd as well as he. On their Approach, he cut his Cables, and put to Sea, about 2 after Noon they began an hot Engagement, which laſted till 8 in the Night, that the *Herbert* blew up, and all her Men loſt, but 6 or 7 that were in the Pinnace, ſome whereof I ſaw afterwards at *Muskat*. The other was lately, *in Anno* 1720. when two of our *Eaſt-india* Ships were watering there, with an *Oſtend* Ship in their Company; they agreed to ſtand by one another in caſe of Aſ-ſaults, or engaging with the common Enemy, but when two Pirates drew near, the *Greenwich* and *Oſtender* weighed, and ſtood to Sea, and left the *Caſſandra* to ſhift for her ſelf, who was obliged to engage the ſmalleſt Pirate (being a Ship of 24 Guns, *Dutch*-built) in the Bay, and ſoon after they began, the *Caſſandra* went aground on ſome Rocks, and the Pirate ſtriving to board her, was alſo taken up by ſome Rocks, not above 20 Yards from the *Caſſandra*. The Pirate's Head lay towards the *Caſſandra*'s Broadſide, and they pelted one another furiouſly, many falling on both Sides, but the Pirates, finding too hot Work on their Decks, were forced to quit them, and run down into the Hold for Shelter. Captain *Mackraw*, who commanded the *Caſſandra*, ſeeing the other Pirate approach near him, and manning all his Boats to reinforce his Comrade, thought it a good Time for him, and who elſe could get aſhore, to embrace the Opportunity, and accordingly they got into their Boats, and ſaved their Lives. The Inhabitants ſhewed much Humanity to the Diſtreſſed, and carried them above a Dozen of Miles up in the Country, for Fear the Pirates, in their mad Fury, ſhould have murdered the poor Men that eſcaped from their Ship. The Pirates, ſoon after they had Poſſeſſion of the *Caſſandra*, got her aflote again, ſhe having received little or no Damage; they alſo got their own Ship off, but ſhe was very much ſhattered, and diſabled in her Maſts.

CAPTAIN *Mackraw*, being a Gentleman that was well verſed in Converſation with Men of any Temper, ventured on board the Pirates, and they were ſo much taken with his Addreſs, that they made him a Preſent of that Ship which he had ſo bravely battered, to carry him and his Crew to *India*; in the mean while, the *Greenwich* came to *Bombay* in *September*, who brought the Account of the Loſs of the *Caſſandra*, and in *November*, Captain *Mackraw* arrived himſelf with his new Ship, and his Ship's Company all in Rags, but were ſoon equipp'd by the Benevolence and Generoſity of the Governor Mr. *Boone*, who was a Gentleman of as much Honour and good Senſe, as any that ever ſat in that Chair.

Mohilla is but a little diſtant from *Johanna*, pretty well inhabited, but the People not ſo well civilized as *Johanna*; and the Kings of theſe neighbouring Iſlands have continual War. The *Johanna* Men, by the Aſſiſtance of Commodore *Littleton*, landed on *Mohilla*, and made great Slaughter and Devaſtations; but what his Policy was in breaking the Neutrality that the *Engliſh* held among thoſe Iſlanders, I know not. *Mayotta* lies about 35 Leagues from *Johanna*, and is the largeſt of the inhabited Iſlands, but being ſurrounded with dangerous Rocks under Water, it is not much frequented, and ſo the Manners of the Inhabitants not ſo well known. The Religion of thoſe Iſlands is *Mahometan*, but there are very few Zealots among them; and ſo I leave them, and return to Cape *Guardafoy*, and travel up the *Red Sea*.

THE Navigation of the *Ethiopian* Seas is very dangerous, and their Maps very deficient; for I ſaw a *Dutch* Skipper at *Mocha*, who had Orders to ſail from *Batavia* towards *Mocha*, in the Month of *January*, and to navigate to the North End of *Madagaſcar*, and from thence to the *Red Sea*, he aſfirmed to me, that he ſaw ſeveral large Iſlands, and many Rocks and Sands in thoſe Seas that were not placed in his Maps, for which Reaſon he was obliged to anchor in the Nights, when he could have Anchor Ground; and that the Currents run very ſtrong to the Southward, among thoſe Banks and Rocks.

CHAP. III.

Gives a Deſcription of Zeyla's *Sea-coaſt, and of a Part of* Ethiopia, Zuakin *and* Upper Egypt.

BUT to return again to Cape *Guardafoy*, from thence up to *Zeyla* is about 120 Leagues. The Coaſt is inhoſpitable as well as the People. There are only two Places in all that Tract that affords freſh Water, one is a little to the Eaſtward of Mount *Felix*, but in *Arabick* it is called *Baba-fileck*, or, *The Mountain of Camels*, where there is a ſmall freſh Water River; the other is called *Khagi* 10 Leagues more Weſterly; it may be eaſily known by the Side of a Hill cloſe to the Sea, whoſe North Aſpect is of white Sand, that ſhews at a Diſtance like a Sail, but may be ſeen in that Figure 10 Leagues off. Several Ships from *India*, that have been neceſſitated to call at thoſe Places for Water, have been cut off; and one poor Man they ſurprized with his own Boat that he ſent for Water. The Boat's Crew were ſurprized whilſt filling Water, them they killed, except two Boys whom they ſaved; they then came off in the Night, and thoſe in the Ship not examining them in Time, they boarded the Ship, and took them all unarmed, and killed every Man, and carrying the Ship cloſe to the Shore, they unladed her, and then ſunk her. The two Youths who gave the Account of that tragical Accident, were brought to *Aden*, which lies oppoſite to that Place, and were ſold for Slaves. A *Surat* Ship being there, bought the Youths, and brought them to *Surat*.

THERE is no anchoring on that Coaſt above a Mile off Shore the Sea is ſo deep; and above *Zeyla*, in a deep Bay oppoſite to *Babelmandel*, which makes the Entry into the *Red Sea*, there is a large River that diſimbogues into the Sea, but tho' the Mouth be large, yet it is ſo deep, and full of Banks and Rocks, with ſuch Whirl-pools, that no Ship dare go near it. At that River begins the *Ethiopian* Shore, ſhewing many high

Mountains, which are eaſily ſeen from the *Arabian* Shore: And all the Coaſt from this River, as far North as *Zuakin*, which is near 200 Leagues, is called the *Ethiopian* Coaſt.

AND tho' I never was on that South-weſt Coaſt of the *Red Sea*, and know but few that traffick there, except *Romiſh* Prieſts, yet I'll venture to relate what I learned from them. There are two or three ſmall Ports between *Zeyla* and *Moſſava*, but an inconſiderable Trade, being moſt in Slaves of both Sexes, which the *Ethiopians* bring to *Mocha* for a Market, where I have ſeen a Drove of thoſe unfortunate Creatures carried like a Flock of Sheep, moſt Part of them inſenſible of their own Miſery, and the higheſt Bidder carries the Bargain. They alſo bring ſome Elephants Teeth, the beſt that ever I ſaw, and ſome Oſtriches Feathers.

Moſſava is ſituated on the North-weſt End of a large Iſland, and affords a very good Harbour for Shipping of any Size; it has a Gariſon of about 250 *Turks* in a Caſtle built formerly by the *Portugueze*, who, according to their impolite Cuſtom, oppreſs Strangers as well as Natives, that come there to trade.

THE Country produceth low Gold, Elephants Teeth, Slaves, and ſome Coffee, but of a larger Grain than what grows on the Land oppoſite to it in *Arabia*, at *Betlefackee*. The current ſmall Money of *Ethiopia* is Salt, which is dug out of the Mountains as we do Stones from our Quarries, which they

they break in Pieces of ſeveral Sizes, the largeſt weighing about 80 Pounds, the others in 40, 20, 10, or 5 Pounds, and are ſo expert in dividing it, that they err not above 5 *per Cent*. more or leſs in their Calculation of Weight; 20 Pounds is in Value about 1 Shilling *Sterl.* and thoſe Pieces of Salt is the current Money in their Markets for Proviſions, and likewiſe for Cloth, when they buy a Yard or two at a Time; and when a Merchant has got any conſiderable Quantity by him, there are Bankers to give Gold for it.

The Religion on the Sea-coaſt is *Mahometan*, but within Land *Cophties*, who are circumciſed *Chriſtians*. The Males they circumciſe ſometimes at 8 Days old, but that Ceremony is often delayed till 40 Days, and ſometimes not till the ſeventh or eighth Year of their Age. They circumciſe Females as well as Males. The Circumciſion, they think, is neceſſary in Memory of *Jeſus Chriſt*, and on a certain Day yearly, they immerſe themſelves in Rivers or Lakes, in Remembrance of *Chriſt's* Immerſion or Baptiſm. They forbear eating ſome Beaſts Fleſh, according to the *Moſaical* Law. They hold from *Saturday*'s Noon to *Sunday*'s Noon their Sabbath. They receive the Sacrament ſtanding, and only in the Church, and the Wine only from the Deacon's Hand in a Spoon. Their Prieſts eat no idle Bread, but maintain themſelves by Labour. They have many Biſhops, but one they call *Abunah* above the reſt, he is held in great Veneration, and when he goes abroad, he has

has great Attendance, and rides on a Mule, with a Croſs in his right Hand.

They enter their Churches bare-footed, becauſe God commanded *Moſes to put off his Shoes, for the Ground he ſtood on was holy.* They allow but one Wife, but as many Concubines as they pleaſe. They allow of Repudiation, but neither Party can marry again, till the Term of three Years be expired, and if the Parties are not reconciled in that Term, they think the Breach too big ever to be cloſed up again.

They have all the canonical Books of our Scriptures, and ſeveral more. They reckon the Prophet *Iddo* one of the greater Prophets, and put him in the Claſs with *Iſaiah, Ezekiel, Eliſha, Elijah* and *Daniel,* and that he wrote 14000 Prophecies, many of which they have at this Day; that his Prophecies of *Jeſus Chriſt,* were clearer, or more diſtinct than any the other Prophets left behind them; but the Subſtance of their practical Religion conſiſts in their Faſts and Feaſts, for they do not much trouble themſelves about the Doctrine of Faith, Repentance and good Works, which makes them very diſſolute in their Lives.

We *Europeans* generally call the King of *Ethiopia, Preſter John,* but his Subjects know no ſuch Appellation; 'tis true, he is Supreme in eccleſiaſtick as well as civil Affairs. His Dominions are very large, and he has many Tributaries, who ſtile themſelves Kings, and act deſpotically. The Royal Family are all kept

at

at *Amara*, which is a pleaſant round Hill, ſituated in 12 Degrees North from the *Equator*, tho' I ſaw an old *Portugueze* geographical Deſcription of *Ethiopia*, place it under the *Equinoctial*. The Hill is walled round with a high Wall, at leaſt 12 Leagues in Circumference, which cuts off all Communication with Strangers or Mal-contents. Within the Walls are Palaces, Gardens, Orchards, Woods for wild Game, Rivulets and Ponds for Fiſh, and all that the Clime can afford to make it pleaſant; there the Youths of the Royal Family ſtudy what Arts and Sciences are proper to their Quality, or according to the Knowledge of their Teachers.

THEIR Empire is hereditary, but not in a direct Line, the Succeſſion being kept in the ancient Family, which they reckon up as high as *Solomon*, but on the Demiſe of one Emperor, they make Choice of a Royal Youth out of the Paradiſe of *Amara*, ſo he that behaves beſt in that State of Probation, or has the beſt Friends to recommend him, ſucceeds without Contention, which political Cuſtom makes their Youths very tractable and ſtudious. There are none reckoned Princes of the Blood after ſecond Couſin-germans, and it ſeems they have ſomething like the *Salick* Law in Force amongſt them, for their Hiſtories mention no Female Reign ſince *Candace*'s Time, if *Ethiopia*, as it now is, was her Country.

THEY are very neſty in their Apparel and Diet, for tho' their Country is well ſtored with Fire-wood, yet they do not take Pains

to

to drefs their Meat by Fire, but having killed their animal Food, before it be well cold, they mince it, and mix Salt and a fharp hot Bark of a Tree well powdered, and make the Morfel up in fmall Balls about the Bignefs of a Wall-nut, and greedily eat it: But the Princes eat in State, for they being feated on a Matt fpread on the Ground, his favourite female Slave or Concubine makes up thofe Balls of Flefh or Fifh feafoned with the aforefaid Sauce of Salt and Bark, and fqueezes them into fafhionable Morfels, his Highnefs gapes like a young Crow, and fhe throws it cleverly in, which he prefently devours. The Commons eat of the fame Sort of Viands with the Grandees, but many of both Sexes die by Excoriations of the Guts and the right Inteftine; but whether their Diet be the Caufe of their Diftemper, I leave to Phyficians to determine, who generally are the beft Judges. They have a good pleafant Liquor made of Hony and Potatoes, which they caroufe in plentifully, and often get drunk by it, and then they are rather mad than inebriated, which renders them very quarrelfom and furious; their Hony, as it is very plentiful in their Country, fo it is the whiteft, hardeft and beft tafted that ever I met with.

I had the above Relation of *Abafina* from four *Romifh* Priefts, who had their Miffion there for 8 Years together, but made but few Profelytes: They had been meddling in State Affairs, and, for Fear of lofing their Heads, they fled, and left two of their Brethren, being

ing old, and not fit for Travel; what became of them they knew not; but those four transgressed their Superior's Orders, and left their Stations, and travelled three or four hundred Miles to the Sea-coast, and got a Passage over the *Red Sea* to *Mocha*, where I entertained them about four Months: They also told me, that seven tributary Kings had lost their Heads in six Months Time, for Mal-administration or Treason, and if my Guests had not removed their Quarters when they did, they had been honoured with the Name of *Roman* Martyrs, *in Anno* 1714. The Country abounds plentifully in Wheat, Rice, Barley, Legumens or Pulse of several Sorts, notwithstanding they eat their raw Meat without Bread. Their Woods abound in Elephants (reckoned the largest in the World) also some Lions and Tigers, and innumerable Troops of Wolves, Monkeys and Ostriches, all much larger than in other Countries. The aforesaid Priests also told me, that the Head of *Nilus*, which the Ancients so much sought for, is in this Country, about the Latitude of 6 Degrees North, and about 400 Miles from the lower End of the *Red Sea*. How far the *Ethiopian* Coast stretches to the North-ward, I know not, but it has no Seaports to the Northward of *Mossava*, and the next Country to it is the barbarous *Zuakin*, whose Inhabitants are very different both in Complexion and Customs from the *Abasines*, whose Colour is only as black as Soot, but the *Zuakins* are as black as Jet, and their Skins as ſoft as Velvet.

THEIR Religion is ſtill Paganiſm, tho they don't worſhip Images. They ſhew outward Civility to *Europeans*, but kill them, and feaſt on their Fleſh, when any are unfortunately ſhipwrack'd on their Coaſt. At firſt they ſhew a ſeeming Humanity, allowing them a convenient Place to lodge in, with Plenty of animal Food to eat, and ſometimes entertain them with their Muſick, and then deſtroy the fatteſt, as they have Occaſion to feaſt on them, an Inſtance whereof I had from a Miſſionary at *Mocha*, *in Anno* 1712. *viz.*

A *Turkiſh* Galley bound from *Moſſava* to *Judda* in *Arabia felix*, had on board about 20 *European Turks*, and one *Italian* Prieſt, as Paſſenger; that Galley was drove aſhore on the Coaſt of *Zuakin* by a Storm, the Galley was loſt, but all the Men got ſafe aſhore, and found the abovementioned Entertainment. They had not been long aſhore, till ſome People of Diſtinction viſited them, and ſeemed to condole their Misfortune, but withal, told them in *Arabick*, that the King had a great Deſire to ſee ſome of them, and they choſe the youngeſt and plumpeſt of the *Turks* to ſhew to the King, who very willingly went away with them, but none came back to bring News how they were entertained at Court; and every fourth or fifth Day, another of the beſt favoured and beſt fleſhed were carried from their Comrades, on the ſame, or ſuch like Errand, till near one Half were

were carried away, thoſe that remained had no Suſpicion, but were lulled aſleep by the good Words and good Treatment they received daily; But one Day, an *Abaſine*, who had fled his Country for ſome Miſdemeanour, came to viſit them, and, in Diſcourſe, they told him how courteouſly they had been entertained by the hoſpitable Natives, and how many of their Company had gone to the King, but that none returned. The *Abaſine* told them, that they were treated after the common Cuſtom of that Country, that when any white Men were ſhipwrack'd on their Coaſt, they found ſuch Treatment as they had, to make them fat, and then to kill and eat them, by cutting ſuch Morſels of the Body as they had preſent Occaſion for, and kept Life as long in the poor Victim as they could; and that very Morning a *Janiſary* had been carried on the aforeſaid Errand, and had one Leg cut off, and the Half of a Thigh, and he ſaw them roſting and broiling the Fleſh as he happened to paſs in his Way to viſit them, and told the diſconſolate *Turks* that remained, that if one or two would accompany him a little Way in the Evening, he would convince them of the Truth of that he told them, but they muſt immediately after return to their Lodging. The Prieſt was one that went to behold the ſad Spectacle, whom they found not quite dead, tho ſpeechleſs, on which the *Abaſine* went ſpeedily away, as the others did to acquaint their Fellows what they had ſeen. Aſſoon as they made their Report,

port, they were under the greatest Consternation, and unanimously resolved to flee to the Woods that very same Night, and trust the wild Inhabitants rather than the crueller Beasts, the *Zuakins*. And the Woods are plentifully inhabited with Lions, Tigers, large Monkeys, but above all with Wolves. The Priest took his Way in the Dark along the Sea-shore to the Northward, but knew nothing of his Fellows, which Way they took, or how they fared. In the Day-time he sculked in Caverns and Hollows of Rocks, which that Sea-coast abounds in, and is not so much frequented by the brutal *Cannibals* as the inland Parts; sometimes he sallied out to get Shell-fish, or what else he could get to eat, and in the Night he travelled, so that after seventeen Nights and Days hard Fatigue, he arrived at a Village in *Upper Egypt* inhabited by *Mahometans* and *Cophties*, who relieved him, and sent him to *Grand Cairo*, from whence he wrote to a Missionary at *Mocha, in Anno* 1714. who resided with me, and gave him the above Account, with the Addition of a very strange Paradox, *viz.* That himself being then about 28 Years of Age, (when he fell on the Coast of *Zuakin*) his Hair was of a dark brown, but when he arrived in *Cairo*, his Hair was turned to a very light gray, and continued so till the Time he wrote to his Friend at *Mocha* of that tragical Adventure.

THERE are no Sea-ports from *Zuakin* on the South-west Side of the *Red Sea*, till we

come

come to *Seues*, which lies near the Head of the Bay of that Sea, which sends his opposite Shores down to the South-eastward, as far as *Babelmandel*.

Sues, or *Seues* seems to be the *Ezion-geber*, or *Eloth*, from whence *Solomon* sent his Ships to *Ophir*, for I have conversed with several Pilots of that Navigation, who assured me, there is no clean Bottom for Anchoring, but *Seues*, on that Part of the Coast, for most Part of the *Red Sea* is incumbred with Coral Rocks under Water, and pestered with Banks, which make the Navigation very dangerous. At present, *Seues* is the only Sea-port for *Grand Cairo*, from whence it is three Days Journey by Land, with a Caffilla or Caravan, but on Horse-back but two short Days. In *Cairo* the *English* and *French* keep their Consuls, for the Support of the Trade of their respective Countries.

In Anno 1714. Mr. *Farrington* was Consul for the *English*, he had a very fair Character from all People, as well Merchants as the Religious that came from *Cairo* to *Mocha*, which made me presume to trouble him with a Letter, giving him the best Account I could of the State of Merchandize in *India*, and to have his Advice, whether it might be practicable to cultivate a Trade from *India* to *Seues*, which Letter he very civilly answered, and next Year it came to my Hand, but he disswaded me from any Attempt that Way; because of the intolerable Avarice and Insults of the *Turkish Bashaws*, and other

Officers of Note, with the Contempt they have for Merchants, eſpecially *Chriſtians*, he aſſured me, that it is impoſſible to be a Gainer by ſuch Commerce.

CHAP. IV

Gives a little Deſcription of the Coaſt of Arabia *the* Happy, *from Mount* Sinai *to* Mocha, *with ſome Obſervations on the Religion, Cuſtoms and Laws, as they are now eſtabliſhed.*

OVER againſt *Seues*, on the *Arabian* Shore, ſtands Mount *Sinai*, about 5 or 6 Leagues from the Sea; and on its Southweſt Side, near the Bottom, is the Monaſtery of St. *Katharina*. The Mount is much revered by the *Jews*, and the Monaſtery by the *Chriſtians*; it is very ancient, and held in ſome Veneration by the *Mahometans*, whoſe Pilgrims to *Mecca*, from *Egypt*, *Turkey* and *Paleſtine*, paſs cloſe by, both in their going and returning, as do likewiſe their Caffillas, and other Paſſengers, that go on Traffick to *Judda*, a City four Days Journey from *Mecca*, where *Mahomet* lies interred: And the great Concourſe of Pilgrims (from all Parts where his Religion is ſpread) brings a great Trade thither.

THERE is a Tradition, that, as *Mahomet* was going on an Expedition to *Paleſtine*, he called at that Monaſtery for Refreſhments, and the

the Monks generously assisted him; and in Acknowledgment of their Civility, he gave them a Charter, which they still keep, wherein he gave them many Immunities, and laid his heavy Curse on all, who should, after that Time, dare to molest that Monastery.

THE Building is strong and high, and no Gate or Door to enter in to it, but one, which stands about ten Yards high (in the Wall) from the Ground. It has a large Inclosure adjoyning to it, with an high Wall, to keep the wild *Arabs* from robbing them of their animal Provisions; for they are such vile Thieves, that they had rather venture to ly under the *Anathema* of their Prophet, than to keep their Hands from Robbery.

ITS present Possessors are *Nestorian* and *Jacobin* Monks, who are maintained by the Charity of Passengers, and a little Revenue that belongs to the Monastery. The *Christians*, in that Part of *Arabia*, are *Nestorians* and *Jacobins*, whose Priests may marry, and they allow of no Images but the Cross, and many other Things repugnant to the *Romish* Tenets.

Judda is the next Place of Note below St. *Katharina*. It is a small, but well fortified City, belonging to the *Turk*. It stands close to the Sea, and is governed by a Bashaw, who keeps a Garison in it, with four or five Galleys to cruize on the *Red Sea*, to hinder the Passing of all Ships or Vessels up the Sea, without first calling at *Judda*.

THE inland Country about it, belongs to a Sheek, who pretends to be a Descendant of *Mahomet*. He has the Title of *Xeriff* given him, to distinguish his Eminency from other Sheeks. And, altho' he be so near akin to the Prophet, yet he squeezes above 100000 Pounds *Sterl.* yearly out of the Pilgrims, who go to worship at his Ancestor's Tomb. And so much Gain he can make of their Folly.

IT is between this Country and *Sinai*, that the famous Balm of *Gilead* grows. It is reported to proceed from a Shrub, the Bark of which is slit, and Vessels set under the Wound to receive it, as it drains from that Wound. The wild *Arabs* about *Sinai*, have a Tradition, that *Abraham* was their Countryman, and are not a little proud of that Honour; but if it was so, that he was their Sheek, as they alledge, they neither follow him in Morals or Religion.

THE Sea-coasts of *Arabia felix*, from *Judda* to the Southward, as far as the Latitude of 15 Degrees, are governed by several Sheeks, who are so avaritious, that no Pilgrims can pass through their Dominions, but Beggars; for if Strangers carry any Thing of Value about them, or if they have good Clothes, they are stript of all, and about a Yard of coarse Cloth given them to cover their Nakedness; and Lectures of Humility and Devotion are preached to them, that whoever goes on so solemn an Errand, ought to shew, by their outward Appearance, that the

the inward Man is humble, and that those who love Riches, ought to sequester themselves from the World, before they approach that holy Place, where, after the Muftee (or his Deputy, the Fackee) had bestowed a Benediction on them, if they had any Grace, they would never covet Riches again.

THE *Immaum* of *Mocha*'s Dominions reach along the Sea-coast from the Latitude of 15 Degrees, to the Southward, as far as *Babelmandel*, very barren and inhospitable, affording neither fresh Water, nor Wood for Shipping, either for Drink or Fuel. Only on the Island of *Commera*, which lies about 5 or 6 Leagues from *Betlefackee*, there is both a good Harbour, and Plenty of Provisions for Strangers, as well as for the Inhabitants, whose Temperance makes them easily satisfied, both with their coarse Diet and Apparel.

Betlefackee is the first Town of Note (near the Sea-coast) of the *Immaum*'s Dominions. It stands about 25 *English* Miles from the Sea, and it is the greatest Market for Coffee in the World. It supplies *India*, *Persia*, *Turkey* in *Asia*, *Africa* and *Europe*, besides *England*, *France* and *Holland*, with Coffee-beans. Other Goods and Merchandize may be bought and sold on Credit, for a certain Time; but Coffee is always bought for ready Money. The *Europe* Shipping lades yearly at *Mocha*, (from whence *Betlefackee* is about 100 *English* Miles) about 2000 Tuns, rather more than less, and the other

Nations above 20000 Tuns more. The whole Province of *Betlefackee* is planted with Coffee Trees, which are never ſuffered to grow above 4 or 5 Yards high; and the Bean or Berry grows on the Branches and Twigs, firſt green, then red, at laſt a dark brown Colour. The Berries cling to the Branches like ſo many Inſects, and when they are ripe, they ſhake off.

Zibet is the next Town, and ſerves for a Sea-port for *Betlefackee*. It was large, and famous in ancient Times for Trade, but in the fourteenth Century, the *Turks* over-ran all the Coaſts of the *Red Sea*, and made them Tributaries to them. They ruined all the Trade from *India* to *Zibet*, and ſettled their *Emporium* at *Aden*, about 35 Leagues without *Babelmandel*, to the Eaſtward: And the *Immaum* holds his Kingdom in Feoff from the *Turk* at this Time; and when the *Turks* come to *Betlefackee*, none dare break the Price of the Market, nor buy before they are firſt ſerved.

THE *Immaum* or King keeps his Court generally at a Town called *Mohaib*, about 200 *Engliſh* Miles to the Eaſt, North-eaſtward of *Mocha*. He has little Splendor about it, and he that reigned *in Anno* 1714. was about 80 Years of Age. His Government has been of a long Time very ill managed. His Luſt having the Aſcendant over his Reaſon, he had ſeldom leſs than Three hundred Wives married to him, of the moſt beautiful young Women in his Dominions. He often marries one,

one, at one New-moon, and, on the next New-moon, remarries her to one of his Minions, and bestows a good Patrimony on her to help her off; so that with his own frequent Marriages, and those of his Minions, he exhausts all his Revenues, and is always necessitous, which forces him on many unjust and mean Ways to exact Money from his miserable Subjects. And, *in Anno* 1720. their heavy Burdens made them rebel, and involved the whole Country in a civil War. One Part was for deposing him, and another for keeping him on the Throne; but what the Event was I never heard.

THE *Turks* being baffled in several Projects and Expeditions from *Aden*, and that they could not well maintain their Ground in that Part of *Arabia*, (being so very far distant from their own Dominions) without much Charge and Trouble, they, in the latter End of the sixteenth Century, withdrew their Garison from *Aden*, and left it, with all its Fortifications and Buildings, to the *Immaum*, who finding *Aden* to ly inconvenient for the Trade of the *Red Sea*, because of the fresh Winds usually blowing at its Mouth, in both Easterly and Westerly Monsoons, made him remove the Trade about 15 Leagues within its Mouth, in a Bay, not very commodious for Shipping, to a Fishing Town called *Mocha*.

CHAP.

CHAP. V

Gives a Deſcription of the Immaum *of* Mocha's *Country, particularly of* Mocha *its Situation, Laws, Cuſtoms and Commerce; with ſome hiſtorical Obſervations.*

MOCHA, upon the foregoing Account, was built for an *Emporium* or Mart for the Trade of *India* to the *Red Sea*, and was mightily forwarded by the Perſwaſion of a *Sheek*, who bore the Character of a Saint amongſt his Country-men. His Name was *Sheek Seddley*; and he pretended to propheſy, that *Mocha* ſhould be a Place of great Trade to the Country, and conſequently of great Profit to the *Immaum*. They had ſuch a Veneration for him, that the greateſt Moſque in the Town, and the greateſt Gate, bear his Name, and did, even in his own Lifetime, ſee the Town walled, tho' but very weakly. It is ſituated cloſe to the Sea, in a large, dry, ſandy Plain, that affords no good Water within 20 Miles, all the Wells nearer the City being brakiſh, ſo that nothing of Fruits grows near it, but a few Dates and Water Melons. The Water for drinking comes from *Moſa*, about 20 Miles off, as I ſaid before, and by that Time we get it to the Town, it coſts us as dear as ſmall Beer is ſold for in *England*. Thoſe who are obliged to drink of the Wells near the Town, are in Danger of having a long ſmall Worm breed in their Legs or Feet, that inflames the

the Place where it breeds, which is accompanied with extreme burning Pains. In 5 or 6 Days it appears between the Cutany and outward Skin, and then puts its Head thro', which when the Patient obſerves, he takes hold of it with a Pair of Tweezers, and pulls it very gently out, about an Inch or two at a Time, in 24 Hours, and rolls it round an Hen's Quill, or ſome other Thing of that Thickneſs. It is no thicker than the Treble String of a Violin; and I have ſeen of them, after they have been pulled out, about two Foot and an half long. While it is in the Leg, it is daily covered with a Plaiſter, and, if it chance to break in the Operation, the Patient will be troubled with intolerable Pains for a long While; and ſometimes they are crippled by it. But the *Moſa* Water, coming from Springs amongſt the Mountains, is very ſweet and wholeſom.

Mocha is a Place of good Trade, notwithſtanding its bad Situation; for, beſides the Commerce with *Sues* and *Judda*, the *Engliſh* and *Dutch* Companies have their Factories there, beſides a Trade from *India*, carried on by *Engliſh* free Merchants, *Portugueze*, *Banyans* and *Moors*, and by Veſſels from *Boſſorah*, *Perſia* and *Muskat* in *Arabia petrea*. The Country, of itſelf, affords or produces very few valuable Commodities, beſides Coffee, and ſome Drugs, ſuch as Myrrh, *Olibanum* or Frankincenſe from *Caſſin*, and *Aloes Soccatrina* from *Soccotra* liquid Storax, white and yellow Arſenick, ſome

ſome Gum *Arabick* and Mummy; with ſome Balm of *Gilead*, that comes down the *Red Sea*. The Coffee Trade brings in a continual Supply of Silver and Gold from *Europe*, *Spaniſh* Money, *German* Crowns, and other *European* Coins of Silver; alſo Zequins, *German* and *Hungarian* Ducats of *European* Gold; and from *Turkey*, Ebramies and Mograbies, Gold of low Matt.

THE Pirates, for many Years, infeſted the Mouth of the *Red Sea*, committing frequent Robberies and Barbarities. Captain *Evory* was the firſt that led the Way, *in Anno* 1695. and the Pirates finding great Booties, purchaſed with ſmall Danger, from the Traders into the *Red Sea*, had a Project to be Maſters of the Key of that Door, ſo they found the Iſland *Prim*, which lies within Gun-ſhot of *Babelmandel*, to have a good commodious Bay for the Security of their Shipping; upon which Conſideration, they began to build regular Fortifications, and dig for freſh Water, and, with much Labour, they dug thro' an hard Rock, 15 Fathoms deep, but found none, but brakiſh Water; wherefore they deſiſted, and removed to St. *Mary*'s Iſland, on the Eaſt Side of *Madagaſcar*, as I obſerved before, and are ſince removed, for more Security, over to the main Iſland, and there they fortify themſelves by Marriages into the noble Families of that great Iſland, from whence they come into *India*, and cruize in thoſe Seas. *In Anno* 1696. they met with a Ship from *Bombay*, commanded by one *Sawbridge*,

bridge, who was carrying *Arabian* Horſes for *Surat*. After they took the Ship, *Sawbridge* began to expoſtulate with them about their Way of Life. They ordered him to hold his Tongue, but he continuing his Diſcourſe, they took a Sail-needle and Twine, ſewed his Lips together, and ſo kept him ſeveral Hours, with his Hands tied behind him. At length they unlooſed both his Hands and Lips; and carried him on board their Ship, and, after they had plundred *Sawbridge*'s Ship, they ſet her on Fire, and burned her and the Horſes together. *Sawbridge* and his People were ſet aſhore near *Aden*, where he died preſently after.

CAPTAIN *Evory* was not ſo inhumane; for the Year before, he took a large Ship belonging to the *Mogul*, and got a Booty of 2600000 Rupees, which amount to, in *Sterling* Money, about 325000 Pounds. He freed the Ship, and let her go, without torturing the People; but carried a young *Mogul* Lady with him, and ſome of her female Servants, who had been at *Mecca* to perform a Vow, laid on her by her Mother on her Death-bed.

BUT, to return again to *Mocha*, from my long Digreſſion: The Town is large, but meanly fortified; and, from the Sea, it has a fine Aſpect. The Buildings are lofty, and make a much better Appearance without than within. The Steeples of five or ſix Moſques raiſe their Heads pretty high above the reſt of the Buildings. Their Markets are well ſtored with animal Proviſions, ſuch as Beef,

Mutton

Mutton of Sheep and Goats, Lamb and Kid, Camel and Antelopes Fleſh, Dung-hill Fowls, *Guinea* Hens, Partridge and Pigeon. The Sea affords Variety of Fiſh, but not ſavoury. I believe their Unſavourineſs proceeds from the extreme Saltneſs of the Sea-water, and the Nature of their Aliment. The Town is well furniſhed, all the Year round, with good Fruits, ſuch as Grapes, Peach, Apricocks and Quinces, of which they make Store of Marmelade, both for their preſent Uſe and Exportation, tho' near the Town, there is not a Tree or Shrub to be ſeen, but a few Date Trees. And they ſeldom have more than two or three Showers of Rain in a Year, and often no Rain in two or three Years; but amongſt the Mountains, about 20 Miles off, ſeldom a Morning paſſes without a moderate Shower, which makes the Vallies very prolifick in Fruit and Corn, ſuch as the Soil will bear; but they have no Rice, tho Plenty of Barley and Wheat.

THE Governor of *Mocha*, and the Officers of the Town, are Merchants, when they think to get good Bargains, and are very ready to break their Contracts, both in Payment of their Debts, and in the Time of Payment. Some Inſtances whereof I ſaw. And, *in Anno* 1716. I had an experimental one; for the Deputy-governor having bought a Part of my Cargo, agreed to pay me the firſt Day of *June*, according to our *Æra* and Computation. At the appointed Time I demanded my Money; but he told me, that notwith-

ſtanding

ſtanding he had agreed at that Time to pay me, yet the Cuſtom was not to pay before the Middle of *July*, and Cuſtom muſt be obſerved before Contract; beſides, the King having much Need of Money, ſent preſſing Demands on the Town for Money, as faſt as it came in by Cuſtoms and other Subſidies; therefore he could not, nor would not pay me before the cuſtomary Time, nor would he clear my Account Cuſtoms (which is a Part of his Office) before that Time. I often ſolicited him to clear my Account, and pay the Balance; but to no Purpoſe. I then fell on a Project to frighten him into Compliance. I went very calmly to him, and told him, that I had ſome Goods left, which would be proper for the inland Markets, and that I would let him have a Penyworth of them. He knew the Goods were proper enough, as I had told him, and ſo came to my Houſe, which was four Stories high. I carried him up to the higheſt, and, having ſeated him in a ſmall Balcony, I ſhewed him the Muſters of my Goods, and askt Prices which he thought too high; and, becauſe we could not agree, he was for going abruptly away, and ſo got on his Feet: But I being much too ſtrong for him, took him by the Shoulders, and forced him to ſit down again, and ordered my Linguiſt to tell him, that, before we parted, he muſt clear my Account Cuſtoms, and give me Bills, on the King's Banker, for the Balance, otherwiſe I would teach him to fly from the Balcony to the Ground, be the Conſequence

Consequence what it would. He had never been so treated before, and Fear seized him so, that he could not speak for a little Time, but, recovering a little, ordered his Clerk, who was in the Room with us, to make up my Account, and draw Bills immediately, who readily obeyed Orders; and, in Half an Hour, we became good Friends again. The Noise of this Action run like a Squib thro' the Town, and, before I came to the Banker with the Bill, (which was for about 1200 *L. Sterl.*) he was apprised how I had served the Deputy-governor, and, upon presenting it, accepted it to be paid in seven Days; but withal desired, that I would constantly keep two *European* Seamen at his Door, with Arms, and, as Money came in, they were to receive one Bag, and the King's People another, till the Sum should be completed: And accordingly in seven Days I got every Peny, and sent the Governor word, that I wanted to wait on him, in order to take my Leave. He returned me Answer, that I should be very welcome; and accordingly I went, and he received me very civilly; and, all the while I staid, he passed Jokes on his Deputy about the Fright I had put him into.

THE King's Customs are very easy, being but 3 *per Cent.* from *Europeans*, and 5 on *Gentiles*; and the Custom-house as easy, for they only desire to see the Musters of Goods, and the Quantity of Goods in each Parcel or Bale, and to cause some, that they choose, to be opened; and if they find the Quantity and Quality

Quality agree with the Invoice given in, the Remainder of the Cargo is carried directly from the Landing-place, to the Ware-houses, without more Trouble; and, after Sale, they receive an Account from the Seller, and rate the Customs accordingly.

THEY are very ignorant in History and natural Philosophy; for they tell, that *Alexander* the *Great* was *Mahomet*'s General, tho' they lived about 900 Years distant from one another; and that, having a Mind to transport his Army over the Mouth of the *Red Sea*, from *Babelmandel* to *Zeyla*, in order to conquer *Ethiopia*, he went about building a Bridge there; and, there being seven Islands in these Streights, called the *Seven Stones*, he placed them there for a Foundation to build on: And they are of Opinion, that the World is supported on the Horns of a great Bull, who sometimes shakes his Head, which they assign to be the Cause of Earthquakes, which frequently are felt there.

THERE are Abundance of Beggars in *Mocha*, and in most other Towns in *Arabia*, who brag of the Sanctity and Verity of their Religion; and, for Proof, when they pass in the Streets, they are always bawling out, that there is but one God, and *Mahomet* his Prophet and best beloved Servant; and, carrying a Piece of Iron like the Tooth of an Harrow, in their right Hand, they strike it with great Force into the Cavity of the Eye, and yet the Eye is not blemished, nor the Eyelids, or Skin about the Eye, seem to be hurt; and

and they often let the Iron hang down, as if the Point was faſtned to the Corner of the Eye next the Noſe. As for mad People of either Sex, they venerate them, believing them to be inſpired, or actuated by a prophetick Spirit.

THEIR Religion is *Mahometiſm*, and are ſuperſtitiouſly rigid in their Way, but abominable Hypocrites; for, in their Promiſes, which they ſeldom keep, with lifted up Eyes, they call on God to be Witneſs to their Sincerity: But in no Part of the World is Juſtice bought and ſold more publickly than here; and the Judge, who generally is the Governor of the Place, whilſt he is paſſing unjuſt Sentences, looks as grave as an old Cat, declaiming againſt Partiality.

In Anno 1716. I ſaw Juſtice executed on a notorious Criminal, guilty of no leſs than Robbery and Murder. A poor Peaſant had raiſed a Stock of 500 Dollars, amongſt his Friends and Neighbours, and was on his Way to *Mocha*, to lay it out in Merchandize proper for the Parts he lived in. A Villain, who knew of his Journey, and the Stock he carried, way-laid him, and cut his Throat from Ear to Ear, and then ſtabbed him in the Breaſt with his Dagger, and ſo poſſeſt the Money, and went off with it. Some Paſſengers, coming that Way ſoon after, found the mangled Corps, not quite cold, went and informed the Neighbourhood of the Tragedy. On Information, they went and viewed the Carcaſe, and knew it. They gave the Account

Account to the murdered Person's Relations, who lived but a little Way off, and they buried the Corps.

SOME Months after, one of the Relations being at *Mocha*, chanced to see his dead Kinsman's Ring on the Murderer's Finger, and challenged it; for it is the Custom of all the eastern Countries, both the *Mahometans* and *Gentiles*, to wear Rings. They wear no Gold Rings, but Silver among the *Mahometans*, and the *Gentiles* commonly wear Gold. The Person who knew the Ring, informed the *Cadjee* or Judge what had past, and the *Cadjee* ordered the Murderer to be apprehended, and brought before him; and ordering him to be searched, to see if farther Proof could be found about him, the very Purse that the Money was in, was found in his Bosom. However the Murderer denied all, but was sent to Prison, and fettered, till other Persons were sent for that were particularly well acquainted with the Defunct. Five or six Evidences who were sent for, appeared, and the Ring and Purse being produced, they swore, that they knew them to be with the unfortunate Defunct when he set out on his Journey for *Mocha*; and he at length confest the Fact himself. The Judge, and the rest of his Court, desired him to return the Money, and they would solicite the murdered Person's Relations to spare his Life, it being in their Power to take away or save his Life; but he absolutely denied the returning back any Part of it, and impudently asked the Judge, how he thought his Wife and Children ſhould be ſupported, if he ſhould return the Money.

THREE Months had paſſed in unfruitful Perſwaſions, but finding him obſtinate, they bid him prepare to die next Day about Noon. And accordingly, with a Guard of about 500 Horſe and Foot Soldiers, he was carried without the City, with his Hands tied behind him; and, about 200 Yards from *Sheek Seddley*'s Gate, he was delivered to the Defunct's Relations, who firſt gave him a deep Stab under the left Pap, and one of the Relations ſtanding behind, pulled back his Head, while another cut his Throat from Ear to Ear, and ſo left him with all their Speed. For aſſoon as the Mob ſaw him killed, they aſſaulted the Executioners with Stones and Brickbats ſo furiouſly, that the Guards had much ado to ſave them from being murdered; for there is a Paſſage in the *Alcoran*, importing, that whoever ſpilt a Believer's Blood, is accurſed, and ought to be ſtoned to Death.

THE Soldiery of *Mocha* are very inſolent and licentious; for, in the Months of *May*, *June* and *July*, the Air being fired with Heat, and the greateſt Concourſe of Strangers come to Town, either about Traffick, or getting Paſſage by Sea to foreign Countries, and about that Time Caſh is plentieſt in Town, then thoſe undiſciplined Cowards ſeldom fail to ſet Fire to ſome Huts that the labouring People live in, and they being built of a few Spars, covered with the Bran-

ches

ches and Leaves of Date Trees, which are very combustible Materials, the Flame soon grows fierce and violent, and very often penetrates thro' the Doors and Windows of Merchants Houses, tho' built of Brick. And, in the Consternation, when People are intent on saving what they can, by removing their Goods from their burning Houses to the Streets, those Varlets plunder publickly there with Impunity; and, altho' those Villains are detected in setting Fire to Houses and plundering, and Complaints made of them to the Governor, those Grievances are so far from being redressed, that I have known a Complainer well bastonaded for detecting the Rogues. When I traded there, I always kept a Part of my Ship's Company ashore for a Guard, and I acquainted the Governor, that if any Person came thro' our Street in the Night with Fire in their Hands, as they often did thro' several other Streets where Merchants kept their Ware-houses, I would order my Men to fire on such Fire-carriers, which kept me pretty secure from them.

The largest City in the *Immaum* of *Arabia felix's* Dominions, is *Sounan*. It is 15 Days Journey North-east from *Mocha*. It drives a great inland Trade, and is the Mart for many of the *India* Goods that are brought to *Mocha*. The Mechanicks of different Trades have each their peculiar different Street; so that whatever Commodities Strangers may want, they readily know where to find them. And in all the Streets there are Brokers for

Wiyes, ſo that a Stranger, who has not the Conveniency of an Houſe in the City to lodge in, may marry, and be made a free Burgher for a ſmall Sum. When the Man ſees his Spouſe, and likes her, they agree on the Price and Term of Weeks, Months or Years, and then appear before the *Cadjee* or Judge of the Place, and enter their Names and Terms in his Book, which coſts but a Shilling, or thereabout: And joyning Hands before him, the Marriage is valid, for better for worſe, till the Expiration of the Term agreed on. And if they have a mind to part, or renew the Contract, they are at Liberty to chooſe for themſelves what they judge moſt proper; but if either want to be ſeparated during the Term limited, there muſt be a Commutation of Money paid by the ſeparating Party to the other, according as they can agree; and ſo they become free to make a new Marriage elſewhere.

CHAP

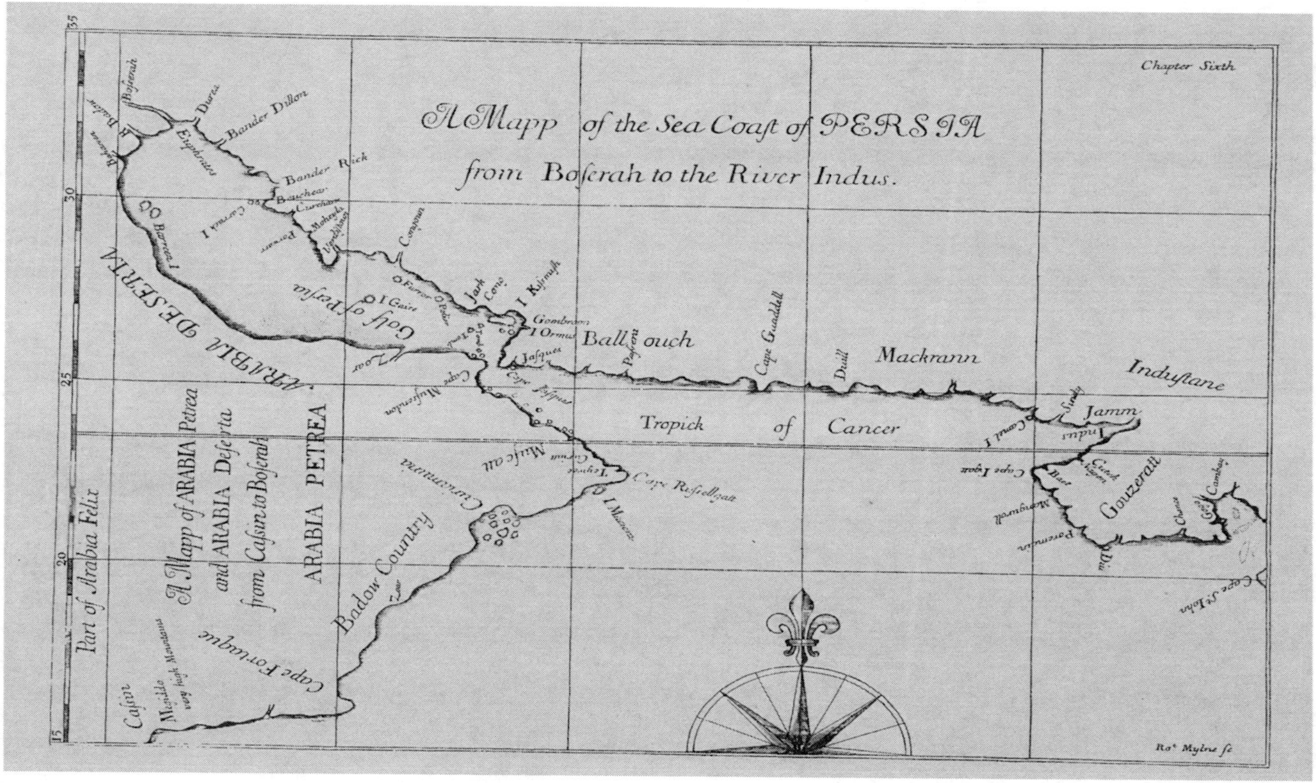
Chapter Sixth
A Mapp of the Sea Coast of PERSIA
from Bosserah to the River Indus.
Bosserah
Dorea
Bander Dillon
Euphrates
Bander Rick
Carrack I
Barreen I
ARABIA DESERTA
Gulf of Persia
I Gaire
I Kishmish
Gombroon
I Ormus
Jasques
Ball ouch
Cape Guaddell
Dull
Mackrann
Industane
Jamm
Indus
Carnal I
Tropick of Cancer
Cape Mussendon
Cape Jasques
Muscatt
Cape Rassellgatt
I Mazeira
Curia Muria
Badow Country
Cape Forteque
Cape Jagat
Gouzeratt
Mangurell
Poremain
Diu
Chaca
Cambay
Cape St John
ARABIA PETREA
A Mapp of ARABIA Petrea and ARABIA Deserta from Cassin to Bosserah
Part of Arabia Felix
Cassin
Megaldo very high Mountains
Robt Mylne sc
35
30
25
20
15

CHAP. VI.

Contains a Description of Aden, *with some historical Remarks about the* Turkish *Expedition from thence into* India: *Also an Account of the Sea-coast of* Arabia petrea, *as far as* Muskat *and* Bassora; *with a particular Account of an* English *Ship lost on the Island of* Maceira.

THE eastmost Town of Note in the *Immaum* of *Mocha*'s Dominions on the Sea-coast, is *Aden*, built by the *Turks*, in the fourteenth Century, as has been hinted before. It is built on the East Side of a barren Island, and has no fresh Water but what the Rains afford them, which they keep in Cisterns. The *Turks* had great Designs when they built it, for they thought of driving the *Portugueze* out of their Settlements in *India*, and to have possest them themselves. Accordingly about the Middle of the sixteenth Century, they made an Expedition into *India*, against the *Portugueze*, but were unsuccessful, and so have never attempted since to settle in *India*. It continued many Years after the Stapple Port for the *Red Sea* Commerce, but the Charges of keeping it, so far from the *Turkish* Dominions, made them leave it to the *Immaum*, as was already observed, and he removed the Trade to *Mocha*.

IT has a good Road for Shipping in the Westerly Monsoons, and a pretty good Mould, or Bason, for the Easterly, close to the Town, and

and the Road is not Half Gun-ſhot from it. It has been well fortified, being naturally ſtrong in its Situation; but the *Badows*, or wild *Arabs*, who inhabit about the Sea-coaſt of *Arabia petrea*, have ſeveral Times taken, and plundred it, ſince it fell into the *Immaum*'s Hands. The Country adjacent produces Barley, Wheat and Legumen, and Store of Fruits and Roots, Camels, Aſſes, Mules and Horſes, all very finely ſhaped and mettleſom; but Money being pretty plenty in that Part of the Country, their Horſes are very dear, for 50 or 60 *L. Sterl.* is reckoned but a ſmall Price for one. They have alſo Plenty of Sheep, with large broad Tails, that reach almoſt to the Ground, and their Goats are the fineſt, both for Beauty and Taſte, that ever I ſaw. And they have Poultry and *Guinea* Hens in Abundance. And the Sea affords Variety of good Fiſh. The *Immaum*'s Dominions reach about 20 Leagues to the Eaſtward of *Aden*, along the Sea-coaſt; but there are no Places of Trade till we come to

Caſſin, that lies almoſt under the Meridian of Cape *Guardafoy*, and under the prodigious high Mountains of *Megiddo*, on the Coaſt of *Arabia*. I have ſeen thoſe Mountains, in a clear Day, above 40 Leagues off.

THE Religion of *Caſſin* is *Mahometan*, and the civil Government *Democracy*. Death is capital, and is puniſhed with Death, but not by the civil Magiſtrate; for the Tribe or Clan of the Defunct purſues the Murderer or Homicide, and when they have found him, he he is immediately beheaded, and his Head put upon the Point of a Lance, and brought to his Relations in Triumph, with Musick and Dancing. And the Tragi-comedy ends in Feasting.

THE Product of the Country (besides the common Roots, and Fruits and Animals) is Myrrh and *Olibanum* or Frankincense, which they barter for coarse Calicoes from *India*; but they have no great Commerce with Strangers. Nor has *Doffar* any better Trade, but is more noted for Barbarity to those they can circumvene. I knew an *English* Ship *in Anno* 1705. that called there for fresh Water, and the Natives came flocking on board with animal Provisions to sell or barter. They found the *English* supinely negligent, and, being but six or seven in Number, they mixt with them, and suddenly stabbed them all; but did no Harm to the *Indian* Seamen and Merchants, who were about 40 in Number. They took every Thing out of the Ship, and then burnt her.

Curia Muria is another Port on that Shore, but of small Account. It is in the Middle of seven Islands, each having a very high Mountain, which makes them conspicuous from the Sea. There are none that frequent it but Trankies, that navigate from the Gulf of *Persia* to the *Red Sea*, who call there for fresh Water and Recruits of Provision. The Inhabitants, along all that Coast, are *Badows*, who wear no Clothes above the Navel. Their Hair grows long, which they plat, and wreathe about their Heads. The next remarkable Place is *Maceira*, a barren uninhabited Iſland, lying about 5 Leagues from the Continent, and within 20 Leagues of Cape *Raſſelgat*. It has dangerous Sholes lying on its Weſt End, which reach above 30 Leagues along the Shore to the Weſtward, and ſo far in the Sea, that the Land (tho' pretty high) cannot be ſeen, before the unskilful or unwary Pilot feels the Rocks with his Ship's Keel. The Inhabitants on the main Continent, ſeem to be Sorcerers; for about the Year 1684. a Ship from *London*, called the *Merchants Delight*, Captain *Edward Say* Supercargo, this Ship unfortunately run aſhore on the Iſland in the Night, being very dark, notwithſtanding they kept their deep Sea Lead going every Half Hour; yet they were ſo lucky as to run her faſt a-ground between two Rocks very cloſe to the Shore. In a few Minutes the Ship was full of Water, but, being dry on the upper Decks, the People kept on them till Day-light, and then they diſcovered about 4 or 500 wild *Arabs*, with ſome Tents pitched at a little Diſtance from them.

THE *Arabs*, by Signs, ſhewed themſelves ready to aſſiſt the diſtreſſed *Engliſh*, and being excellent Swimmers, ſwam to the Ship, and brought the End of a Rope aſhore. There was one on board, whom I was afterwards well acquainted with, who, before that, had ſailed ſome Years in *India*, and had learned the *Induſtan* Language, and ſome *Arabick*; he he ſerved for an Interpreter. They bid the *Engliſh* hoiſt their Boats out, and come aſhore without Fear, which they accordingly did, with their Arms. They told the *Engliſh*, that they were not come there to rob them, but to aſſiſt them for reaſonable Rewards, and that they would take no Advantage of the ill Circumſtances they were in, but would make a fair Contract with them, and perform their Part, as ſhould be ſtipulated in their Agreement. The *Engliſh*, tho' very diffident of the treacherous *Arabs*, were obliged to covenant, and agree, that whatever was ſaved of the Treaſure, Cargo, or the Ship's Furniture, ſhould be equally divided, and the *Engliſh* to have the Choice which Part they might have a mind to; and that the *Arabs* ſhould tranſport the *Engliſh*'s Part to *Muskat*, about 60 Leagues off, Freight free.

Assoon as the Contract was made, the *Arabs* went couragiouſly to Work, and, in a Week or ten Days, got every Thing aſhore that was portable, and they, according to Agreement, divided the whole into two equal Parts, and gave the *Engliſh* their Choice, and then got Trankies, (or Barks without Decks) and ſhipt what belonged to the *Engliſh* for *Muskat*. All the while they were getting the Goods aſhore, they treated the *Engliſh* with excellent Mutton, both of Sheep and Goat, and laid in Proviſion for their Paſſage to *Muskat*, free of Charge to the Supercargo.

After

After the Interpreter aforesaid was grown familiar with those *Arabs*, that were so kind and benevolent, he askt them why so many of them had assembled on that barren Island. They answered, that about eight Days before the Ship was lost, a *Fakee*, who is an ecclesiastick Officer in their Church, prophesied, that near such a Time, a Ship would be lost there, and pressed them to go to the Assistance of the ship-wrack'd People, who would be glad to come under Contract with them, to have one Half of what was gotten out of the Wrack; and conjured his Auditory to perform their Part faithfully, which accordingly they did; tho' at other Times the *Badows* are perfidious, treacherous and cruel.

Cape *Rasselgat* lies about 16 Leagues to the Eastward of *Maceira*, and the Sea-shore is clear of Danger; and just within the Cape, to the Northward, is a Village called *Teywee*, which stands on the Side of a small River, near the Sea; but is best known by a little Mountain (close by it) shaped like an high-crown'd Hat. And about 16 Leagues farther to the Northwestward, is *Curiat*, a large Village in a Valley close to the Sea. To the Northward of it is a very high large Mountain, whose Foot is washt by the Sea, and there are 40 Fathoms within 200 Paces of it. It may be seen above 40 Leagues from the Sea. There are neither Trees nor Grass to be seen along the Sea-coast, but at *Curiat*; and yet the Country has Plenty of Cattle, great

great and ſmall, with Variety of Fruits and Roots from the Vallies, and Fiſh from the Sea. Their Wells are dug in the Vallies very deep before they come to Springs, but the Water is very good.

CHAP. VII.

Treats of the Kingdom and City of Muskat, *and of their religious and civil Cuſtoms; with ſome hiſtorical Account of their Wars and Oeconomy. And a little Account of the Sea-coaſt of* Arabia deſerta, *as far as* Baſſora.

MUSKAT lies about 22 Leagues to the North-weſtward of *Curiat*, and is the Mart Town of *Arabia petrea*. It is built on the Bottom of a ſmall Bay, that almoſt has the Shape of an Horſe Shoe. It was built and fortified by the *Portugueze*, in the fifteenth Century, but taken from them about the Year 1650. The King of that Province (for tho' there be many Kings in *Arabia*, yet none aſſumes the Title of King of *Arabia*) having War at that Time with the *Perſians*, had raiſed an Army of 40000 Men to inſult the Sea-coaſt of *Perſia*; and had provided a ſufficient Number of ſmall Veſſels, called Trankies, for their Tranſports His Army lay at a little Diſtance from *Muskat*, and his Fleet at *Muttera*, a ſmall Bay about a Mile from the Entrance of *Muskat* Harbour. The

King

King ſent a civil Meſſage to the *Portugueze* Governor, deſiring the Liberty of his Markets to buy Proviſions.

THE inſolent Governor, thinking himſelf ſafe within a walled Town, with many ſmall Forts to annoy any Enemy that could come to attack the Walls of the Town, inſtead of returning a civil Anſwer to the King's Requeſt, ſent a Piece of Pork wrapt up in Paper, as a Preſent to the King, and bid the Meſſenger tell him, that if he wanted ſuch Proviſions, he could furniſh him. The Meſſenger, not knowing what was in the Paper, carried it to his Maſter, with the rude Anſwer. Now Pork being forbidden the *Mahometans* as well as *Jews*; they hold it in Abomination, and conſequently it aggravated the deſigned Affront. The King was much ſurprized at the Governor's ill Manners, but diſſembled his Reſentment, in Expectation to find a proper Time at his Return from his *Perſian* Expedition, to correct the Governor's Inſolence, or revenge the Affront put on him: But the whole Army being enraged at the Affront, breathed nothing but preſent Revenge. And the Queen, who was of the *Seid* Extraction, who are a Tribe or Family deſcended from *Mahomet*, by *Fatima* his Daughter and *Alli* his Apoſtle, being of a maſculine fiery Temper, reproached the King for not reſenting ſo groſs an Affront, ſwore by her Anceſtor the Prophet, that ſhe would never ſtir out of the Tent ſhe then ſat in, till *Muſkat* was taken from the *Portugueze*. All the

Army

Army applauded the Queen, and threatned to mutiny, if they were not forthwith led by their Officers to the Scalade of the City Walls. And at laſt the King finding that no Perſwaſions could cool their Fury, tho' the Day was far ſpent, ordered them to be led on. The *Portugueze* flank'd them, from their Forts on the Mountains, with Plenty of great and ſmall Shot; but the *Arabs* never looked back, nor minded the great Numbers of their dead Companions, but mounted the Walls over the Carcaſes of their ſlain. About Sun-ſet they drove the *Portugueze* from two of the City Gates, and purſued their Enemy ſo hard, that not one eſcaped, tho' they fled in great Haſte towards the great Fort, where the Governor ſtaid. That Fort is built on a Rock almoſt ſurrounded by the Sea, and has no Way to get up to it, but by a Stair-caſe hewn out of the Rock, above 50 Yards high, and not above two or three Perſons can aſcend a-breaſt. The *Arabs* thought it impracticable to attack it, ſo made a Blocade of it. In the Attack of the Town, the *Arabs* loſt between 4 and 5000 of the beſt of their Forces; and the *Portugueze*, in their Forts, were reduced to 60 or 70. Thoſe in the ſmall Forts were obliged ſoon to ſurrender for Want of Ammunition and Proviſions; and all were put to the Sword, except thoſe, who, to ſave their Lives, promiſed to be circumciſed, and abjure the *Chriſtian* Religion. Thoſe in the great Fort held out about ſix Months, under great Want and Fatigues; and all

all Hopes of Relief being cut off, they resolved on a Surrender, on which Motion, the imprudent Governor, who was the sole Cause of their Calamity, leapt down a Precipice into the Sea, where the Water being very shallow, he was dasht to Pieces on the Rocks.

THE little Garison would fain have come to a Capitulation, but the *Arabs* would grant them no Terms, but that they must yield, or be starved ; and tho' the Terms were hard, yet they thought best to surrender, and all were put to the Sword, except a few who embraced *Mahometism*, which in all were eighteen Persons. And this Relation I had from a very old Renagado, who was at the Tragedy, being then a Soldier, who reckoned himself about 100 Years old, and, by his Aspect, could not be much less.

THE City of *Muskat* is very strong, both by Nature and Art ; but the Buildings very mean, as most Fabricks are under the Oeconomy of a People who abominate Luxury and Pride, as the *Muskat Arabs* do. The Cathedral built by the *Portugueze*, still retains some Marks of its ancient Grandeur, and is now converted into a Palace for the King, when he resides there, which is generally a Month or two yearly. The Wall of the Town that faces the Harbour, has a Battery of large Cannon, about 60 in Number, and there are 8 or 10 small Forts built on the adjacent Rocks or Mountains, which guard all the Avenues to the Town, both by Sea and Land ; and there are none permitted to

come

come in or go out of the Harbour between Sun-set and Rising.

THE Pirates that infested the *Indian* Seas at the latter End of the sixteenth Century, made a Breach between the *English* and them. The Pirates having made Prize of one of their Ships, they retaliated on the *English* private Shipping: They seized Captain *Morrices*'s little Ship, and detained him and all his Crew as Slaves, and would never ransom them. *In Anno* 1705. they took Captain *Murvel* in a rich Ship from *Bengal*, bound to *Persia*; but that might be attributed to Pusillanimity, in not offering to make a Defence.

THEY put their Slaves to no Manner of Labour, and allow them a Soldier's Pay for Subsistence; and what they can earn otherwise by Industry, is wholly their own.

THERE are neither Trees, Shrubs nor Grass to be seen on the Sea-coast from *Curiat* to *Muskat*, and but a few Date Trees in a Valley at the Back of the Town, and yet there is not the least Want of them felt in the City; and it has as good Markets for Wheat, Barley and Legumen, and for excellent Fruits, Roots and Herbage, and good Cattle, both great and small, as any where in *India*, where the Soil is most luxurious. And the Sea furnishes them with Plenty and Variety of excellent Fish. Their Cattle look to be very lean, but when killed, they are very fat and good, affording a great Deal of Tallow. They are not well stocked with Fowl, but those they have, are very good.

FROM

FROM *May* to *September* the Heats are exceſſive in the Town, ſo that none appear on the Streets, from 10 in the Morning till 3 or 4 after Noon. Their *Bazaars* or Markets are all covered with Date Tree Leaves, ſpread on Beams of the ſame Tree, that reach from Houſe to Houſe-top; and the Houſes being all flat on their Tops, terraſſed with Clay and Straw mixt, in the aforeſaid Months every Body lodges on them in the Nights; for below Stairs they cannot ſleep for Heat, and the Nights afford plentiful Dews, that ſometimes weet them thro' their thick Cotton Quilts; and theſe Dews are reckoned very ſalubrious.

THE Reaſon of ſo intenſe Heats proceeds from the Nearneſs of the Sun in thoſe Months, who ſends his Beams almoſt perpendicularly down on the Sides of the Mountains, which being all naked, and nothing but an hard black Rock appearing, the Sun heats them to ſuch a Degree, that between 10 and 11 in the Forenoon, I have ſeen the Slaves roſt Fiſh on them. And the Horſes and Cattle, who are accuſtomed to that Food, come daily, of their own Accord, to be ſerved their Allowance, and when they have breakfaſted, retire again to Shades built for them; and yet their Beef and Mutton, that are partly nouriſhed by that Sort of Food, have not the leaſt Savour of Fiſh. And the Reaſon why Fiſhes are ſo plentiful and cheap in the Markets, is by the eaſy and odd Way they have in catching them, or rather conjuring of them; for I have ſeen

a

a Man and two Boys catch a Tun Weight in an Hour or two. The Man ſtands on a Rock, where the Sea is pretty deep near it, and calls *Tall, tall*, for a Minute or two, and the Fiſh come ſwarming about the Rock. The two Boys, in a little Boat, ſhut them in with a Net about 20 or 30 Yards long, and 3 or 4 deep, and, drawing the Net near the Rock, keep all in; and, when People come for Fiſh, he asks them what Sorts they want, and puts an Hoop-net, fixed to the End of a Pole, into the Water, and ſerves every Body with what Kind they ask for; and when he has done, he hales out his Net, and gives the reſt their Liberty.

THEIR eſtabliſhed Religion is *Mahometan*, of the Sect of *Alli*. They hinder no Body, of what Perſwaſion ſoever, to go into their Moſques, even in Time of divine Service. And their *Molahs* or Prieſts often preach themſelves into violent Paſſions, eſpecially if the Subject of their Sermon be about the Verity of their Religion; and then they'll challenge the Prieſts of any other Religion whatever, to confirm theirs with as good Evidences as they can; for, being well verſed in Legerdemain Tricks, (which all we *Chriſtians*, except one Set of our Prieſts, are ignorant of) they'll take live Coals out of the Fire, and ſeem to eat them, with as good an Appetite as a School-boy can eat a *Bergamy* Pear; which Trick the poor deluded Auditory takes for a Miracle, to confirm the anctity of their Religion.

The King keeps his Court generally at *Nazawa* or *Reyſtock*, two Towns four or five Days Journey from *Muskat* within Land. He has no ſplendid Equippage, and his Garb very plain, and no finer than an ordinary Soldier's is. He has about 100 of his own Slaves armed with Matchlocks and ſhort broad Swords, for his Guard, who always attend on him. He, nor his Subjects uſe no Tables, but plain Mats ſpread on the Ground, ſerve for Table and Chairs. Their Viands are a Diſh of Rice, either plain, or made in Pillaw, and a Diſh or two more of ſtew'd or fryed Fleſh, Fiſh or Fowl, placed near the Diſh of Rice: And he, with his Table Companions, ſit on the ſame Mat, with their Buttocks on their Heels, and, in that Poſture, they feed very plentifully. Their right Hand ſerves them for Spoon, Knife and Fork, except when they eat Broth or Milk, and then they have large wooden Spoons. Their uſual Drink is Water, or ſowre Milk, and in hot Weather Sherbets.

They make no great Difference about Table Gueſts; for the King and a common Soldier, the Maſter and Slave, ſit promiſcuouſly, and dip in the ſame Diſh: But Women never eat in Company with Men. The Mens Apparel is a Pair of Breeches down to their Ancles, with a looſe Veſt on their Backs, with very large Sleeves, and the Body of the Veſt girded about their Bodies with a Saſh, and a large Turband careleſly wreath'd about their Heads, and a Poniard, or a ſhort broad

broad Sword ſtuck into their Girdle perpendicularly; their Shoes clumſily made, and very low and ſtiff at the Quarter-heels; and thus a Gentleman is equipped; but in cold Weather they uſe Camelins, a ſort of looſe Coat, without Sleeves, made of Camels Wooll. Their Women wear Breeches to their Heels, of finer Stuffs, and better Colours than the Men. The Body of the Veſt made for their Uſe, is ſtrait, but ſhort waſted, and gathered above the Navel in Plats, which makes the lower Part look like a Petticoat. Their Shoes are ſhap'd like the Mens, flat and broad.

THE Reaſon why their Shoes are made ſo, is for their eaſier ſlipping off or on, when they enter, or come out of a Room, that they may not dirty the Carpets or Mats wherewith the Rooms are ſpread, which ſerve them for Beds in cold Weather. And, except ſome large round Pillows of broad Cloth or Velvet, ſtuft with Cotton, for the Eaſe of thoſe who ſit on the Carpets or Mats, to lean upon as they ſit croſs-legg'd, there is no other Furniture in a Room.

OVER all the three *Arabias*, their Cuſtom in treating Strangers or Friends, is the ſame; for aſſoon as every one is ſeated, a Servant brings a Pot of Coffee, and ſerves it about in ſmall Cups, that contain not a Quarter of a Gill; but aſſoon as one Cup is out, they fill again, and perhaps a third Time: Then a Pipe of Tobacco is preſented, their Pipes differing much from ours in *Europe*, in Shape and Magnitude; which Service laſts till near the Time of breaking up Company, when comes in a little Pot of hot burning Coals, on which they throw ſome Chips of Agala-wood, or ſome Powder of Benjoin, Myrrh or Frankincenſe, which produce a thick Smoke, that incenſes or perfumes the whole Room. And, as I obſerved before, it is the Cuſtom of wearing very great Sleeves to their Garments. They open their Sleeves as wide as they can, and hold them over the Smoke, which perfumes their Arms, Shoulders, Neck and Beard. And the laſt Courſe is ſome Roſe-water to beſprinkle the Company, which is the Signal to be gone every one about their Buſineſs; ſo, without any Forms of Ceremony, every one walks off.

THE Products of *Arabia petrea* for Exportation, are but few, as Horſes, Dates, fine Brimſtone, ſome Coffee, but not ſo good as at *Mocha*; ſome Ruinoſs, which is the Root of a ſmall Shrub, that dies Crimſon, and ſome Pearl. Their Manufacture is ſome coarſe Cotton Linen and Camelins, which they conſume moſt in their own Country; but the *Badows* need none, ſince they wear none. The *Arabs* wear no Pearl or Gold; but the Women of Diſtinction wear Pearl of a ſmall Price, tho' I ſaw one there as big as a large Hazel-nut, exactly round, and of a fine Water. It was valued at 1000 Tomans, which is above 3000 *L. Sterl.* I have ſometimes gone in a Boat to ſee them dive for Pearl, and have bought ſome Pearl Oyſters of them; but the Divers are Cheats, putting the Oyſters

Oyſters in the Sun, which makes them gape, and then the Rogues rummage them, and ſhake out the Pearl; and, after they are robbed of their Treaſure, they put them into Water again, and they cloſe. I bought at Times above 100 Oyſters, and got nothing; they coſt me but ſeven Pence half Peny a Piece. At laſt I found one that had an Excreſcence growing to the Shell on the Inſide, which I carefully took off; and, at *Carwar* in *India*, I ſold it for 9 *L. Sterl.*

THE Women in this Country have ſome peculiar Privileges beyond the Men; for if one complain that a Man has offered Violence to her Perſon, without further Proof than her Word of Honour, he is puniſhed with 100 Baſtinadoes on the Soles of the Feet, or put into a Dungeon under Ground, which has only an Hole at the Top, big enough to receive a Man; and when he is in, there is a Stone put over the Hole, too big to be removed by a ſingle Perſon, and there he muſt ſtay three Days, and as many Nights, without Meat or Water, or Room to ly at his Length. And if a Wife complain of her Husband for Unkindneſs in any Kind, particularly of *due Benevolence*, as by Law eſtabliſhed in the *Jewiſh* and *Mahometan* Churches, the Husband muſt undergo the Puniſhment of the Dungeon. But if a Lady treſpaſſes, and her Spouſe detect her Crime, he has the Law in his own Hand, and may chaſtiſe her with the Whip ſeverely; but muſt not touch her Life, on Pain of Death.

THE *Muskat Arabs* are remarkable for their Humility and Urbanity. I had one Inſtance of their Civility. As I was one Morning walking the Streets, I met accidentally the Governor of the City, by them called the *Waaly*, and, according to my Duty, I went into the Door of a Shop, to let him and his Guards have the Street, which generally are narrow; but he obſerving, by my Complexion and Garb, that I was a Stranger, made his Guard go on one Side, and beck'ned me to come forward, and ſtood till I paſt by him. And for an Inſtance of their cool Temper, in hearing Debates and rectifying Miſtakes between Parties diſagreeing about Commerce: The before mentioned Interpreter at *Maceira*, was Commander of a Ship from *India*, and had freighted her to *Muskat*: The Freighter, who was a *Mahometan*, delayed paying the Freight, long after it was due by the Tenor of the Charter-party; upon which he being in Paſſion with the Freighter for his continued Delays, went to the *Waaly* to complain. He obſerving by the Gentleman's Countenance, that his Mind was diſcompoſed, anſwered him, that being at that Time very buſy about ſome of the King's Affairs, he had not Time to ſend for his Freighter, but deſired that he would come ſome other Time, and he would hear him, and order the Payment. The Delays ſtill continuing, the Captain went again in an angry Mood to make his Complaint, but was ſtill put off with gentle Excuſes: But at laſt addreſſing the

Waaly

Waaly with Coolneſs, he was deſired to ſit down, and he would ſend for the Freighter, which accordingly he did; and, on his Appearance, the *Waaly* askt him why he did not comply with his Contract, as was ſtipulated by Charter-party; and his Excuſes being thought inſufficient, he was ordered to make Payment forthwith, or go to Priſon; but the Freighter choſe rather to bring the Money, and end the Diſpute. The Captain askt the *Waaly* why he did not do him Juſtice ſooner, who received for Anſwer, that it was his own Fault, for coming drunk to make Complaint. The Captain proteſted that he had not been drunk in many Years; but the *Waaly* replied, that he ſaw him drunk with Paſſion, which was the moſt dangerous Sort of Drunkenneſs.

THE Countries to the Southward of *Muſkat*, as far as *Curia Muria*, are under the Dominions of *Muskat*, and the *Sheeks* or Princes are their Tributaries. The Land is mountainous; but the Plains and Vallies very fertil and well watered, and conſequently well peopled. And, to the Northward of *Muskat*, the ſame Chain of rocky Mountains continue as high as *Zoar*, above Cape *Muſenden*, which Cape and Cape *Jaques* begin the Gulf of *Perſia*, on the *Arabian* Side. About *Zoar* begins the Deſert, that runs as far northerly as *Aleppo*. The Monntains near the Sea, are ſandy, and the Vallies and Plains ſteril, and ill inhabited, and as ill watered.

About the Year 1620. *Persia* was in a flourishing Condition, and was a Terror to all its Neighbours. *Shaw Tamas*, Son to the famous *Shaw Abass*, was then King, and being of a martial Disposition, had a Design to annex all the *Arabian* Coast opposite to *Persia*, to his own Dominions, and accordingly transported from *Cong*, a City of his own that lies on the Sea-shore, an Army of 35 or 40000 Men to conquer it. The Army met with no Opposition in landing, and they soon over-ran the Country wherever they went; but they had not been long in Pursuit of their Conquest, till Provisions began to be scarce in the Army, which, with the Scarcity of fresh Water, and the intolerable Heats, both of Sun and Winds, brought a Contagion on the *Persians*, that killed the better Half of them, and obliged what was left to return back to *Persia* by Shipping, as they had come from it.

Those barren Coasts are needlesly secured by sandy Banks, that run 10 or 12 Leagues off from the Shore, which would make Navigation impracticable, if it should meet with Encouragement; but the two Islands of *Bareen*, lying in the Latitude of 29 Degrees 30 Minutes, almost in the Bottom of the Gulf, and belonging to the Crown of *Persia*, have the best Pearl Fishing in the World.

About the Beginning of this Century, the *Muskat Arabs* took Possession of *Bareen* Islands; but the honest Pearl Fishers deserted it whilst the *Arabs* kept Possession, who finding

finding that their new Settlement could not defray the Charge of keeping, without the Pearl Fishers, they left it; and the Fishers, who are mostly *Arabs*, returned to their Industry, and continue the Fishery.

THE great *Turk* gives Laws to all the Countries that ly between the River *Euphrates* and *Ethiopia*; but there are many Sheeks who inhabit those Deserts, that make but small Account of him or his Orders, because the Sterility of their Country makes them secure from great Armies coming amongst them, and a small one dares not venture amongst them as Enemies. They being naturally Thieves, rob Friend or Foe, or one another; so that few People of Substance have any Commerce with them.

THERE are no Towns of Note between *Muskat* and *Bassòra*, but *Zoar*, and but very few inconsiderable Villages; but there are two or three pretty convenient Harbours for Shipping. The southermost is about 6 Leagues to the Southward of Cape *Mosenden*, called *Courforcaun*. It is almost like *Muskat* Harbour, but somewhat bigger, and has excellent fresh Water in deep Wells, about a Quarter of a Mile from the Landing-place. The Village contains about twenty little Houses; yet there are pretty good Refreshments to be had there. Cape *Mosenden* is of itself but a good Number of small high Islands lying near one another, but they appear like a Promontory on *Terra firma*. And up to the Westward of the Cape there is another Harbour,

bour, whose Name I have forgot; but there are good fresh Water and animal Provisions to be had there. And now having described *Muskat* and its Territories as well as I can, I'll make one Observation more, and proceed on my Travels.

EVER since the *Portugueze* left *Muskat* to the *Arabs*, there has been a continual War; but in the main the *Arabs* have been the Gainers, yet they have been obliged to build and buy Ships of Force to confront the *Portugueze* at Sea, and to keep their Coasts free from their Insults. Their Fleets have often met, and had some Engagements, but few Ships have been taken or sunk on either Side; but Merchant Ships of both Sides have been taken. The *Portugueze* use their Captives with great Severity, making them labour hard, and inure them to the Discipline of the Whip; but the *Arabs* use theirs with very much Humanity, only making them Prisoners at large, without putting them to hard Labour, and allow them as much Diet Money as their own Soldiers receive, and that is duly paid them twice a Month. And if any of the *Portugueze* are Artificers or Mechanicks, they may freely work at their Trade, to earn Money to redeem themselves.

In Anno 1715. the *Arabian* Fleet consisted of one Ship of 74 Guns, two of 60, one of 50, and 18 small Ships from 32 to 12 Guns each, and some Trankies or rowing Vessels from 4 to 8 Guns each, with which Sea Forces they keep all the Sea-coasts in Aw, from Cape *Co-*

merin

merin to the *Red Sea*. They have often made Deſcents on the *Portugueze* Colonies on the Coaſt of *India*, deſtroying their Villages and Farms, but ſpare the Churches, for better Reaſons than we can give for plundring them. They kill none in cold Blood, but uſe their Captives courteouſly. *In Anno* 1695. they quarrelled with the *Carnatick Rajah*, a potent Prince by Land; yet they came with their Fleet, and plundred and burned the Towns of *Barſalore* and *Mangulore*, two of the beſt and richeſt Towns on that Coaſt. And now I leap from *Muskat* to

CHAP. VIII.

Gives an Account of Baſſora *City, and that Part of* Arabia deſerta; *with Remarks on its Government and Commerce, and ſome Occurrences, both ancient and modern, that have happened to it*; *with ſome Account of the famous River of* Euphrates.

BASSORA is the eaſtmoſt City or Town in the *Turkiſh* Dominions, ſtanding about two Miles from the famous *Euphrates*, and has a ſmall Rivulet that waſhes its Walls on the Weſt Side, and diſcharges its Waters into the *Euphrates*. This City ſtands about 30 Leagues from the Sea, and it is alledged, was built by the Emperor *Trajan*, and had the Honour to be the Birth-place of another *Roman* Emperor, *Philip* ſirnamed the *Ara-*

bian:

bian: But at first it was built along the Side of the River, and the *Vestigia* of its ancient Walls are still to be seen from the aforesaid Rivulet, a League down the Banks of *Euphrates*, which disembogues her Waters, by four or five Mouths, into the Gulf of *Persia*; but none navigable for Ships of Burden, but that Chanel that leads to *Bassora*. At the City it is a short Mile over at high Water, and it keeps about the same Breadth to the very Mouth of it.

THE River abounds in Fish, but none good, except a small Shad about the Bigness of an Herring. And there is great Plenty of wild Fowl, such as Swans, Geese, Duck, Teal, Wigeon and Curlews; and the Fields have Plenty of Partridge of several Kinds, Plover, Snipes, Doves, Pigeons and large Larks, whose Flesh is very savoury, and their wild Notes grateful to the Ear. They have also Birds of Prey, as Eagles, many Sorts and Sizes of Hawks, and Kites, Crows black and white, and it is observable, that the black keep the *Arabian* Side of the River, and the white the *Persian*, and if any presume to interlope into anothers Province, they raise the *Posse*, and drive them back to their own Territories.

THERE is great Plenty of small Tortois in the River; but none eat them, because they are forbidden in the *Levitical* Law, to which the *Mahometans* adhere much in Point of eating. They have also many Species of wild Beasts. Wild Swine are very numerous, and

and their Flesh is very sweet and juicy, but no Fat to be seen about them. And the Peasants come often to Town to invite *Christians* to kill them; for they make sad Havock of their Corn and Roots. And if a *Christian* kills any, they'll bring them to their Houses on Asses or Mules, for a very small Reward, notwithstanding there is a positive Command in the *Alcoran*, that forbids them to touch Swine's Flesh.

THEY have Plenty of black Cattle, wild and tame, and good Milk; but they make but scurvy Cheese of it, and no Butter, because they make the Fat of their Sheeps Tails serve in their Kitchens instead of Butter; and they keep no Tea-tables for the Consumption of fresh Butter. And Coffee, which is much in Use, is the constant Companion of a Pipe of Tobacco, which is taken by the Ladies as well as Gentlemen. In the Desert, which is very near the Town, there are wild Camels, Horses, Asses, Goats, Lions, Leopards, Panthers and Foxes, which they hunt on Horse-back, with Sword and Lance, and on Foot with Fowling-pieces. They have Plenty of delicious Fruits, as Pomegranates, Peaches, Apricocks, Quinces, Olives, Apples, Pears, Nectarines and Grapes that are as sweet as the Juice of the Suggar-cane, and their Spirits are so weak, that they'll produce neither Wine nor Vinegar: But the most plenty and useful of all their Fruits, are their Dates, which support and sustain many Millions of People, who make them their daily Food,

Food, and they are wonderfully nourifhed by them. *Baſſora* exports yearly for foreign Countries, above 10000 Tuns of Dates, which employ Abundance of Seamen for their Exportation, befides many more Poor in gathering and packing them in Mats made of the Leaves of the Date Tree, and likewife in drying them. I bought about 160 Pound Weight of wet Dates for 2 *ſh.* 3 *d. Sterl.* and fometimes they are cheaper.

THE Ruines of the famous *Babylon* ly about 200 *Engliſh* Miles up the River from *Baſſora*; and at *Bagdat*, which is 12 Miles below it, the Ruines appear to be a Mountain, and are the Habitation of wild Beafts and Serpents. Whether *Bagdat* was built out of its Ruines, or no, I know not; but 'tis reported, and generally believed that it was. It is now a prodigious large City, and the Seat of a *Beglerbeg*, who governs a very great Province. The Bafhaws of *Baſſora*, *Comera* and *Muſol* (the ancient *Nineveh*) are fubordinate to him, and are able to bring 150000 Men into the Field.

Comera ftands on the Banks of *Euphrates*, about 80 Miles above *Baſſora*, and, by common Tradition, is the Place where holy *Job* dwelt. It abounds in all Things that *Baſſora* produces, *viz.* Fruits, Roots, Herbs and Animals: Befides, it is very fruitful in producing Wheat, Rice, and Pulfe of feveral Species. There is a Garifon of 10000 Janifaries continually kept there, and 8 or 10 River Gallies, well furnifhed, to aw the circumjacent

cent Countries, who are apt to rebel. And *Bassora* has 3000 Janisaries and 5 Gallies for the same Account. The Bashaws of the Gallies are not subordinate to the Bashaws of the Cities; but he of the Gallies has the Command of the circumjacent Countries, laying on of Taxes, and raising Subsidies at his Pleasure, as he of the Cities has Power to oppress the Citizens: And their Avarice and Severity often cause Mutinies and Blood-shed. One of those Mutinies happened at *Bassora*, *in Anno* 1721. for the Bashaw of the City having married a Lady out of the *Grand Seignior*'s *Seraglio*, and that Monarch having some Deference for her on Account of Consanguinity, her Husband was put into the Bashaw's Ship to get Money to support his Lady's Extravagancy; and finding that fair honest Ways would be a long While in raising such Sums as he thought would be sufficient for that End, opprest both City and Country to fill his Coffers. The poor opprest Merchants, Mechanicks and Peasants plied him with Complaints on his Soldiery, who, they thought, robbed them, since the Exactions were new. They gave in Remonstrances of their Grievances, and petitioned for Redress; but the Persons sent with those Addresses, had the Bastinado for their Impertinence. Upon this the distressed City and Country made their Address to the Bashaw of the Gallies, who knew they had just Cause of Complaint. He wrote to the *Beglerbeg*, and informed him of their Case and Condition, and obtained a severe

vere Reprimand; for he of the City, inſtead of Amendment, added Cruelties to Oppreſſion, and murdred many who would not, or could not pay what they were ſeſſed at, which unheard of Barbarities made above 50000 of the City and Country betake themſelves to Arms, and march out, with the *Mufti* or high Prieſt at their Head; and he had a green Flag, which is *Mahomet*'s Banner, before him, carried by a Prieſt; and he and his Army encamped near the Baſhaw of the Gallies his Houſe, which ſtands about two Miles below the City, by the River Side; and the Baſhaw of the Gallies joined them with 1000 Janiſaries. The *Mufti*, according to Cuſtom, plied his ſpiritual Artillery, and excommunicated the Baſhaw of the City, and all that adhered to him. This Mutiny continued ſome Days; but I heard of no Bloodſhed, and only opprobrious Language paſt. But the Town began to feel Want, for the Peaſants would bring no Eatables to the City; but the *Mufti*'s Hoſt were plentifully ſupplied. All Shops being ſhut up, and all the Markets unprovided, made the Baſhaw of the City begin to think what the End would be, if the Mutiny continued any longer; ſo he got ſome Country Gentlemen, who were of neither Faction, to go to the *Mufti* and the Baſhaw of the Gallies, as Mediators; and accordingly they went, and were handſomly received, and, in their Oration on the preſent Poſture of Affairs, made the *Mufti* and his Party incline to Peace, pro-

providing that about a Dozen of Incendiaries might be delivered to them, to receive condign Puniſhment for their Faults. All the proſcribed, but one, by the Interceſſion of Friends, were pardoned; but they would hear of no Peace till the other was made a Sacrifice to their juſt Reſentment: for this Villain would accoſt a Merchant in the Street, and, after common Compliments were ended, he would ask them what became of the Diamonds, or other Jewels, that they had ſhewn him ſuch a Time. The innocent Merchant, who perhaps never had any Jewels, being ſurpriſed at his Queſtion, would deny that ever they had any ſuch as he ſpake of. Then the impudent Fellow would tell them plainly, that without they would bribe him with a round Sum, he would inform the Baſhaw, that he had ſeen ſuch Quantities of rough Diamonds, or other valuable Stones, in their Poſſeſſion, and if they could not be found entred in the Cuſtom-houſe Books, they muſt expect to ſuffer what Puniſhment the Baſhaw would pleaſe to inflict for defrauding the King of his Cuſtoms. Some out of Fear would comply, and give a Sum, others again ſtood on their Innocence, and would not give him Money; and they were ſure to be informed againſt, and brought before the Baſhaw, and, upon that Villain's Evidence, were generally fined about double of what he askt of them; ſo that beſides the great Sums that came into the Baſhaw's Coffers by that Raſcal's Ingenuity, he had accumulated twenty five Bags to himſelf, each Bag containing 500 Crowns, and all this in the Space of three Years that he had been in *Baſſora*; for he came from *Conſtantinople* one of the Baſhaw's Retinue, hardly worth an *Aſper*, and at his Death ſo much ready Caſh was found in his Houſe, which fell into his Maſter the Baſhaw's Hands: For after this Villain was culled out to be ſacrificed to the juſt Reſentment of the People, and found that they would not be appeaſed without having his Life, he fell at his Maſter's Feet for Protection. The cunning covetous Baſhaw bid him convey what Money he had to his Houſe, and he would take Care of it for the Uſe of his Wife and Children, and would ſend him ſecretly out of the Town, and get him ſafely conducted to *Comera*. He ſwallowed that Bait, and delivered his ill-gotten Money to his Maſter, who protected him but one ſingle Day, and then told him, that the People's Clamours were ſo great, that he could protect him no longer; and accordingly he was delivered to the enraged Mob, who forthwith ſtrangled him, and threw his Body on a Dung-hill by the Side of an High-way, where I ſaw it two Days after. And the Mufti and Baſhaw made Matters up for the Eaſe and Satisfaction of the People, who grew quite tired of their Diviſions.

Baſſora was many Years in the Hands of the *Perſians*, who gave great Encouragement to Trade, which drew many Merchants from foreign Parts to ſettle there, and particularly

cularly from *Surat* in *India*. But *in Anno* 1691. a Pestilence raged so violently, that above 80000 People were carried off by it, and those that remained fled from it, so that for three Years following it was a Desert, inhabited only by wild Beasts, who were at last driven out of the Town by the circumjacent wild *Arabs*, who possest it about 12 Months, and were in their Turn driven out by the *Turk*, who keeps it till this Day; but its Trade is very inconsiderable to what it was in the Times that the *Persians* had it, and the Reason is, that the *Turks* are very insolent to stranger Merchants. *In Anno* 1721. I had an Instance of their arbitrary Insolence, for I sold a considerable Quantity of Pepper, which some stranger Merchants bargained to take at 28 *Mamoodies* * a *Maund Attarie*, without Deductions. The Bashaw being made acquaint with the Contract, sent Orders, that the Pepper must be delivered to two Minions of his at 24 *Mamoodies*, and allow them † *Turk* and *Burk*, which is a Piece of Stone or Brick between a Pound and an half or two Pounds Weight, into the Scale with the Standard Weights, besides the Tare of the Bags. I at first refused to comply with the unjust Order, and stood out three or four Days, but at last was advised by some *Surat* Merchants (who were there, and had met

† F 2 with

* 28 *Mamoodies* are 17 *s.* 6 *d.* A *Maund Attarie* is 28 *lib.*
† *Turk* and *Burk* is a customary Donation, such as Tret in *Britain*.

with as great Oppreſſions) to obey, leſt I ſhould run the Riſque of being plundred by the Soldiery.

THERE are many *Jews* in *Baſſora* who live by Brokrage and exchanging Money; but the *Turks* keep that Set of People very low, for Reaſons of State. There are alſo about 200 *Chriſtians* of the *Greek* Church, but no Prieſts of that Communion, wherefore ſome *Roman* Miſſionaries officiate there. The *Greek* Clergy are very indifferent about gaining Proſelytes, and, to nouriſh their Flocks, will not run the Riſque of Martyrdom, ſo they keep none of their Prieſthood at *Baſſora:* But when I was there, three *Romiſh* Prieſts of the *Carmelite* Order had the Superintendency of that Church. Theſe ſanctified Raſcals were a Scandal to *Chriſtianity*, by making a Tavern of their Church; for having more Indulgence from the Government than the *Mahometans*, in moral Matters, they abuſe it to the vileſt Uſes, in ſelling Arrack, which they diſtil from Dates, and procuring Birds of Paradiſe for the Uſe of their Cuſtomers. The *Mahometans* again are forbidden ſtrictly the Drinking of Wine or diſtilled Liquors, both by their eccleſiaſtick and civil Laws; for the Heat of the Sun, and the dry ſandy Soil create much aduſt Choler in their Brains, that when they are heated by drinking ſtrong Liquors, they become furious and miſchievous to one another, and, in thoſe mad Fits, wound and kill their Fellows. Thoſe ſcandalous Prieſts had been often reprimanprimanded by the Government, for abusing the Indulgence they had, but to little Purpose, for their Trade was very gainful; but, upon a drunken Quarrel between two Seamen of mine, wherein one was dangerously wounded with a Knife, and the other, for Fear of Punishment, turned *Mahometan*, being before a *Portugueze Christian*, the Bashaw sent an Officer and Soldiers to enter the Church, and all the Houses appertaining to it, with Orders to break their Stills and Jars, with the rest of the distilling Utensils, and to pour out all the Arrack they found, on the Ground, which was accordingly done; and, in the Search, the Soldiers met with a fine Silver Watch, and about 400 *Spanish* Dollars, which they carried off with them. The Priests petitioned the Bashaw to have the Watch and Money restored; but were answered, that they preacht much on the Contempt of worldly Riches, and if his Soldiers had made them practise what they preacht, they ought to be thankful, and to let the despicable Money continue in Hands that profest their Love of it, and knew much better how to use it than Priests, and so dismist them, with Threats of harder Penalties on their next Transgression: But the Sweets of worldly Gains soon made them forget the Admonition given them by the Bashaw, as well as their heavenly Promises and Oaths made at their Admission into their holy Order; and, like a Dog to his Vomit, returned back to their old Trade of debauching *Christians*,

Jews, *Mahometans* and *Pagans* with Liquors, and ſet up Stills for that Purpoſe once more.

NOTWITHSTANDING that the *Turkiſh* Government is ſo well eſtabliſhed by Severity, and even Cruelty when their Laws are tranſgreſſed, yet the *Arabs*, who are the natural Lords of their own Country, are not to be rigorouſly dealt with, for they are a People very bold, revengeful and cunning. While I was at *Baſſora*, a Parcel of Janiſaries were ſent to the Iſland of *Gabon*, which lies between the City and the Mouth of the River *Euphrates*. The Weſt End is waſhed by a Branch of the River, which runs into the Sea, and the North Side by the main River for 25 Leagues, till it diſembogues into the Sea by the Chanel for Shipping. It being pretty well inhabited, and the Baſhaw impoſing exorbitant Taxes on thoſe poor Iſlanders, which they either would not, or could not pay, ſent the aforementioned Janiſaries to dragoon them into Compliance. They firſt built a Sconce, and fortified it, both to ſecure themſelves from ſudden Attacks or Surprize, as well as to hold what they might diſtrain from the poor Peaſants. Many of thoſe poor Wretches having experimented the *Turkiſh* wholeſom Chaſtiſements of plundring and baſtonading thoſe who ſcrupled to obey, or were not able to pay what they were taxed, making their Complaints to one another, and bewailing the Miſery that they underwent by the inexorable Janiſaries, took Counſel to ferret them off their Iſland at the

the Hazard of their Lives, rather than continue under the unsupportable Yoke they were in; wherefore about three hundred of them prepared for an Attack on the Janisaries little Fort, with no other Weapons than Lances and Swords. There were about forty Janisaries in the Fort, well armed with Guns; but the *Arabs* defeated the Design of Powder and Ball, by making up great Bundles of Straw, that covered them intirely from Head to Foot whilst their Faces were towards their Enemy. They waited a convenient Time when the Wind was pretty high, and marching towards the windwardmost Part of the Fort, set Fire to their Straw, whose Blaze and Smoke kept the Janisaries clear from molesting them to windward. There were some Shades within the Fort, built of Date Tree Leaves, for lodging the Garison, but they took Fire also; and five or six Barrels of Powder blowing up, destroyed most of the Janisaries, and some few who leapt down the Outside of the Wall, were killed with the Sword; so that, between Fire and Sword, not one escaped. I saw some of the slaughtered and half-burnt Carcases brought up to the City next Day after the Tragedy was acted; but the Commotions that had happened before in the City, made the Bashaw bridle his Resentment, since it was his own Avarice that begat both Mutinies.

THE Horses in this Part of *Arabia* are very well shapt, and mettlesom, and the Men the moſt dextrous in managing them that ever I ſaw. They ſhoot with Bow and Arrow, and throw their Lance at full Speed, and very ſeldom miſs the Mark. They will ſtoop at full Speed, and take up an Hare as ſhe runs, with their Hands, or throw a Lance in the Air, and catch it before it comes to the Ground: And indeed the moſt of their Exerciſe, whilſt young, is in managing their Horſes.

THEY have many Boats on the River, of ſeveral Shapes and Dimenſions; ſome are made of Wood, with high broad Boughs, and very long, others are very ſhort: Their Rudders are in Breadth a Quarter Part of their Keel's Length, but not intire of one Piece as ours are, and they daub them over Outſide and Inſide with Bitumen, without caulking them; others are Baskets made of Reeds, perfectly round, with two Sticks laid athwart croſs-ways their Bottoms to keep them open. They are alſo daub'd on the Outſide and Bottom with Bitumen. And this Sort they make uſe of to tranſport Goods from Place to Place. Bitumen is a thick ſulphurous and unctious Matter, generated in the Earth there, and boils up of its own Accord to the Surface; and ſometimes it is ſo hot, that it ſcalds the Hands or Feet of them that go to gather it. And there are ſome hot Pits in the Ground, that putting a Pot over them, they'll boil Meat. There is alſo Oyl of *Peter* in thoſe Grounds, which is very good in healing rheumatick Pains.

CHAP.

CHAP. IX.

Gives a Description of the Sea-coast of Persia, *from* Euphrates *to* Gombroon, *with the Places of Commerce on the* Persian *Side of the Gulf.*

THEY have a Tradition, that between *Bassora* and *Comera* was *Job*'s Habitation, if he had any; but that is out of my Sphere, and so I'll travel down the *Euphrates* again towards *Persia.*

FOR above 20 Leagues to the eastward of the Chanel for Shipping, or from *Margan* Point, the Land is very low and marish, and is overgrown with Reeds and Shrubs, which, in the Month of *August*, are very dry by the extreme Heats of *June* and *July*; and the Winds blowing fresh, put them in so great Agitation, that by Friction they take Fire; so that before we see any Land, we see great Smokes by Day, and great Fires by Night, of 4 or 5 Leagues long. But at *Durea*, which I take to be the eastermost Branch of the River, the Land is pretty high, and some Date Trees to be seen from the Sea. And the first Mountains that appear in *Persia*, are those of *Bander-dillon*, which is a large Town on the Sea-coast. It has large Plains near it, that produce Plenty of Wheat and Barley, and have good Pasturage for Horses and Cattle. As also does *Bander-rick*, another Sea-port Town, and may be seen plainly from the Sea; but the Bay is shallow so far off, that

that a Ship cannot come within three Leagues of it; however it has pretty good inland Trade, by reason of its Vicinity to *Shyrash*, the second Town in *Persia* for Magnitude, from whence it is but six Days Journey for Beasts of Carriage.

Bowchier is also a maritim Town, about 12 Leagues to the Southward of *Banderrick*. It stands on an Island, and has a pretty good Trade, both by Sea and Land.

THE Islands of *Carrack* ly, about West North-west, 12 Leagues from *Bowchier*. One of them has no Inhabitants but Deer and Antelopes. The southermost has between 2 and 300 poor Fishers on it, who serve Shipping with Pilots for *Bassora*. It affords good Mutton and Fish, and Potatoes and Onions, with good Water. The Anchoring-place is at the North End of the inhabited Island, in 12 Fathoms Water. Their Language is *Arabick*, and Religion *Mahometan*.

ABOUT 7 Leagues to the Southward of *Bowchier*, on the Sea-coast, is *Curchoir*, where are the Ruines of a large Castle and Pier that jets a pretty Way into the Sea. They were built by the *Portugueze*, who kept a Garison there, and had Gallies continually cruizing about in the Bottom of the Gulf, to compel all Ships that traded there, or to *Bassora*, to pay 10 *per Cent*. Toll or Customs to them. There is nothing else to invite Observation for Travellers, from *Curchoir* to *Congoun*, which is about 30 Leagues, but

high

high, dry, barren Mountains, and hideous Precipices.

Congoun ſtands on the South Side of a large River, and makes a pretty good Figure in Trade; for moſt of the Pearl that are caught at *Bareen*, on the *Arabian* Side, are brought hither for a Market, and many fine Horſes are ſent thence to *India*, where they generally ſell well. And four Days Journey within Land, is the City of *Laar*, which, according to their fabulous Tradition, is the Burying-place of *Lot*, and they pretend to ſhew his Tomb ſtill; but they do not know a Word about the poor Woman his Wife. That there are many Mountains of Rock Salt there, is very certain.

THE next maritim Town, down the Gulf, is *Cong*. where the *Portugueze* had lately a Factory, but of no great Figure in Trade, tho' the Town has a ſmall Trade with *Banyans* and *Moors* from *India*. The many Inſults the *Muskat Arabs* give it with their Fleet, frighten Merchants of conſiderable Stocks from frequenting it. After the *Portugueze* loſt *Ormus*, and a Peace made with *Shaw Abaſs* the King of *Perſia*, they were permitted to ſettle at *Cong*. But that King built the City of

Gombroon, or, as the Natives call it, *Bander Abaſſi*, or the Sea port of *Abaſſi*. This City ſtands on a Bay, about 4 Leagues to the Northward of the Eaſt End of the Iſland of *Kiſmiſh*, and 3 Leagues from the famous *Ormuze*, which the *Engliſh* had ſo great an

Hand

Hand in reducing to the Obedience of *Shaw Abaſs*. What Time the *Portugueze* ſettled on *Ormuze* I know not, nor could I ever learn from the *Perſians* that I converſed with, when they did ſettle; but finding it a convenient Place to tyrannize over the Traders into the Gulf of *Perſia*, they built a large Fort on the Eaſt End of it, almoſt environed by the Sea that waſhes the Fort Walls. This *Gombroon* was formerly a Fiſhing Town, and, when *Shaw Abaſs* began to build it, had its Appellation from the *Portugueze* in Deriſion, becauſe it was a good Place for catching Prawns or Shrimps, which they call *Camerong*. The *Engliſh* and *Dutch* have their Factories here, which bring a good Commerce to it; and the *French* formerly had their Factory too. It is ill ſeated, and wants almoſt every Thing that contributes to the Support of human Life, except Fiſh and Mutton; yet, for many Years, it has been well peopled by reaſon of its Trade, which has filled the Pockets of many Merchants, who, at their firſt ſettling there, were very empty. They have no drinkable Water within three Miles of the Town, except a few Ciſterns, which are dry above one Half of the Year: And the Hills, near it, are barren, and the very Rocks taſte of Salt. And, when Rain falls, which is but ſeldom, the Rivulets (which are filled by the Waters running down the Hills into low Grounds) bear a Cruſt of fine white Salt on their Sides, but is bitteriſh, by reaſon of too much Nitre

and

and Sulphur in its Composition. People of Distinction and Fortune keep a Camel or two daily employed in bringing them fresh wholesom Water from *Asseen*, about 15 Miles from the City, because the Water of *Naban*, which is three Miles off, is not accounted salubrious. There is an high Mountain that lies North from *Gambroon*, about 8 Leagues, whose Reflection of Heat on the lower Ground, in the Summer Months, almost fires the Air, which creates much Uneasiness and Unhealthfulness to the Inhabitants of *Gombroon*; wherefore most of them retire into the Country, to pass the Heats of *June*, *July* and *August*, whose Heats affect the Sea, in so much that in *August* there comes a Stink from it, that is as detestable as the Smell of dead Animals on the Land; and vast Quantities of small Shell Fish are thrown on the Shore by the Surges of the Sea; from them I judge the intolerable Stink proceeds. It tarnishes Gold and Silver, as bad as the bilge Water of a tight Ship.

About 10 Miles from *Asseen*, at the Foot of the aforesaid Mountain, is a Place called *Minoa*, where are natural cold and hot Baths, which cure Itches, Poxes, Leprosy and rheumatick Pains, only by bathing, for they are not drinkable; and some that try to drink them, and get a few Spoonfuls down, find them powerful Emeticks. There are two or three little Choulteries or Shades built for Patients to rest in; but there are no People that inhabit near it, so that whoever goes there,

there, muſt carry all Neceſſaries or Conveniencies along with them.

At *Aſſeen* there are many Gardens, where the Inhabitants of *Gombroon* retire to in the hot Months; but the *Engliſh Eaſt-india* Company's is the beſt, and beſt cultivated. It produces Plenty of *Seville* Oranges, whoſe Trees are always verdant, and bear ripe and green Fruit, with Bloſſoms, all at once. In the hot Seaſon it is well watered from its Wells, ſo that Roots and Herbage are plentiful, and good in their Seaſons, which ſupply the Factory at *Gombroon*: And there is pretty good Fowling and Hunting in that Plain, but the Road to the Town is only paſſable for Men, and Aſſes or Camels, but not for Horſes: Nor are there any Houſes on the Road, but one *Fackire*'s or Beggar's Lodge. But *Naban* is a Village pretty well peopled, and has one Tree, or rather a Wood ſprung from the Root of a Tree, whoſe Branches ſpread wide, and from them other Branches deſcend to the Ground, and take Root, and the Branches of them ſpread as the firſt did, that it became near three hundred Yards from one End to another, and could ſhelter 10000 Men from the Heat of the Sun. The Leaves are large and thick, and it bears a red Berry, only uſeful for Crows and Parrots, who alſo build Neſts on the Tree.

Gombroon is very unhealthy for *Europeans*, occaſioned by the ſcorching Heat of Summer, and peircing Cold of Winter; for as thoſe that ſtay there in Summer have Windchimchimnies to cool and fan them, so they are obliged, in Winter, to wear Cloth Coats, lined with Fur, to keep them warm. The *Europeans* often hasten Death sooner than he would come of his own Accord, by Intemperance and Debauchery of several Kinds; and they have a Burial-place pretty near the Town, well stored with Tombs, but never a *Christian* Church in this Town, tho' the *Portugueze* have one at *Cong*, where generally reside a Priest or two, who subsist on Alms and Perquisites. When an *English* or *Dutch* Heretick marry, or bring the Fruits of their Labour to Light unmarried, then the Priest is sent for to make the Infant a *Christian*; but we officiate in Burials ourselves.

THE animal Provisions of Cattle, Sheep, Goat, Fowl and Fish, are all in their Kind good, and pretty cheap; but they kill no Cows publickly, because the *Banyans* from *India*, who make a good Figure in the Town, and are pretty numerous, give the *Shanasheen* or Governor, a yearly Present of Value, to prohibit Cow-killing, for they being all *Pythagoreans* in the Belief of Transmigration, worship that Beast in as great a Degree of Veneration as a *Papist* does the Image of a Saint given him for a Protector. The Devotees of both differ not much in Point of Adoration; for setting aside the Divinity of Cattle, who till the Ground, and nourish them by their Milk, which, they say, is more than a dead Image can do, they have greater Antiquity, and as great Authority as *Christian* Idola-

Idolaters can pretend to. Their Books are as numerous, and their Traditions and Legends as full in relating Prophecies uttered by the Cow, as well as Miracles performed by her, as the others can boaſt of done by their Images; ſo they laugh at a *Papiſt* that calls them Idolaters.

THE Grapes, Melons and Mangoes that ſupply the Market of *Gombroon*, come from the high Mountain beforementioned, or from the Vallies on the North Side of it. In *November* and *December* the Snow falls ſo plentifully on that Mountain, as well as on others to the Southward of it; that it clothes them in white generally till the Month of *March*.

IN *Auguſt* the poorer Sort of People go up the Country to their Date Harveſt; and for a Month's Time that the Harveſt laſts, we can hardly find Boatmen and Porters enow to lade or unlade our Shipping, which often proves very inconvenient for thoſe whoſe Voyage depends on quick Diſpatch. And the Winds blowing then hard at South-weſt from the *Arabian* Shore, bring along with them ſuch Clouds of ſcorching Sands, that the Sun is obſcured by them.

A memorable Accident happened about the Year 1712. to two *French* Gentlemen, who, contrary to the Advice of their Friends at *Gombroon*, would needs travel in the Month of *July*, for *Iſpahan*, the Metropolis of *Perſia*, which lies 700 *Engliſh* Miles from *Gombroon*. The Chief of the *Engliſh* Factory, who was a Gentleman of much Candor and Probity, and

and had travelled that Road ſeveral Times, told them of the Danger of ſuffocating Heats that they muſt paſs through the firſt three Stages of their Journey; for there are ſome deep Caverns in the Sides of ſome Mountains, commonly called by the Inhabitants, *Hell's Mouths*, which ſometimes ſend forth ſuch hot dry Winds, that kill Man and Beaſt, if they do not ſhun them, which is done by falling flat on the Ground, and placing their Cattle's Rumps to the Wind, whilſt they ly on their Bellies. Thoſe Blaſts may be ſeen ſome Minutes before they come near enough to Men or Beaſts to hurt them, and, in a Minute or two, they blow over, being confined to a ſmall Space of Ground to blow on. The general Rule for Travellers, is to ſet out between three and four in the Morning, and travel to Nine, which Rule thoſe *French* Gentlemen obſerved, and being fatigued by their Morning's Journey, aſſoon as they came to a *Caravanſeray*, (which are Lodgings built at every Stage's End, a Stage being about 15 Miles) they were diſpoſed to reſt, and ordered their Servants to make their Beds ready, (for even thoſe neceſſary Furniture Travellers are obliged to carry with them on Carriage-beaſts) and ordered their Servants to call them when Dinner was ready, and withal ordered a Sheet for each of them to be dipt in Water, to lay over them, in order to cool them. One of thoſe hot Blaſts unfortunately came whilſt the Gentlemen ſlept, and had left the Windows of the Room open, and the Wind blowing in at the Windows, ſcorcht them both to Death on their Beds, where the Servants found them when Dinner was ready, and pulling off the Sheets, the Skin and ſome Fleſh came off with them.

I obſerved before, that *Iſpahan* is diſtant from *Gombroon* about 700 Miles, and yet I have known a Foot-poſt bring Letters in 11 Days from thence, tho' the Ways are ſo bad, that Horſes cannot travel it in that Time.

Shyraſh is a large City on the Road, about 550 Miles from *Gombroon*, in a fine, pleaſant fertil Country, that produces Fruits of all Sorts, excellent in their Kinds, particularly Apples, Pears, Plumbs, Figs, Wall-nuts, Cheſnuts, Hazel-nuts, Piſtacio-nuts, and Grapes which afford good Wines, and Raiſins, and is ſo well ſtored with Roſes, that they can yearly export 2000 Cheſts of Roſe-water, beſides ten Times as much ſpent in *Perſia*, *Arabia* and *Induſtan*. A Cheſt contains about 12 *Engliſh* Gallons, carefully put up in thin Flasks or Bottles. The *Mahometans* are forbid to meddle with Wine, therefore the *Armenian Chriſtians* (who are very numerous in *Perſia*) have the Privilege of making Wines, moſt excellent in their Kind; and it is a Queſtion whether the World affords better, for they are excellent Stomachicks, and being ſtrong, they'll bear four Times the Quantity of Water to mix with them, without being flat; and the Mixture has a very fine Flavour. They make alſo Brandy and Vinegar,

negar, but, tho' much ſtronger, not ſo palatable as what *France* produces; ſo that this Country, which formerly was a Kingdom of itſelf, not only produces what is convenient for itſelf, but exports large Quantities of Wines, Brandy, Vinegar, Roſe-water, Raiſins and Figs, with the aforementioned Nuts, which greatly increaſe the Wealth of the Country, which alſo abounds in good Wheat, Peaſe and Barley for its own Conſumption: And their Beef, Mutton and Fowl are exceeded by none in *Europe*.

About 5 Leagues off the Road of *Iſpahan*, are the Ruines of the famous *Perſepolis*, that mad *Alexander* of *Macedon* burnt at the Requeſt of a Strumpet: And, as I have been informed by ſeverals that had the Curioſity to ſee thoſe Ruines, in their Way to and from *Iſpahan*, it has been a large ſtately City. The Fabrick has been noble, by what may be yet ſeen in ſome Parts yet ſtanding, and ſome Paintings on Stone, that ſtill look freſh, in ſpite of Time's Iron Teeth, who defaces and deſtroys moſt ſublunary Things, or alters their Figures ſo much, that they can be known no other Way than by Tradition.

CHAP. X.

Is a Continuation of Obſervations on the Empire of Perſia, *giving an Account of its Magnitude, the Reduction of* Ormuze *to the Obedience of* Perſia *by the Aſſiſtance of the* Engliſh: *Alſo of the late Rovolution by* Meriweys.

THE Empire of *Perſia* is of a large Extent, being limited by *Euphrates* and the *Perſian* Gulf to Weſtward, the *Indian* Ocean, from Cape *Guaddel*, to the Southward, on the Eaſt Side by the River *Indus*, that runs 1200 Miles to the Northward from its Mouths, and on the North, by *Usbeck*, *Tartaria*, *Colchis*, *Mangrelia*, the *Caſpian* Sea and *Georgia*. *Erivan* in *Armenia*, is a Province in the North-weſt of it, as *Cabul* and *Candaha* are on the North-eaſt Side. Towards *Turkey* they ſometimes loſe and get whole Provinces in a Year. About the Beginning of the ſeventeenth Century, *Shaw Abaſs* was King of *Perſia*, a King worthy of Empire, and made himſelf famous by his Valour and Juſtice; but having no Fleet at Sea, the *Portugueze* inſulted his Sea-coaſts, and ſettled themſelves on the Iſland of *Ormuze*, and built a good ſtrong Fort, as is already obſerved, with a pretty large Town, and magnificent Churches. Some Porches and broken Pillars I have ſeen, that ſpeak their ancient Grandeur; and the Caſtle is ſtill good, and well kept. The *Portugueze*, with their

their light Frigats and Gallies, insulted the Sea-coasts of *Persia*, and all the Shipping that had Commerce in the Gulf, for above a whole Century. *Shaw Abass* being tired with the Complaints of his Subjects, and others that had been robbed and insulted by the imperious *Portugueze*, made him very uneasy, and found no Remedy but by encouraging the *English*, who then had a small Factory on the Sea-shore, about 7 Leagues from the Mouth of the Gulf, to the East-ward, called *Jasques*, but were continually disturbed in their Commerce by the domineering *Portugueze* from *Ormuze*.

Sir *Thomas Row* being then Ambassador at the Court of *Persia* for King *James* the First of *England*, to cultivate a Correspondence between the two Kingdoms, *Shaw Abass* broke his Mind to Sir *Thomas*, and proferred any reasonable Indulgence to the *English* that traded into *Persia*, providing they would joyn his Land Forces with theirs at Sea, in *India*, to drive the troublesom *Portugueze* out of the *Persian* Gulf. Sir *Thomas* agreed, that, if *Shaw Abass* would defray the Charges of the Ships that should come to his Assistance, give the *English* a free Trade all over the *Persian* Dominions, Custom free, and grant them one Moiety of the Customs raised by Merchandize in the Gulf, they would not only help to drive the *Portugueze* out of *Ormuze*, but keep two Ships in the Gulf, to protect Trade. All which was agreed to by both Parties, and ſealed and ſigned by the King of *Perſia.*

THE *Engliſh* Forces conſiſted of five Ships, about 40 Guns one with another, and were well mann'd. The King of *Perſia* ſent an Army of 40 or 50000. with Trankies for Tranſports, to land them on *Ormuze.* The *Engliſh* ſoon deſtroyed the *Portugueze Armado* of light Frigats and Gallies, which were hal'd dry on the Land near the Caſtle. The Caſtle firing briskly on them, ſunk one of the *Engliſh* Ships, whoſe Artillery was carried aſhore, and put in Batteries to annoy the Caſtle, which the Shipping and Batteries did ſo effectually, that, in leſs than two Months, the *Portugueze* capitulated to leave *Ormuze*, with all the Fortifications intire, and to carry nothing away but their noble ſelves. The Plunder, which was very great, was equally divided between the *Engliſh* and *Perſians*; and Tradition reports, that there was ſo much ready Bullion found in the Caſtle, that it was meaſured by Long-boats-full; and one Boat being pretty deep, and an Officer ſtill throwing in more, put the Boatſwain of the Ship, who was in the Boat, into a Paſſion, and made him ſwear, that for every Shovel-full that they threw more in, he would throw two out into the Sea; for he could not tell what would ſatisfy them, if a Long-boat Load of Money would not. On the Reduction of the Iſland and Fort of *Ormuze*, the *Portugueze* withdrew their Men from the Forts of *Laracka*, another Iſland

ſland 4 or 5 Leagues from *Ormuze*, and from *Kiſmiſh* Fort, that lies on the Eaſt End of that Iſland, and retired to *Muskat*. *Shaw Abaſs* was punctual in obſerving the Agreement with the *Engliſh*; and it was punctually kept by the ſucceeding Kings, till about the Year 1680. the *Engliſh* Company failed on their Part of keeping the Gulf clear of Inſults; and the *Perſians*, finding that the *Engliſh* Company's Forces were now too ſmall for the increaſing Power of the *Arabs* their Neighbours, took away the half Cuſtoms, and allow them 1100 *Tomaans*, which is about 3300 Pounds *Sterling* a Year; but I am afraid that that is alſo loſt by the late Revolution in *Perſia*.

When *Shaw Abaſs* demiſed, his Son *Shaw Tomas* ſucceeded him, who was a Son worthy of ſuch a Father. He died about the Year 1630. He was a very valiant and fortunate Prince in his Wars with *Turk* and *Mogul*, and a great Lover of Juſtice; for whoever broke the eſtabliſhed Laws, were ſure to ſuffer the Penalty annext to them. One Inſtance of that he ſhewed on a Baker; for, being once detected in making his Bread lighter than the Standard, he was ſeverely fined; but, on his being detected and convicted a ſecond Time, he was condemned to be bak'd in his own Oven, for a Terror to others, who might flatter themſelves with breaking the Laws with Impunity.

After *Shaw Tomas*, the ſucceeding Kings have been debauch'd with Ignorance of their own Affairs, Voluptuousness and Indolence, leaving the Reins of Government in the Hands of Parasites, or Eunuchs and Concubines, who never fail to bring their Master into Contempt, and the People into Murmurings and Rebellions. A very flagrant Instance is to be seen in *Meriweys*'s Revolution.

THE whole Reign of the last *Sophi*, or King, was managed by such Vermin, that the *Ballowches* and *Mackrans*, who inhabit the Sea-coast from Cape *Jasques* to *Indus*, observing the Weakness of the Government, threw off the Yoke of Obedience first, and, in full Bodies, fell in upon their Neighbours in *Carmania*, who were thriftier and richer than the maritim Freebooters, and plundred their Fellow Subjects of what they had got by their painful Industry. There was no Want of Remonstrances and Petitions put into the Court to put a Stop to those Enormities, but no Redress could be had. The *Usbecks* came also on their neighbouring Province of *Muschet*, and committed many Depredations; and when Letters came from the Governor of that Province, to acquaint the King of the *Usbecks* Incursions, he happened then to be at Play with a young Cat, that hunted a Feather that he kept in Motion with a Thread. One of the Pages acquainted him, that a Messenger was come in great Haste from *Muschet*, with Letters to the Vizier, who was at the Chamber Door, to know what his Majesty would please to order in that Juncture. He answered, that assoon as he had

had done playing with his Cat, he would ſend for the Vizier, and conſult of that Matter; but he never thought more of it. This Indolence made many Thefts, Robberies and Murders to be committed throughout the Country: Nay, his own Guards went out in Troops, and way-laid Merchants going or coming to or from *Iſpahan*, robbed them, and often murdered them; and when Complaints were made, and Proof offered, yet no Redreſs could be had, which made moſt People believe, that ſome Court Favourites were Encouragers of the publick Calamities. *In Anno* 1716. I carried ſome *Armenian* Merchants from *Perſia* to *Surat*, who aſſured me, that there was a Deſign to depoſe the King, and ſet up his Son, or invite the *Muſcovite* into the Province of *Casbin*, whoſe Shores are on the *Caſpian* Sea, and where a foreign Army may eaſily be brought into their Ports by Sea: And certainly there was ſuch a Deſign; for *in Anno* 1719. the Plot of depoſing the King was found out, and the *Attamadoulet* or Vizier was deeply concerned in it. He was *Meriweys*'s, or *Meir Mahoumud Shaw*'s Father, the Son being then *Chawn*, or Prince of *Candahaar*. The King was ſolacing himſelf in a Garden near the City of *Iſpahan*, when he was appriſed of the Plot, which was to be executed the ſame Night it was diſcovered. He immediately ſent for the *Attamadoulet*, pretending Buſineſs of Importance about ſome Frontier Provinces; and the old Gentleman not dreaming of of the Discovery made, came to the King, who taxing him with the Plot, made no Difficulty to confess that it was of his own Contrivance, to save the Country from Ruin, which was inevitable, if he continued in Supineness, which had affected him near 40 Years, and there was no Sign of Amendment, notwithstanding his Remonstrances and Admonitions all that while, and now that he was detected, he knew the worst that could befal him, was to be sacrificed for the Good of his Country, which he took to be rather glorious than dishonourable. The King ordered some Bars of Iron to be heated, and his Eyes kept open till the Irons were gently moved near the Eyes to dry up the Moisture, which is the royal Punishment in *Persia*, for disobedient or rebellious Princes; so the old Man being made blind, his Treasure was seised, but his Palace and Gardens allowed him, and an Allowance suitable to his Dignity. He had in Gold and Diamonds, to the Value of 800000 *Tomaans* or 2400000 Pounds *Sterling*; and some said he had more in his Son's Custody: But how true these Reports are, I am no proper Judge, either to believe or reject; but some Bars of his Gold I saw at *Gombroon*.

BEFORE this Conspiracy of the *Attamadoulet* happened, the *Muskat Arabs* came with a Fleet, and landed 5 or 6000 Men on *Ormuze*, and besieged the Castle; but could not take it in three Months, and being tired with Fatigue, they left it. But *in Anno* 1720. *Meri-*

Meriweys hearing how the King had used his Father, made the whole Province of *Candahaar* rebel, and wrote Letters to the *Chawn* of *Samachie* to come into Alliance with him and his Confederates the *Ballowches* and *Usbecks*, who readily embraced his Propositions in Hope of Plunder. In 1721. *Meriweys* began his March towards *Isfpahan*, with an Army of 45000. and paid honestly for what his Army had Occasion for in his March, declaring, that he did not take Arms for their Hurt or Destruction, but to free *Persia* from the Folly and Tyranny of a doting Fool, who was incorrigible by fair Means. The *Usbecks* entred the Provinces of *Muschet* and *Tesd*, with 40000. and acted like Robbers. Another Army of 40000 went out of *Samachie*, and ravaged *Erivan*; and the *Ballowches* entred the Province of *Carmania*, and plundred the Country, and at last took the City. Then they marched towards *Laar*, and took the Town, but not the Fort: And there twelve *Hollanders*, who were sent from *Gombroon* to convey down some Treasure belonging to their Company, behaved themselves to Admiration. They were lodged in a *Caravanseray*, where the *Ballowches* came with about 300 to attack them, but they had a brave warm Reception, and left about four Score of their Number dead on the Spot, without the Loss of one *Dutch* Man: But not thinking themselves and their Treasure safe where they were, they desired Admittance into the Fort, which was readi-

ly

ly granted, and there they alſo behaved themſelves ſo well, that the *Ballowches* marched away without the Booty they came ſo far for. The *Dutch* ſtaid there above a Month, and in that Time came a Detachment of 4000 Horſe to plunder *Gombroon.* We heard of their Deſign about ten Days before they came, and ſo we and the *Dutch* fortified our Factories as well as poſſibly we could, planting little Falconets on the Top of our Walls in Swivels, and beating out Ports in our Walls, to ply great Guns, to ſcour the Avenues to our Factories. Mean while the *Perſian* Governor fired Guns every Night, to let the Enemy know he was a brave Fellow: However they had a Mind to ſee, and, on the 15 of *December*, they appeared near the Town, on a ſwift March towards it, which ſcared the Governor ſo much, that, tho' there was an high Mud Wall between him and them, he got on Horſe-back, and fled to a Fort on the Sea-ſhore, leaving a few Guns, loaded as they were, to the Enemy.

THE *Ballowches* came firſt to the Weſt Quarter of the Town, where our Factory ſtands, and ſoon made Paſſages through the Mud Walls. They hewed down all that came in their Way, particularly old People and Children, and came in a confuſed Haſte to attack our Factory, down ſome Lanes; but we gave them a warm Welcom with our great Guns and ſmall Shot. They ſoon found their Miſtake, and retired in as great Haſte as they came. Some of their Musketeers got into ſome

ſome ruined Houſes, and fired on us; but we being barricadoed, they did us little Damage, and had our Men obſerved their Orders better, we had come off with leſs. Our Firing laſted about three Hours, in which Time we loſt three or four, killed by their own Raſhneſs in ſtanding open to the Enemy, when they might have done better Service under Cover of our Barricadoes. We had alſo ſeven wounded, but none mortally, but one who was a Factor, who received a Shot in his right Hand, which threw him into a Fever, of which he died in ſeven or eight Days. The Agent being gone to *Iſpahan* ſome Weeks before we had any Advice of the *Ballowches* coming, had carried twenty Soldiers along with him for a Guard, and left but ſix in the Factory, beſides Cooks, and a few Servants. I ſaw the Factory in Danger if they ſhould be attacked, ſo I reinforced it with thirty ſix of my beſt Men, and another ſmall *Engliſh* Ship from *Bombay*, aſſiſted with eight or nine of his, ſo that when the Enemy came, we were about fifty ſtrong. The Seaſon being very cold, made our Duty hard, for we lay in our Arms every Night for 10 or 12 Nights that the Enemy lay in the Town. They had a Conſultation next Day after their Repulſe, how they might make another Attack; but none would undertake to lead their Men on, and ſo the Day after Conſultation, they went to attack the *Dutch*, who were three Times ſtronger than we, and they met with the ſame kind Reception we

gave

gave them; but they had a Ware-houſe within Piſtol-ſhot of their Factory, with Goods to the Value of 20000 Pounds *Sterling* in it, which the *Ballowches* broke into, and plundred. The *Dutch* loſt twelve Men, and had eight or ten wounded: So finding our Factories were not to be taken without the Danger of much Blood-ſhed, they went a plundring the Town for eight or nine Days, and carried away, in Money and Goods, above 200000 Pounds, beſides 14000 Captives, and as many Beaſts of Carriage, and ſo went off about five or ſix Miles from the Town, which they laid in Aſhes before they left it. They continued in our Neighbourhood, with their Plunder, about a Month, I ſuppoſe till they received new Orders how to diſpoſe of themſelves.

NOTWITHSTANDING ſuch numerous rebellious Armies were a Foot, threatning Deſtruction to the State, the indolent King being lulled aſleep in Security, did not offer to raiſe any Forces for the Defence of himſelf and Country, but ſaid to his Cabinet Counſellers, *that he was ſure his Enemies would leave him* Iſpahan, *and that one City would be enough to maintain him and them his Counſellers*: But when *Meriweys* came within three Days Journey of the City, he raiſed about 50000 of the Citizens, and ſent to the *Engliſh* and *Dutch* Agents, to joyn their little Forces to his, to manage the Artillery, and to lend him ſome Money to ſupport and pay his new raiſed Army. The latter deſired

red to be excuſed in both; but the *Engliſh* complied, and were very active in defending the City, when *Meriweys* came to beſiege it: And when he approached within a Mile or two of the City, the King ſent his raw Army out to fight *Meriweys*; but in their March, *Meriweys*'s Men having made a long Trench a pretty Way from their Front, and hid a large Quantity of Gun-powder in it, and then filled it up again, which Ambuſcade the King's Army fell into, and, after a good Number of them had paſt it, Fire was ſet to it, and blew up and ſcorched many of the King's Men, which ſo frightned the reſt, that they turned Tail, and fled without ſtriking one Stroke, ſo *Meriweys* made an eaſy Conqueſt of the City, and found the King weeping, and deſerted by his baſe and treacherous Courtiers. But *Meriweys* ſoon put an End to his Melancholy, by ordering his Head to be ſtruck off, which was forthwith executed, and put on the Point of a Lance, and carried thro' the City three Days ſucceſſively, as a Spectacle. The Prince royal, or the young *Sophi* ſeeing his Father's Affairs in ſo wretched a Condition, had left the City, and went to *Taurus* or *Teverize* before *Meriweys* came. *Meriweys* carried himſelf mighty civilly to the Citizens, but made the *Engliſh* Priſoners, and ſeized what Money and Goods could be found of theirs, and alſo the *Dutch* Company's Effects, but not their Servants Perſons. It was reported, that the *Engliſh* loſt about 60000 Pounds, and the *Dutch*

210000

210000. But the Truth of these Reports are best known to themselves.

WHEN the old King had a Mind to honour the *English* Factory with a Visit, as I saw in a Letter from Mr. *Bruce* the Company's Agent, that he sometimes did, and one particularly in his Agency, he magnifies the Honour done to his Masters, above what the *Dutch* could ever obtain. He relates how he and all the Factory, great and small, were ordered to leave their House, and Chamber Doors and Ware-houses all open, for his Majesty and his *Seraglio* Companions to ramble thro', and take such Things as best pleased him and his Minions; and there was a Table left in the Dining-room, spread and furnished with the richest Sweet-meats and Fruits.

I believe the Company was not very ambitious of having many such Honours conferred on them, since they were obliged to pay for them. And when the King has a Mind for some new Concubines, he issues out Orders for all Men and Youths to depart out from their Houses in the Street, that he is pleased to visit, and to leave all the Ladies in Possession till his Majesty surveys them; and the Penalty of Disobedience is Death. He generally makes his Progress thro' the *Armenian* Quarters, because the fairest and most beautiful are amongst their Children.

THE Religion, by Law established for near eleven Ages, is *Mahometan*, of the Sect of *Alli*; but the ancient Religion was *Parsi*, or Worshippers of the Sun and Fire. The Founder

der of it was *Zoroaster*, whom they still venerate. About the ninth Century of the *Christian Æra*, the *Mahometan* Zealots, according to the laudable Way of some *Christians*, raised a Persecution against the *Parsis*, whose wholesom Severities made many Proselytes; but some obstinate Rogues, who would not change for a worse, were lawfully murdered, or obliged to run their Country, so that at present there are but few left in *Persia*, and those that are left, are protected by their Poverty and Habitations, which are in Deserts or Hills little frequented.

THERE are vast Numbers of *Armenian Christians* in *Persia*, whose Religion is tolerated. Their former Country of *Armenia* is now the Province of *Erivan*. There are many substantial Merchants of *Armenians*, who inhabit *Julfar*, a Town near *Ispahan*, and they send Factors all over *India* to carry on Trade; and some come to *Europe* on that same Account.

THE *Mahometans* in *Persia*, to encourage Proselytes to their Religion, have a Law, that if a Son of an *Armenian* turns *Mahometan*, all the Father's Estate becomes his, and all who continue *Christians* are excluded, which sometimes makes great Divisions and Alterations in a Family.

IN Baptism they immerse, but do not sprinkle. The Priest must officiate in his sacerdotal Garb, with a Crown on his Head, and must have two Assistants in holy Vestments also, but without Crowns. Their titulary Saint is Saint *Gregory*, of whom they tell many ſtrange Stories; but whether true or falſe I know not: But I am ſure he has plagued them with Faſt-days, for they faſt one Half of the Year at leaſt.

HAVING made what Obſervations I could of the Empire of *Perſia*, I'll travel along the Sea-coaſt towards *Induſtan*, or the *Great Mogul's* Empire. All that Shore, from *Jaſques* to *Sindy*, is inhabited by uncivilized People, who admit of no Commerce with Strangers, tho' *Guaddel* and *Diul*, two Sea-ports, did, about a Century ago, afford a good Trade.

CHAP. XI.

Treats of the Mogul's *Dominions on the River* Indus, *particularly of the ancient Kingdom of* Sindy *its Product and Commerce, Religion and Cuſtoms of the Inhabitants; with a Deſcription of the River* Indus.

SINDY is the weſtmoſt Province of the *Mogul's* Dominions, on the Sea-coaſt, and has *Larribundar* to its Sea Mart, which ſtands about 5 or 6 Leagues from the Sea, on a Branch of the River *Indus*, capable to receive Ships of 200 Tuns. It is but a Village of about 100 Houſes, built of crooked Sticks and Mud; but it has a large Stone Fort, with four or five great Guns mounted in it, to protect the Merchandize brought thither, from the Robberies of the *Ballow-*

ches

thes and *Mackrans* that ly near them, to the Westward, and the *Jams* to the Eastward, who being Borderers, are much given to Thieving, and they rob all whom they are able to master. The former are revolted Subjects of *Persia*, and the other are Subjects of the *Mogul*; but being secured from the Aw of an Army's coming to chastise their Insolency, by the marish Grounds they live in, and the rapid Tides of *Indus*, they make but little Account of their Sovereign's Power or Orders, and so they commit Depredations on the Caffillas that pass to and fro between *Tatta* and *Larribundar*, notwithstanding a Guard of 100 or 200 Horse are sent along with them, by the *Nabob* or Vice-roy of *Tatta*, for Protection; but often those Protectors suffer the Caffillas to be robbed, pretending the Robbers are too numerous to be restrained by their small Forces, and afterwards come in Sharers with the Robbers.

Tatta is the *Emporium* of the Province, a very large and rich City. It is about three Miles long, and one and an Half broad, and is about 40 Miles Distance from *Larribundar*, and has a large Citadel on its West End, capable to lodge 5000 Men and Horse, and has Barracks and Stables convenient for them, with a Palace built in it for the *Nabob*. All Goods and Merchandize imported or exported between *Tatta* and *Larribundar*, are transported on Carriage Beasts, such as Camels, Oxen and Horses. The Country is almost level, and overgrown with Shrubs and Buſhes, very fit to cover an Ambuſcade, which the aforeſaid Robbers often make uſe of, and ſuddenly ruſh out on a Caffilla, and whilſt the Guards and Carriers are fighting in one Place, either of Front, Flank or Rear, the Robbers drive away the Beaſts with their Packs. *In Anno* 1699. a pretty rich Caffilla was robbed by a Band of four or five thouſand Villains: The Guard, conſiſting of 250 Horſe, were intirely cut off, and above 500 of the Merchants and Carriers, which ſtruck a Terror on all that had Commerce at *Tatta.*

IT was my Fortune, about four Months after, to come to *Larribundar*, with a Cargo from *Mallabar*, worth above 10000 *L.* I could find no *Tatta* Merchants that would meddle with my Cargo before it was carried to *Tatta*; but agreed on the Prices of moſt of the Species of my Goods: And finding no other Remedy but travelling by Land, in a Caffilla of 1500 Beaſts, and as many, or more Men and Women, beſides 200 Horſe for our Guard, about the Middle of *January* we ſet out; and after we had marched about 16 Miles, our Scouts brought in News of the *Ballowches* and *Mackrans* being juſt before us, in great Numbers. I had thirteen of my beſt Firemen with me in the Front, where my Beaſts were. We being all mounted on little Horſes, alighted, and ſet our Beaſts on our Flanks and Front, to ſerve us for a Barricadoe, to defend us from Sword and Targetmen, which were the principal Strength of the Robbers, and we, at the ſame Time, had Room

Room enough to fire over our Barricadoe. We were not long in that Posture, till the Enemy sent an Herald on Horse-back, with his Sword brandishing, and when he came within Call of us, he threatned, that if we did not instantly surrender at Discretion, we should have no Quarters. I had two of my Seamen that shot as well with a Fuzee as any ever I saw, for I have seen them at Sea, for Diversion, knock down a single Sea-fowl with a single Bullet, as they were flying near our Ship. I ordered one to knock down the Herald, which he instantly did, by a Bullet through his Head. Another came presently after, with the same Threatnings, and met with the same Treatment. The next that came, I ordered his Horse to be shot in the Head, to try if we could take his Rider, that we might learn somewhat of the Enemy's Strength. The Horse was killed assoon as he appeared, and some of our Horse got the Rider, and hewed him down, instead of bringing him to us. Our Guard of Horse continually kept in the Rear, but seeing what we had done in the Front, took Courage, and getting in amongst the Bushes, met with some that had a Design to attack our Flank, and soon defeated them, which put the Robbers in such Fear, that they betook themselves to Flight, and our Horse pursuing, put many to the Sword; so when they returned from the Pursuit, we went on in our Journey, and travelling four Miles, came to a Mud-wall Fort, called *Dung-*

ham, a proper *English* Name for ſuch a Fortification. It is built mid-way between *Tatta* and *Larribundar*, to ſecure the Caffilla from being ſet upon in the Night, who all lodge within it, Men and Beaſts promiſcuouſly, which makes it ſo naſty, that the *English* Appellation is rightly beſtowed on it. There are about twenty little Cottages built cloſe to it, who breed Fowls, Goats and Sheep, to ſell to Paſſengers. And theſe are all the Houſes to be ſeen in the Way between *Tatta* and *Larribundar*.

THE News of a Victory that I had over three *Sanganian* Pirates at Sea, on my Voyage from *Malabar* to *Larribundar*, had reacht *Tatta*, before the ſecond Skirmiſh by Land, ſo that when I came to *Tatta*, we were received with Acclamations from the Populace, and the better Sort viſited us with Preſents of Sweet-meats and Fruits, aſcribing the ſafe Arrival of the Caffilla wholly to our Courage and Conduct.

WE were lodged in a large convenient Houſe of 15 Rooms, and had good Warehouſes. The Stairs from the Street, were intire Porphyry, of 10 Foot long, of a bright yellow Colour, and as ſmooth as Glaſs. They were about ten in Number, and led up to a Square of 15 Yards long, and about 10 broad. Next Day we had a Compliment from the *Nabob*, of an Ox, five Sheep, as many Goats, twenty Fowls and fifty Pigeons, with Sweet-meats and Fruit in Abundance. He, at that Time, lay encampt about ſix Miles from the Town,

Town, with an Army of 8 or 10000 Men, with a Design to punish the *Ballowches* and *Mackrans* for robbing the Caffilla, and killing his Men, as is before mentioned. He desired me to let him know when we designed to drink a Dish of Coffee with him, and he would send Horses to bring us to the Camp. I returned Thanks for his Civility, and sent him Word, that I designed to kiss his Hand the very next Day; and he accordingly sent twenty fine *Persian* Horses, well equipp'd, for my Use, ten of which I accepted for myself and Guard to mount, and the other ten were mounted with some of the most considerable Merchants in *Tatta*, who went to accompany me out of Respect; and, to make our Cavalcade appear with the greater Grace, assoon as we came to the Camp Gate, we would have alighted, but an Officer on Horseback told us, that it was the *Nabob*'s Pleasure, that we should be brought to his Tent on Horse-back, and he riding before us, conducted us to the Tent Door, and, assoon as we got from our Horses, I was conducted into his own Pavilion Chamber, where he was sitting alone. The rest that came with me, were not admitted for an Hour after. It would take a great Deal of Time and Room to relate the Compliments and other Discourses that past; but I knew the Custom, not to appear before great Men with an empty Hand. I desired Leave to lay a little Present at his Feet, which he permitted. It consisted of a Looking-glass of about 5 Pounds

 in

in Value, a Gun and a Pair of Piſtols well gilded, a Sabre Blade and Dagger-blade gilded, and a Glaſs Pipe for his Tobacco, and an embroider'd Standiſh for it to ſtand in. He then ſent for all who had accompanied me into the Room, and ſhewed the Preſent I had made him, magnifying every Piece of it; and after ſome Encomiums on my Valour and Generoſity, told me, that I was a free Deniſon of *Tatta*, with the Addition of an Indulgence of being free of all Cuſtom and Tax on all Goods that I had brought or ſhould export, and that whoever bought any Part of my Cargo, and did not pay according to the Agreement made for Payment, I ſhould not be liable to ſeek Juſtice at the *Cadjee*'s Court, but to impriſon my Debtors, and if that would not perſwade them to give Satisfaction, he would ſell their Wives, Children or neareſt Relations to make good their Debt. This Privilege did me ſingular Service when the Term of Payments came, and was obliged to try the Experiment of impriſoning. After three Hours Converſation, we took Leave to go, and he diſmiſt us with much Civility, and told me, that when he returned from that Expedition, he would repay my Viſit at my Lodgings; but in three Months that I ſtaid, he did not return, but often ſent to enquire after my Welfare, and how my Affairs ſtood.

IN travelling from *Dungham* towards *Tatta*, about 4 Miles ſhort of the City, on ſmooth riſing Ground, there are forty two fine large Tombs,

Tombs, which, from the Plain, appeared to be a ſmall Town. They are the Burying-places of ſome of the Kings of *Sindy*, when that Country was governed by its own Kings. I went into the largeſt, which is built in the Form of a Cupola, and in the Middle of it, ſtood a Coffin-tomb, about three Foot high, and ſeven Foot long, with ſome others of a leſſer Size. The Materials of the Cupola were yellow, green and red Porphyry, finely poliſhed, and the Stones ſet in regular Order, Chequer-ways, which Variegation ſtrikes the Eye with wonderful Pleaſure. The Tomb is about 10 Yards high, and 7 in Diameter. I was told, that it was the Burying-place of the laſt King of that Country, who was robbed of his Sovereignty by *Jehan Guire* Grandfather to the famous *Aurenzeb*, in the Beginning of the ſeventeenth Century, who, after he had him Priſoner, bid him ask what Favours he would deſire for himſelf and Children, and they ſhould be granted. He nobly replied, That all the Favour he begg'd, was, that himſelf, his Queen, and their Children, might be buried in that Tomb, which, in Times of Proſperity, he had built for that Purpoſe, and had coſt him two Lack of Rupees, or 25000 *L. Sterl.* which Requeſt his Conqueror could not well refuſe.

Tatta City ſtands about two Miles from the River *Indus*, in a ſpacious Plain, and they have Canals cut from the River, that bring Water to the City, and ſome for the Uſe of their Gardens. The King's Gardens were in pretty

pretty good Condition *in Anno* 1699. and were well ſtored with excellent Fruits and Flowers, particularly the moſt delicious Pomegranates that ever I taſted.

For three Years before I came there, no Rain had fallen, which cauſed a ſevere Plague to affect the Town and circumjacent Country, to ſuch a Degree, that, in the City only, above 80000 died of it, that manufactured Cotton and Silk, and above one Half of the City was deſerted and left empty. And that was one Reaſon why the *Nabob* had placed his Camp in that Place that I went to viſit him at. The Figure of the Camp was a regular Tetragon, and ditched about with a Trench about 3 Yards broad, and 2 deep. The Ground taken out of the Ditch, was thrown upon the Inſide, about 4 Foot high, and regularly built like a Parapet. It had 4 Gates, one in the Middle of each Curtain, and a ſtraight Street from the oppoſite Gates, which made an exact Croſs in Figure, and the *Nabob*'s Tent was pitch'd in the Middle of the Croſs. Each Side of the Tetragon was about 6 or 700 Paces in Length, and the Ditches could be filled with Water from the *Indus*, and let out at Pleaſure, into a large Mariſh about two Miles off the Camp.

The River *Indus* is navigable for their Veſſels, as high as *Caſmire*, that lies in the Latitude of 32 Degrees ; and one Branch runs up to *Cabul* to the Weſtward, and others to *Penjeb*, *Lahore*, *Multan*, *Buckor*, and other large Provinces and Cities to the Eaſt-

Eastward, and all share the Benefits of the inland Navigation. Their Vessels are called *Kifties*, of several Sizes. The largest can lade about 200 Tuns. They are flat-bottomed, and, on each Side, Cabbins are built from Stern to Stem, that overhang about 2 Foot; and, in each Cabbin, is a Kitchen and a Place for Exoneration, which falls directly in the Water. Those Cabbins are hired out to Passengers, and the Hold, being made into separate Apartments, are let out to Freighters, so that every one has a Lock on his own Cabbin and Apartment in the Hold, and has his Goods always ready to dispose on at what Places he finds his Market. And indeed in all my Travels I never saw better Conveniencies of travelling by Water. They have one Mast of a good Length, and a Square-sail to use when the Wind is a-stern, or on the Quarter; but they never hale close by the Wind. They are obliged to carry a great Number of Men for tracting them up against the Stream, when the Winds are against them, so that a Voyage from *Tatta* to *Labore*, they reckon six or seven Weeks long, but from *Labore* back, not above eighteen Days, and sometimes it is performed in twelve.

At *Tatta* the River is about a Mile broad, and, where I tried with a Lead and Line, it was about six Fathoms deep, from Side to Side. The Stream is not very rapid, for its Motion did not exceed two Miles and an half in an Hour. It produces many Species of Fresh-water Fishes, and among them, the best

Carp

Carp that ever I ſaw or taſted. Some of them weigh above 20 Pound Weight, and we have them alive in *Tatta* Market. They have black Cattle in great Plenty, large and good, and moſt excellent Mutton, of 80 or 100 Pound Weight. Their Horſes are ſmall, but hardy and ſwift. Deer, Antelopes, Hares and Foxes are their wild Game, which they hunt with Dogs, Leopards, and a ſmall fierce Creature, called by them a *Shoegooſe*. It is about the Size of a Fox, with long prickt Ears like an Hare, and a Face like a Cat, a gray Back and Sides, and Belly and Breaſt white. I believe they are rare, for I never ſaw more than one. When they are taken out to hunt, an Horſe-man carries it behind him, hood-winkt, and their Deer and Antelopes being pretty familiar, will not ſtart before Horſes come very near. He who carries the *Shoegooſe*, takes off the Hood, and ſhews it the Game, which, with large ſwift Springs, it ſoon overtakes, and leaping on their Backs, and getting forward to the Shoulders, ſcratches their Eyes out, and gives the Hunters an eaſy Prey. The Leopard runs down his Game, which often gives the Hunters a long Chaſe, as well as the Dogs, who will take the Water when the Game betake themſelves to ſwimming, which they frequently do. They have Store of Peacocks, Pigeons, Doves, Duck, Teal, Widgeon, wild Geeſe, Curlews, Partridge and Plover, free for any Body to ſhoot. They have a Fruit, that grows in their Fields and Gardens, called

led *Salob*, about the Size of a Peach, but without a Stone. They dry it hard before they uſe it, and being beaten to Powder, they dreſs it as Tea and Coffee are, and take it with powdered Sugar-candy. They are of Opinion, that it is a great Reſtorative to decay'd animal Spirits.

THIS Country abounds richly in Wheat, Rice and Legumen, and Provender for Horſes and Cattle; and they never know the Miſery of Famine, for the *Indus* overflows all the low Grounds in the Months of *April*, *May* and *June*, and when the Floods go off, they leave a fat Slime on the Face of the Ground, which they till eaſily before it dries, and being ſown and harrow'd, never fails of bringing forth a plentiful Crop.

THE other Productions of this and the inland Country, are Saltpeter, Sal-armoniack, Borax, Opoponax, Aſſa-fœtida, Goat Bezoar, *Lapis tutiæ* and *Lapis laſuli*, and raw Silk, but not fine.

THEY manufacture in wrought Silks, which they call *Jemawaars*, in Cotton and Silk, called *Cuttenees*, and in Silk mixt with *Carmania* Wooll, called *Culbuleys*, in Calicoes coarſe and fine, ſheer and cloſe wrought. Their Cloth called *Jurries*, is very fine and ſoft, and laſts beyond any other Cotton Cloth that I have uſed. They make Chints very fine and cheap, and Coverlets for Beds very beautiful. They make fine Cabinets, both lack'd and inlaid with Ivory. And the beſt Bows and Arrows in the World, are made at *Multan*, of Buffalos Horns. They lack wooden Dishes and Tables, but not so well as in *China*. The Lack is clear enough, but always clammy. They export great Quantities of Butter, which they gently melt, and put up in Jars, called *Duppas*, made of the Hides of Cattle, almost in the Figure of a Glob, with a Neck and Mouth on one Side. They are made of all Sizes, from those that contain 320 *lb.* to those of 5. and that Butter keeps, without Salt, the whole Year round, but, as it grows old, it becomes rank.

THE Wood *Ligna dulcis* grows only in this Country. It is rather a Weed than a Wood, and nothing of it is useful but the Root, called *Putchock*, or, *Radix dulcis*. I never heard it is used in Physick, but is a good Ingredient in the Composition of Perfumes. There are great Quantities exported for *Surat*, and from thence to *China*, where it generally bears a good Price; for being all Idolaters, and burning Incense before their Images, this Root beaten into fine Powder, and an Incense-pot laid over smoothly with Ashes, and a Furrow made in the Ashes, about a Quarter of an Inch broad, and as much in Depth, done very artificially into a great Length, the Powder is put into that Furrow, and fired, and it will burn a long Time like a Match, sending forth a fine Smoke, whose Smell is very grateful, the Powder having the good Qualities of maintaining and delaying the Fire.

THE

THE Religion, by Law established, is *Mahometan*; but there are ten *Gentows* or *Pagans* for one *Mussulman*. But the City of *Tatta* is famous for Learning in Theology, Philology and Politicks, and they have above four hundred Colleges for training up Youth in those Parts of Learning. I was very intimate with a *Seid* who was a Professor in Theology, and was reckoned to be a good Historian. He askt me one Day, if I had heard of *Alexander* the *Great* in my Country. I told him I had, and I mentioned his Battle with *Porus*, and his Victory. He told me, that their Histories mentioned the same, but with some Difference in the two Kings Names, and *Alexander*'s Passage over *Indus*. He said, that their History mentioned *Shaw Hasander* and *Prorus*, and that *Alexander* was a great Magician, and summoning above a Million of wild Geese, they swam his Army over the River, and that *Porus*'s Elephants would never turn their Heads towards the Place where *Alexander* was.

THE *Portugueze* had formerly a Church at the East End of the City. The House is still intire, and in the Vestry are some old Pictures of Saints, and some holy Vestments, which they profered to sell; but I was no Merchant for such Bargains.

THE *Gentows* have full Toleration for their Religion, and keep their Fasts and Feasts as in former Times, when the Sovereignty was in *Pagan* Princes Hands. They burn their dead, but the Wives are restrained from burning

ning with the Corps of their Husbands. There is a very great Consumption of Elephants Teeth, for 'tis the Fashion for Ladies to wear Rings of Ivory from their Arm-pits to their Elbows, and from their Elbows to their Wrists, of both Arms; and when they die, all those Ornaments are burnt along with them.

THEY had several Feasts when I was there, but one they kept on Sight of a New-moon in *February*, exceeded the rest in ridiculous Actions and Expence; and this is called the Feast of *Wooly*, who was a Knight errant in Time of yore, and was a fierce Fellow in a War with some Giants, who infested *Sindy*, and carried away naughty Girls and Boys, and made Butcher Meat of them. This *Wooly*, in a Battle one Day, killed fifty of them, each of them as tall as a Tree, and, after he had dispatcht them, he led them down to Hell, and there they continue bound up to their good Behaviour, and are never to appear again on Earth, for Fear they should scar the King's Liege-subjects, or frighten Children.

IN this mad Feast, People of all Ages and Sexes dance thro' the Streets to Pipe, Drum and Cymbals. The Women, with Baskets of Sweet-meats on their Heads, distributing to every Body they meet. The Men are bedawb'd all over with red Earth, or Vermilion, and are continually squirting gingerly Oyl at one another; and if they get into Houses of Distinction, they make foul Work with

with their Oyl, whose Smell is not pleasant; but in giving a Present of Rose-water, or some Silver Coin, they are civil enough to keep out of Doors. And in this Madness they continue from 10 in the Morning till Sun-set.

THE River of *Sindy* would be hard to be found, were it not for the Tomb of a *Mahometan* Saint, who has an high Tower built over him, called *Sindy* Tower. It is always kept white to serve as a Land-mark. The Bar, going into the River, is narrow, and has not above two Fathoms and an Half, on Spring-tides: But this is only a small Branch of *Indus*, which Appellation is now lost in this Country that it so plentifully waters, and is called *Divellee*, or seven Mouths; but it disembogues itself into the Sea thro' many more.

CHAP. XII.

Gives an Account of the ancient Kingdom of Guzerat, *now a Province annext to the* Mogul's *Dominions, its Situation, Product, Manners and Religion; with some Account of the Pirates that inhabit Part of it, and some Observations on* Diu, *a* Portugueze *City on an Island appertaining to* Guzerat.

THE next maritim Country to *Sindy*, is *Guzerat*. The *Indus* makes it an Island, by a Branch that runs into the Sea at the City of *Cambaya*. This Province, tho'

Vaſſals to the *Mogul*, yet continue in their old Religion of *Paganiſm*, and, for the moſt Part, drive the old Trade of thieving and pirating, for they plunder all whom they can overcome, on both Elements: Nor can the *Mogul* reſtrain them, for their Country is ſecure from the Marches of Armies into it, by reaſon of the many Inlets of the Sea that overflow the low Grounds, and make it ſo ſoft and muddy, that there is no travelling but by little Boats, in many Places.

THE firſt Town on the South Side of *Indus*, is *Cutchnaggen*. It admits of ſome Trade, and produces Cotton, Corn, coarſe Cloth and *Chonk*, a Shell-fiſh in Shape of a Perriwinkle, but as large about as a Man's Arm above the Elbow. In *Bengal* they are ſaw'd into Rings for Ornaments to Womens Arms, as thoſe of *Sindy* wear Ivory Rings. They are in Faſhion in many Countries in *India*. The Province and Town of *Cutchnaggen* are governed by a Queen, who is very formidable to her neighbouring States. The Reaſons they give for chooſing that Sex for their Governeſſes, are, that they'll be better adviſed by their Council than Men, who, by too large a Share of Power and Honour placed on them, become obſtinate in their Opinions, and inſolent in their Behaviour: But Ladies are eſteemed compliſant and gentle.

THE next Province to *Cutchnaggen*, is *Sangania*, which is alſo governed by a Princeſs, for the above Reaſons. Their Sea-port is called *Baet*, very commodious and ſecure. They admit

admit of no Trade, but practise Piracy. They give Protection to all Criminals, who deserve Punishment from the Hand of Justice. All Villains in the Countries about flock thither, and become honest Robbers, so that they are a Medley of Criminals, who flee their Country for Fear of condign Punishment due to their Crimes. This Province produces Cotton and Corn, as all the Kingdom of *Guzerat* does; but they admit of no Trade in their Country, as I observed before, for Fear of being civilized by Example. I had several Skirmishes with them. They, being confident of their Numbers, strive to board all Ships they can come at by sailing. Before they engage in a Fight, they drink Bang, which is made of a Seed like Hemp-seed, that has an intoxicating Quality, and, whilst it affects the Head, they are furious. They wear long Hair, and, when they let that hang loose, they'll give no Quarter.

In Anno 1686. a small Ship of theirs, that mounted 8 Guns, and mann'd with 300 of these furious Fellows, was cruizing on the Coast of *India*, between *Surat* and *Bombay*, and the *Phenix*, an *English* Man of War of 42 Guns, was bound for *Surat*. The *Sanganian* made towards her, and engaged her, but would fain have been gone again when they found their Mistake; but that was impossible. The *Phenix* sent her Boats, well mann'd, to try if they could make them yield, in order to save their Lives; but they scorned Quarter, and killed and wounded many of the *English*, ſo that Captain *Tyrrel*, who commanded the *Phenix*, was forced to run his lower Teer out, and ſink them: And, after their Ship was ſunk, and the Miſcreants ſet a ſwimming, yet moſt of them refuſed Quarter, and only about 70 were taken alive. (I believe Sir *George Bing* can give a better Account of the Story than I, for, if I miſtake not, he was a Lieutenant then on board the *Phenix*, and received a dangerous Wound in the Combat, at leaſt one of his Name, who bore a Commiſſion, did.) *In Anno* 1717. they attackt a Ship called the *Morning Star* in her Paſſage between *Gombroon* and *Surat*. She was richly laden, which they were appriſed of, and two Squadrons were fitted out from two different Ports, to way-lay her, and accordingly ſhe fell in with eight Sail of thoſe Pirates. One was a large Ship of near 500 Tuns, and three others were Ships between 2 and 300 Tuns, and the other four were *Grabs*, or Gallies, and *Sheybars*, or half Gallies. They reckoned in all there were above 2000 Men in their Fleet, and the *Morning Star* but 17 fighting Men, who were reſolved to truſt Providence, and fight for their Lives, Liberty and Eſtate. The firſt Attack was by the greateſt Ship alone, but was ſoon obliged to ſheer off again, with the Loſs of ſome Men, and the Captain of the *Morning Star* was wounded in the Thigh, by a Lance darted at him, that pierced his Thigh through and through. The Pirates were not diſcouraged by this firſt Repulſe, but joyned their

Forces

Forces and Counsels together, and, after a Day's Respite and Consultation, they attackt the *Morning Star* a second Time, the two largest Ships boarding, one on her Bow, and another on her Quarter, and three more boarded them two, and entred their Men over them. The Combat was warm for above four Hours, and the *Morning Star* had seven killed, and as many wounded; but kind Providence assisted her. Whilst she was on Fire in three Places, and had burnt through her Poop and half Deck, she was disengaged of them, and left five of the largest so entangled with one another, that they could not pursue her. So she pursued her Voyage to *Surat*, but having no Surgeon on board, she called at *Bombay*, to get her wounded Men drest and cured. In the Time of the Combat, while the Pirates were on board of the *Morning Star*, twenty one *Indian* Seamen went on board of them, and twenty six Merchants had gone to them, to try if they could perswade them to take a Sum, and not put it on the Hazard of a Battle. All those they detained, and carried along with them, and made them pay above 6000 Pounds for their Ransom, who gave an Account afterwards of great Slaughter done on the Pirates. And the Commodore lost his Head assoon as he landed, for letting so rich a Prize go out of his Hands.

In Anno 1698. one Captain *Lavender*, in the Ship *Thomas*, bound from *Surat* to *Mocha*, encountred four Sail of those Freebooters,

ers, and fought them bravely; but they burnt the Ship and all her Crew, because he would not yield. They are very cruel to those they can master, if they make Resistance; but to those that yield without fighting, they are pretty civil.

THE next Sea-port Town to *Baet*, is *Jigat*. It stands on a Point of low Land, called Cape *Jigat*. The City makes a good Figure from the Sea, shewing four or five high Steeples. It is the Seat of a *Fouzdaar* or Governor, for the *Mogul*. It is a Place of no Trade, and consequently little known to Strangers.

THE next maritim Town is *Mangaroul*. It admits of Trade, and affords coarse Calicoes, white and died, Wheat, Pulse and Butter for Export, and has a Market for Pepper, Sugar and Betlenut. It is inhabited by *Banyans*; and wild Deer, Antelopes, and Peacocks are so familiar, that they come into the very Houses without Fear.

THE next Place is *Poremain*, a pretty large Town on the Sea-shore, and admits of Trade, producing the same Commodities as *Mangaroul*, and its Inhabitants are of the same Religion; but both Towns are obliged to keep *Rasspouts* to protect them from the Insults of the *Sanganians*.

THOSE *Rasspouts* are Natives of *Guzerat*, and are all Gentlemen of the Sword, and are well trained in the Art of killing. They, like the *Switz*, employ their Swords in the Service of those who give them best Pay. They seldom give or take Quarter, and when they go go on an Expedition, they carry their Wives and Children in Carts and Wagons along with them, and if they meet with a Repulse, their Wives will never suffer Cohabitation till they can regain their lost Honour by some noble Exploit.

Diu is the next Port, and is the southermost Land on *Guzerat*. It is a small Island of three Miles long, and two broad, belonging to the Crown of *Portugal*. The City is pretty large, and fortified by an high Stone Wall, with Bastions at convenient Distances, well furnished with Cannon to flank it, and a deep Mote hewn out of an hard Rock, to defend it on the Land Side, which is about one third Part of the City. The other Parts are fortified by Nature, having the Ocean thick set with dangerous Rocks and high Cliffs, who forbid any Approaches on that Side, and a rapid deep River, that affords a good Harbour, on the North-east Side. The Harbour is secured by two Castles, one large, that can bring above 100 large Cannon to bear on the Mouth of the Harbour, to forbid Shipping Entrance without Leave. The other is but small, and is built irregularly on a Rock in the Middle of the River, and Chanels for Shipping to pass by it, within ten Yards of its Wall. It is made use of for a Magazine for Powder and other warlike Stores.

It is one of the best built Cities, and best fortified by Nature and Art, that ever I saw in *India*, and its stately Buildings of free Stone and

and Marble, are ſufficient Witneſſes of its ancient Grandeur and Opulency; but at preſent not above one fourth of the City is inhabited. It contains five or ſix fine Churches, which are great Ornaments to the City, which ſtands on a riſing Ground of an eaſy Aſcent from the great Caſtle; and the Churches, being built wide from one another, and ſtanding gradually higher than one another, make the *Viſto* from the Sea admirably pleaſant, by ſhewing all their beautiful Fronts that Way. And within they are well decorated with Images and Paintings.

THERE is a Tradition, that the *Portugueze* circumvented the King of *Guzerat*, as *Dido* did the *Africans*, when they gave her Leave to build *Carthage*, by deſiring no more Ground to build their Cities than could be circumſcribed in an Ox's Hide, which having obtained, they cut it into a fine Thong of a great Length, and over-reacht their Donors in the Meaſure of the Ground.

AFTER the City was built and fortified, it drew all the Trade from the King's Towns of Commerce thither, which made him heartily repent his Generoſity; and he made Propoſals to the *Portugueze* to reimburſe all the Charge and Expence they had been at, if they would reſtore that Iſland again, but he could never perſwade them to that Bargain, and ſince fair Means would not do, he deſigned to try what might be obtained by Force, wherefore he raiſed a great Army, and beſieged it, but was ſoon forced to draw off again

gain with Loss, for the *Portugueze* large Cannon from their Walls disturbed and distrest his Camp so, that he found but little Safety for himself, and much less for his Host.

THIS City came to such an Height of Trade and Riches in the sixteenth Century, that it drew a very potent Enemy from the *Red Sea*; for, about the Year 1540. the *Turks* designing to have a Footing in *India*, cast their Eyes on *Diu*, as being conveniently situated, and well fortified for their Purpose, so they came in a Fleet of Gallies and Transports 25000 strong, from *Aden*, and landed on the West End of the Island, and laid Siege to the City; but the *Portugueze* sent a Reinforcement from *Goa*, of twenty Sail, some of which were large Ships or Galleons, who carried heavy Metal, with which they battered the *Turkish* Fleet, being small Vessels, that many *Turks* were sunk, and the Bashaw was forced to make off with great Loss and Shame, and leave their battering Artillery to the *Portugueze*, for which Misfortune and Disgrace, he lost his Head when he returned to *Aden*.

BUT about the Year 1670. the *Muskat Arabs* had better Fortune, for they came with a Fleet of Trankies, and took an Opportunity to land in the Night, on the West End of the Island, without being discovered, and marcht silently close up to the Town, and, at Break of Day, when the Gates were opened, they entred without Resistance. The

Alarm

Alarm was ſoon ſpread over the Town, and happy was he who got firſt to the Caſtle Gates, but thoſe who had heavy Heels were ſacrificed to the Enemies Fury, who ſpared none, ſo in a Moment that fair rich City and Churches were left to the Mercy of the *Arabs*, who, for three Days, loaded their Veſſels with rich Plunder, and mounted ſome Cannon in a great beautiful Church, and fired at the Fort, but to little Purpoſe. The Governor, who was in the Caſtle, could ſoon have obliged them to remove farther off the Caſtle, by the Force of his heavy Cannon, yet the Prieſthood forbid him firing at the Church, on Pain of Excommunication, leſt ſome unlucky Shot ſhould ſacrilegiouſly have defaced ſome holy Image.

But the *Arabs*, like a Parcel of unſanctified Rogues, made ſad Havock on the Churches Trumpery, for, beſides robbing them of all the ſanctified Plate and Caſh, they did not leave one Gold or Silver Image behind them, but carried all into diſmal Captivity, from whence they never returned that I could hear of. And as for the poor Images of Wood and Stone, they were ſo rudely treated by thoſe barbarous *Infidels*, that they came well off if they loſt but a Limb, and I ſaw ſome who loſt their Heads: But by the indefatigable Induſtry of the Clergy, their Churches are again as well, or better furniſhed with well carved Images of Wood and Stone than they were before; but I ſaw none of Gold or Silver to ſupply the Places of the poor Captives.

HOWEVER, before the *Arabs* had done plundring, they became ſecure and negligent, which the Governor having Notice of, proclaimed Freedom to all Slaves who would venture to ſally out on the Enemy. Accordingly about 4000 Soldiers and Slaves made a Sally with Succeſs, killing above 1000 *Arabs*, and made the reſt flee from the Town, the Aſſailants loſing but very few; and by that one Sally the Town was regained. Thoſe Slaves are generally *Moſambique* and *Mombaſs Negroes*, whoſe Strength and Bravery I have mentioned before. The City ſtill feels the diſmal Effects of the Loſs it then received. At preſent there are not above 200 *Portugueze* both in the Caſtle and City. The reſt of its Inhabitants are *Banyans* of all Sorts. There may be about 40000. but few of them of Fortune or Figure, becauſe the Inſolence of the *Portugueze* makes it unſafe for money'd Strangers to dwell among them. The King of *Portugal* has about 12000 Pounds *per Annum*, of Poll Money paid into his Treaſury, and the Cuſtoms and Land-tax may come to about 6000 Pounds more: But if that Iſland were in the Hands of ſome induſtrious *European* Nation, it would be the beſt Mart Town on the Coaſt of *India*, for the River *Indus* being near Neighbours, both by *Sindy* and *Cambay*, thoſe Commodities might be imported and exported to Advantage. And that Commerce has raiſed *Surat*.

ALL

All the Country between *Diu* and *Dand* Point, which is about 30 Leagues along Shore, admits of no Traffick, being inhabited by Freebooters, called *Warrels*, and often associate with the *Sanganians*, in exercising Piracies and Depredations. They confide much in their Numbers, as the others do, and strive to board their Prizes, and, assoon as they get on board, they throw in Showers of Stones on the Prizes Decks, in order to sink them that Way, if they don't yield, and they have earthen Pots as big as a six Pound Granadoe Shell, full of unquenched Lime, well sifted, which they throw in also, and the Pots breaking, there arises so great a Dust, that the Defendants can neither breathe nor see well. They also use Wicks of Cotton, dipt in a combustible Oyl, and firing the Wick, and throwing it into their Opposer's Ship, it burns violently, and sets Fire to the Parts that it is thrown on. They have no Cities, and their Villages are small. The best of them stands about 60 Miles to the Eastward of *Diu*, and is called *Chance*. It is built about a League within the Mouth of a River, which has a small Island lying athwart it, about two Miles into the Sea. The Island has good Springs of fresh Water, but no Inhabitants, *In Anno* 1716. the *English* went to burn that Village, and their pirating Vessels, but were unsuccessful in their Undertaking. The *Warrels* occupy all the Sea-coast as high as *Goga*, which lies about 12 Leagues within the Gulf of *Cambay*. And the Coast, from *Dand* Point

to

to *Goga*, is very dangerous, being thick ſet with Rocks and Sand Banks; and a rapid Tide runs amongſt them of 6 or 8 Miles in an Hour, in a Chanel that is 20 Fathoms deep in ſome Places, which cauſes Anchoring to be dangerous alſo.

Goga is a pretty large Town, and has had ſome Mud Wall Fortifications, which ſtill defend them from the Inſults of their Neighbours the *Coulies*, who inhabit the Northeaſt Side of *Guzerat*, and are as great Thieves by Land as their Brethren the *Warrels* and *Sangamans* are by Sea: Nor is there any Land Army that can come into their Country to chaſtiſe them, for there are ſo many Rivulets made by *Indus* and the Sea, that are ſo ſoft and muddy at the Bottom, that there is neither Paſſage for Men nor Horſe to penetrate their Country. And their Towns are invironed with ſuch thick Hedges of green *Bamboos*, which are not to be burned in a ſhort Time, and the People ſo numerous and valiant, that it would be an hard Task to civilize them.

Goga has ſome Trade, admitting Strangers to a free Commerce in ſuch Merchandize as are fit to be imported or exported to or from *Guzerat*. It has the Conveniency of an Harbour for the largeſt Ships, tho' they ly dry on ſoft Mud, at low Water; but the Tides riſing four or five Fathoms perpendicular, afford Water enough at high Water. The Town is governed by an Officer from the *Mogul*, who commands about 200 Men, who are

are kept there for a Guard to it, and are ſubordinate to the Governor of

CHAP. XIII.

Gives an Account of the Cities of Cambay, Baroach *and* Surat; *with ſeveral Occurrences that happened to them.*

CAMBAY, or, as the Natives call it, *Cambaut*, about 12 Leagues from *Goga*, in the Bottom of the Gulf of *Cambay*, on a ſmall River, that is ſent by the Overflowing of the *Indus* into that Gulf or Bay, is a large City, with high Walls, and was formerly the Metropolis of a Kingdom that bore the City's Name; but *Eckbar*, great Grandfather to *Aurengzeb*, ſent his Son, *Jehan Guire*, with a great Army in the ſixteenth Century, and conquered it, and annext it to the Empire of the *Great Mogul*.

It is ſtill a Place of good Trade, tho' not half inhabited, and it contributes very much to the Wealth and Grandeur of *Surat*, to which it is ſubordinate; and its Vicinity to *Amadabant*, from whence it is about 150 Miles diſtant, makes it ſhare the Advantages of that great City, which, in Magnitude and Wealth, is little inferior to the beſt Towns in *Europe*. What it exports by Sea, comes moſt to *Cambay*, and carried by the *Surat* Shipping all over *India*, except what *European* Ships carry for *Europe*.

THE

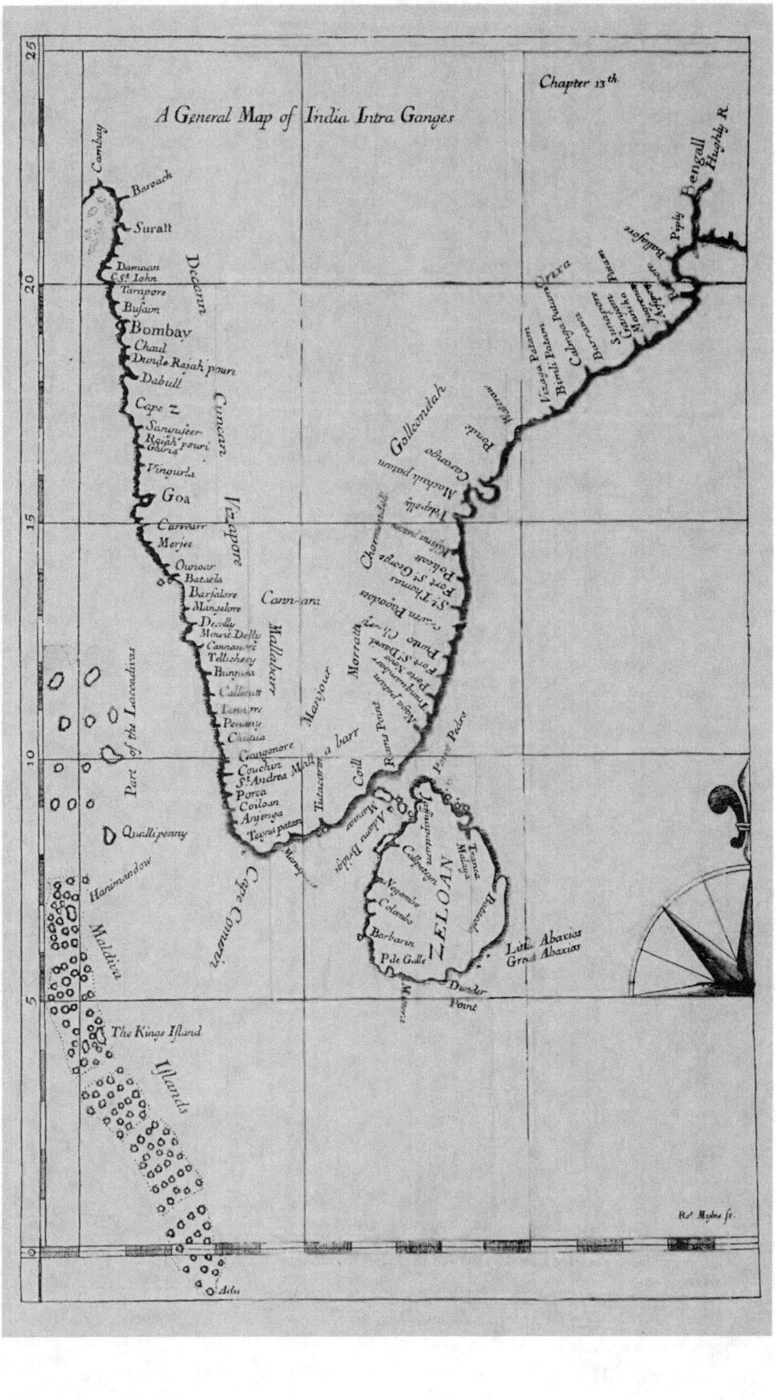
Chapter 13th
A General Map of India Intra Ganges
Cambay
Baroach
Suratt
Damaan
Tarapore
Bombay
Chaul
Dabull
Decann
Cuncan
Goa
Vingurla
Visapore
Merjee
Batacla
Barsalore
Mangalore
Cannanore
Tellichery
Callicutt
Penany
Cranganore
Couchin
St. Andrea
Porca
Coiloan
Anjenga
Canarin
Mallabarr
Part of the Laccadivas
Quallipenny
Maldiva
The Kings Island
Islands
Adu
Cape Comarin
Marrowa
Coll
Ramas Point
Point Pedro
Jaffnapatam
Trinca Malaya
Collapatam
Negombo
Colombo
Barbarin
P. de Galle
ZELOAN
Little Abaxios
Great Abaxios
Dundar Point
Charmondell
Gollcondah
Masulipatam
Caranga
Fort St. George
St. Thomas
Fort St. David
Porto Novo
Tranquebarr
Nega patam
Vizaga Patam
Bimli Patam
Orixa
Ballasore
Bengall
Hughly R.
Piply

The Product and Manufactories of *Cambay* are inferior to few Towns in *India*. It abounds in Grain and Cattle, Cotton and Silk. The Cornelian and Agate Stones are found in its Rivers, and no where else in the World. Of Cornelian they make Rings, and Stones for Signets, and of the Agate, Cabinets, intire Stone except the Lids. I have seen some of 14 or 15 Inches long, and 8 or 9 deep, valued at 30 or 40 Pounds *Sterl.* They also make Bowls of several Sizes of Agate, and Spoons, and Handles of Swords, Daggers and Knives, and Buttons, and Stones to set in Snuff-boxes, of great Value.

They embroider the best of any People in *India*, and perhaps in the World. Their fine Quilts were formerly carried to *Europe*. I have seen some worth 40 *L. Sterl.* and some Cornelian Rings, above double their Weight in Gold. The *Patanners* are their near Neighbours. They are mostly Horsemen, and bold Fellows, who borrow round Sums from the City, by Way of Compulsion, and the *Rasspouts* and *Coulies* make Inroads into this Province, and plunder even to the Gates of the City, and sometimes have surprised, and plundred the City itself, for which Neglect the Governors Heads answered.

In Anno 1716. they were very bold and presumptuous, so that there was a Stop put to all the Commerce of *Amadabant* and *Cambay*. The Governor of *Surat* got an Army of 20000 to chastise and restrain them; but they laid so many Ambuscades, that, in two Months,

Months, the Army was reduced to leſs than Half of the Number, and the reſt were obliged to get Home, with ſorrowful Hearts, to *Surat*.

THE next Town of Note for Commerce, is *Baroach*, a walled Town, ſtanding on a riſing Ground, on the Banks of the River *Nerdaba*. Formerly it was a Place of great Trade, but in *Aurengzeb*'s Wars with his Brothers, about the Year 1660. this Town held out a great While againſt his Army. That Seaſon proving a dry one, *Aurengzeb*'s Folks ſuffered much for Want of freſh Water and Proviſions, but at laſt he took it, and put all to the Sword that had born Arms againſt him, and raz'd Part of the Walls, and pronounced a Curſe on them that ſhould repair them again. But the *Sevajees* Incurſions made him order the Rebuilding them himſelf, and he chriſtned it *Suckabant*, or the *dry City*; but that new Name could not efface the old one, which it yet retains. It is now inhabited by Weavers, and ſuch Mechanicks as manufacture Cotton Cloth. And the *Baroach* Baſtas are famous throughout all *India*, the Country producing the beſt Cotton in the World. This Town is alſo ſubordinate to *Surat*; and formerly the *Engliſh* and *Dutch* had Factories ſettled there, but of late have withdrawn them.

Surat is the next Sea-port. It was built about the Year 1660. on the Banks of the River *Tapta* or *Tappee*, which being diſcommoded with Banks of Sand at *Rannier*, the then Mart Town on this River, the *Engliſh* removed

moved about two Miles farther down the River, on the opposite Side, near a Castl which had been built many Years before, to secure the Trade from the Insults of the *Malabar* Pirates, who used to lord it over all the Sea-coast between Cape *Comerin* and *Cambay.* In a little Time after the *English* had settled there, others followed their Example, so that in a few Years it became a large Town, but without Walls, and so it continued till about the aforesaid Year, that *Rajah Sevajee,* who had never submitted to the *Mogul's* Domination, came with an Army, and plundred it, except the *European* Factories, who stood on their Guard. Them he complimented with the Profer of his Friendship, because perhaps he apprehended, that he could not plunder them without Bloodshed and Loss of Time. However he carried away a very great Booty, which made the Inhabitants petition *Aurengzeb* to secure them for the future, by a Wall round their Town, which Favour he granted, enclosing about 4 Miles to build their City in; but Trade increasing, the Town was too small within the Walls to contain the People that came about Commerce, wherefore several large Suburbs were added to the City for the Conveniency of Mechanicks. The Wall was built of Brick, about eight Yards high, with round Bastions, 200 Paces distant from one another, and each had 5 or 6 Cannon mounted on them. And the rich Men of the Town built many Summer-houses in the

Fields, and planted Gardens about them to ſolace themſelves and Families in the Heats, which are pretty violent in *April*, *May* and *June*.

THE City flouriſhed in Trade till *Anno* 1686. that the *Engliſh* Company diſturbed its Tranquillity by an unjuſt War they made on *Surat*, but pretended it was not with the *Mogul*, who had given them many Indulgences, which War I'll remark when I treat of *Bombay*, but that War was ended *in Anno* 1689. neither to the Profit nor Honour of that *Eaſt-india* Company. *In Anno* 1695. Captain *Evory* a Pirate diſturbed the Trade and Tranquillity of the Town with four ſmall Ships, taking one of the *Mogul*'s Ships, with a great Booty in Silver and Gold, and a *Mahometan* Lady, as I obſerved before on the Commerce of the *Red Sea* and the Iſland of *Madagaſcar*. And ſince that Time this City has felt many Convulſions in its Trade.

In Anno 1705. when *Aurengzeb* began to be crazy with old Age, the circumjacent *Rajahs*, with an united Force of fourſcore thouſand Horſe, came and beſieged *Surat*, and plundred all the Villages in the plain Country; but having no Artillery, they could do but little Harm to the City itſelf, beſides ſtraitning it a little for Proviſions, but the City having their River and Sea open, that Difficulty was removed by plentiful Supplies brought them from *Guzerat*.

THESE Freebooters go under the general Appellation of *Gennims*, but they are compoſed

posed of the aforementioned *Warrels*, *Coulies*, *Rassbouts*, *Patanners* and *Gracias*. These *Gracias* were formerly the landed Men of this Country, and, upon their Submission to *Ecbar*, the then Emperor of *Mogul*, articled to have the Ground Rents paid to them and their Posterity; but the *Nabobs* often defraud them, and they, to put the Governors of Towns and Villages in mind of the Contract, come in great Numbers, and plunder, or lay them under Contribution.

But whilst this rabble Army lay before the Town, the Citizens built Sconces in convenient Places, about half a Mile without the Wall, to protect the Suburbs, and all those Sconces had Cannon mounted on them, which kept the *Gennims* at a Distance; and, after the Sconces were finished, they built a good high Wall between each Sconce, that encompassed the whole Suburbs, which Wall is about five Miles in Length from the Bank of the River above the Town, to that Part that terminates below the Town; and all the Inclosure is well inhabited. The Inhabitants are computed at 200000 Souls, and amongst them are many very rich, both *Mahometans* and *Gentiles*. *Abdul Gafour*, a *Mahometan* that I was acquainted with, drove a Trade equal to the *English East-india* Company, for I have known him fit out in a Year, above twenty Sail of Ships, between 300 and 800 Tuns, and none of them had less of his own Stock than 10000 Pounds, and some of them had 25000; and, after that foreign Stock was ſent away, he behoved to have as much more of an inland Stock for the following Year's Market. When he died, he left his Eſtate to two Grandſons, his own Son, who was his only Child, dying before him. But the Court had a Fling at them, and got above a Million *Sterl.* of their Eſtate.

THE Trade of *Surat* was, and ſtill is very conſiderable, for, from *Anno* 1690. to 1705. the Revenues ariſing from the Cuſtom-houſe, Land Rents and Poll Money, *communibus annis*, came to 1300000 Rupees, which is *Sterl.* 162500 *L.* And the Revenue of *Amadabant* is generally reckoned ten Times as much as *Surat.* The Cuſtoms in the King's Books, are but 2 *per Cent.* for *Mahometans*, and 5 *per Cent.* for *Gentiles*. The Land pays three Quarters of its Product in Corn, and the Poll about a Crown an Head; but the Rich generally aſſiſt the Poor, ſome paying for 10. ſome for 100. and ſome for 1000. This Account I had from an Officer, called the *Vaccanaviece*, who is obliged yearly to take in the Accounts of the Collections, and ſend them to Court. Beſides the current News that monthly occur in his Diſtrict, he ſends to the Vizier by Poſt.

THE Poſt in the *Mogul*'s Dominions goes very ſwift, for at every Caravanſeray, which are built on the High-roads, about ten Miles diſtant from one another, Men, very ſwift of Foot, are kept ready. The Letters are incloſed in a gilded Box, which he that carries holds over his Head when he comes near

near the Seray, and giving Notice of his Arrival, another takes it, and runs to the next, and so on, Night and Day, at 5 or 6 Miles in an Hour, till it is carried where directed to, so that in eight Days, Advices are brought from the farthest Parts of that large Empire, to Court. And those Curriers are called *Dog Chouckies*.

In the City of *Surat* there are as many different Religions as in *Amsterdam*. That by Law established, is *Mahometan*, of *Hali*'s Sect, and they are called *Moors*. Then there are *Persians* and *Turks*, and some called *Musey*, who observe *Moses*'s Law as well as the *Alcoran*, and another Sect called *Molacks*, who observe some ancient *heathnish* Customs and Feasts; but all the others reckon them *Hereticks*. They have a yearly Feast, but the Time of its Celebration is only known to themselves, wherein, after much Mirth and Jollity, each Sex withdraw to a Room. The Women take each an Handkerchief, (or some such Sign that may be again known) and go in the Dark promiscuously among the Men, and, without speaking, ly down together on Mats or Carpets spread for that Purpose, and enjoy one another's Company some Hours, then withdraw to their own Room, leaving their Signals with their Bedfellows, who know whom they have been caressed by: but very often they find incestuous Embraces, which at that Feast are only lawful. *Aurengzeb* made it Death to be found at those Meetings, yet that execrable

Rite is ſtill continued and practiſed. And *Abdul Gafour*, the rich Merchant aforementioned, was a Diſciple of that Sect.

THE *Banyans* are moſt numerous in this City, and are either Merchants, Bankers, Brokers or Pen-men, as Accountants, Collectors and Surveyors, but few or none Handycrafts, except Taylors and Barbers. They have 85 different Sects among them, that do not eat with one another. The greateſt Part of the eaſtern Religion is in Forms of Worſhip, and abſtaining from certain Meats; and their Prieſts differ as much in thoſe Points, and ſome others of Doctrine, as *Papiſts* and *Proteſtants* do, for the *Brahamans* or *Bramanes* are the Prieſts of the major Part of thoſe Sects, who gull the People when any are dangerouſly ſick, by perſwading them to leave Legacies to their Church, as ſome pious *Chriſtians* do among us, and when they obtain a Legacy, they gratefully acknowledge the Receit of it, by putting a Scroll of Paper into the dead Perſon's Hand, containing an Account of the Legacy, with a Bill at the Bottom, to receive ten Times the Value in the other World, from ſome eminent Saint that deals in ſuch Bills of Exchange in Paradiſe. They have Patriarchs and Biſhops to ſuperintend the inferior Clergy, who, by Virtue of a divine Right, live ſplendidly and luxuriouſly on the Oblations of the People.

THE other Sects are taught by the *Talapoins*, who declaim againſt that *papiſtical* Polity

lity, and preach up Morality to be the best Guide to human Life, and affirm, that a good Life in this World, can only recommend us in the next, to have our Souls transmigrated into the Body of some innocent Beast, or to rest in Paradise.

Their Priests indeed shew much Self-denial, for they live on Alms, and their *Pontificalia* is a white Sheet that covers their Bodies, from the Shoulders downwards, a black Staff about 5 Foot long in their Hand, and a small earthen Pot, with some powdered Saffron and Oyl, to mark those on the Forehead that have received their Benediction that Day. When they go abroad, the old carries a Novice in his Company, to teach him Divinity and Morality by Example. They seldom speak in the Streets, but look gravely and demurly, and they extend their Charity even to Beasts and Birds. They suffer their Hair to grow as low as their Shoulders, and have no other Covering on their Heads, and keep their Beards shaved.

Another Sort of them are Doctors of Physick, who pretend to do great Cures by Amulets, Philtres and Prayers. They have some Skill in Simples and Minerals, which make them in great Esteem; but when their Skill in Physick produces not the promised Effects, then they perswade the Patient, that they ly under the Displeasure of some angry Deity, who must be appeased by Oblations and Penances, which they turn to good Account, by ordering the Offerings and Penance to be light; and when that Trick fails, they leave their Patients to work out their own Salvation the beſt Way they can.

THERE is another Sort called *Jougies*, who practiſe great Auſterities and Mortifications. They contemn worldly Riches, and go naked, except a Bit of Cloth about their Loyns, and ſome deny themſelves even that, delighting in Naſtineſs and an holy Obſcenity, with a great Shew of Sanctity. They never cut nor comb their Hair, and beſmear their Bodies and Faces with Aſhes, which makes them look more like Devils than Men. I have ſeen a ſanctified Raſcal of 7 Foot high, and his Limbs well proportioned, with a large Turband of his own Hair wreathed about his Head, and his Body bedawb'd with Aſhes and Water, ſitting quite naked under the Shade of a Tree, with a *Pudenda* like an Aſs, and an Hole bored through his Prepuce, with a large Gold Ring fixed in the Hole. This Fellow was much revered by Numbers of young married Women, who, proſtrating themſelves before the living *Priapus*, and taking him devoutly in their Hands, kiſt him, whilſt his bawdy Owner ſtrokt their ſilly Heads, muttering ſome filthy Prayers for their Prolification.

THE Auſterities of the *Jougies* are beyond Belief to thoſe who have not been Eye-witneſſes of them. Some ſtand on one Foot ſome Years, with their Arms tied to ſome Beam of an Houſe, or Branch of a Tree over their Heads, and continue in that Poſture

ſture, except when Nature calls for Exoneration, for others feed them whilſt they ſtand. Their Arms in Time ſettle in that Poſture, that ever after they become uſeleſs, and are not to be brought again into their natural Poſition. Some ſit in the Sun-ſhine, with their Faces looking upwards, till they are incapable of altering the Poſture of their Necks, their Gullet ſwelling almoſt as thick as their Heads; and they alſo take no Suſtenance with their own Hands. Others clinch their Fiſts, and ty them in that Poſture, till their Finger Nails come through the Back of their Hands. And their Faſtings are as incredible. I ſaw a Woman of about 30 Years of Age, who made a Vow of faſting three Months, to avert ſome impending Calamity threatned by Heaven, that ſhe pretended to foreſee. The Governor of *Surat* being a zealous *Mahometan*, (who generally diſcourage *Gentiliſm*, and ſtrive to detect their *Leger de main* Miracles) ordered the ſaid Woman to be put into a Priſon without Windows, without any other Suſtenance than fair Water, and to be well guarded by *Mahometans*, to avoid Impoſture. About 80 Days after ſhe was impriſoned, I and ſeveral other *Europeans* paid her a Viſit, and got the Door opened to obſerve her Aſpect. We found her in Health, but very weak, and her Pulſe beat very low. Her Keepers declared, that ſhe had taken no Suſtenance, but a very ſmall Quantity of Water, all the While they had the Overſeeing of her, nor did ſhe ever deſire any Food.

She

She told us, that three or four Years before, ſhe had faſted ſixty Days on the ſame Account.

Yet *in Anno* 1721. the Governor detected a great Piece of Impoſture of the *Jougies*, who paid pretty dear for their Impudence. One of thoſe ſilly Zealots, who pretended to more Sanctity than his Neighbours, gave out, that he would be buried (in a Grave 10 Foot deep) alive, and that he would appear at *Amadabant*, which is diſtant from *Surat* about 200 Miles, within the Space of 15 Days. The Grave was dug, and he went in, and had ſome Reeds placed about a Foot or two over his Head, to keep the Mould off that was to be thrown over him. There was a large Jar of Water ſtanding under the Shade of a great Tree, about ten or twelve Yards from the Grave, where a good Number of *Jougies* had for ſome Time taken up their Quarters, they were Accomplices in the Impoſture, and, by their pretended Sanctity and great Intereſt with Heaven, had gull'd many poor People into a Belief of their Story, and many brought Preſents to them. But the Governor of *Surat* ordered a Party of Soldiers to ſee the *Jougie* interred, and to ſee that no Impoſture ſhould be uſed about his pretended Reſurrection, and to ſearch well, that there ſhould be no ſubterraneous Communication between the Grave and any Place that might be ſuſpected above Ground, and accordingly ſearching narrowly, they ſuſpected ſome Place about the Root of the

Tree might afford a Passage, ordered the *Jougies* to remove a little out of their Way, which they did willingly, and, finding no Visto that might be suspected, they ordered the *Jougies* to remove their great Water Jar, which was near full of Water; but the *Jougies* clamoured loud against that Breach of their Privilege, in touching their Water: But their Noise made the *Mahometans* Suspicion grow stronger, and the Jar was either removed or broken; and behold, where the Jar stood, they discovered a Mine that reacht within 2 Foot of the Grave, which Cheat being thus detected, the angry Soldiers fell to Work with their broad Swords, to try if their Sanctity was Proof against sharp Steel, but found, by an Experiment of laying a Dozen or more dead on the Ground, and twice as many maim'd with Wounds, that they were as easily killed or wounded as other honest Folks. The poor Miracle-monger lost his Head in the Fray. That spoiled his Journey to *Amadabant*, and, which was worse, brought great Scandal on the whole Order.

I was one Day walking by the Side of a great *Tank* or Pond near *Surat*, in Company with an *English* Lady, and seeing a young *Jougy* sitting by the Tomb of a celebrated *Cutteree*, who are a Sect that bury their dead, the Youth seemed to be very devout in Prayer; but, by the Lady's Order, I interrupted him, and, asking him why he prayed there, and to whom did he direct his Prayer, he answered that he prayed to God to to make him as good a Man as he was who lay interred there. I askt him where God was, at which he ſeemed to ſmile, and askt me, where is he not? and ſo continued a little Space in Prayer, and, when he had done, he took ſome Flowers and Grain, with a little Water, and beſprinkled the Tomb, and, making ſome decent Cringings towards the Tomb, took a formal Leave to go his Way.

CHAP. XIV.

Is a Continuation of my Obſervations of the Religions and Cuſtoms uſed in Surat *and the adjacent Country.*

THE great God, whom all adore, they call *Quedaa*; but they have many inferior Deities, and of them *Mahadow*, or, as they expreſs it, *Maadow*, is the ſecond in Place and Dignity. *Ramm* is the third, and *Brahma* the fourth. And *Parvette* is a Goddeſs much venerated, and is ſuppoſed to be the Wife of *Maadow*. The inferior Deities or Saints are very numerous; but the Images of *Gunies*, *Jagarenat*, *Ruſtum*, *Gopalſami* are moſt worſhipped in their Temples, as reckoned to have moſt Intereſt with the ſuperior Deities.

THE Marriages of the *Gentiles* in *India*, are celebrated with much Pomp. They begin in the Forenoon to ſend a long Train of People with covered Diſhes or Baskets on their

their Heads, with Presents from the Bridegroom to the Bride, and, before the Present march Hautboys, Drums and Trumpets. After the Presents march some female Slaves for the Bride and Bridegroom's Use. After the Slaves comes an empty *Pallankeen* to transport the Bride from her House to her Husband's. At Night the Bride and Bridegroom are carried in State thro' the Town, with Torch-light and Musick before them, and Fireworks played off as they pass in the Streets, and the Parents of the married Couple send Presents to their Friends. They have no Choice in their Marriages, for that is left to the Parents or nearest Relations; and they are married before they can be capable either to choose or refuse, being often married at six or seven Years of Age; but they do not cohabit before the Bride be about 12. and the Bridegroom 16. As to their Burials, some burn and some inter; but Children under 4 Years of Age are all buried. And the Wives are not permitted to burn with their Husbands; but, when once she is a Widow, she never can marry again, but lives to bewail her Widowhood, and perhaps her Virginity, all her Days.

They marry but one Wife, except in Cases of Barrenness or Adultery, tho' there are no Laws against Polygamy. They abhor Buggery and Sodomy, and the *Mahometans* for that Account, because they use them. They eat twice a Day, but the Husband and Wife eat separate; and they wash before and after

after Meat. And the *Europeans* there follow that cleanly Cuſtom.

THE *Parſees* are numerous about *Surat* and the adjacent Countries. They are a Remnant of the ancient *Perſians*, who rather chooſe to be baniſht their Country than change their Religion; for in the ſeventh Century of the *Chriſtian Æra*, when *Mahometiſm* over-ran *Perſia*, the Spirit of Perſecution came there, and ſome 4 or 500 Families were put on board of Shipping, and ſent to Sea, without Compaſs or Pilot; and they, ſteering their Courſe Eaſtward (in the Southweſt Monſoons) from *Jaſques*, in about 20 Days, fell in with the Coaſt of *India* in the Night, and the firſt Thing they ſaw was a Fire aſhore, which the Exiles ſteered towards, and accidentally ſteered into the River of *Nunſaree*, about ſeven Leagues to the Southward of *Surat*, and were welcomed to Land by the Crowing of a Cock. *Zoroaſter* was their Founder, and taught them to adore the Sun and Fire, that produced and maintained all ſublunary Beings. Their ſeeing the Fire on their Approaching the Land, confirmed their Belief, in the Opinion that Adoration was due to it, for which Reaſon they never extinguiſh Fire by its oppoſite Element Water; and even if their Houſes are a burning, they'll uſe no Water to quench the Flames, but throw Earth or Duſt to put it out. And becauſe the Cock ſaluted them firſt, after they had paſt through a dangerous

Sea,

Sea, and were secure in a River, they will neither kill, nor eat the Flesh of a Cock.

When they came ashore, the charitable *Indians* flockt about them, and there being some among them that could speak some *Indian* Languages, related what hard Usage they had met with in their own Country, and that Providence having directed them to the *Indian* Country, they begged Leave to settle among them, and by their Behaviour they would shew their Gratitude for relieving distrest Strangers, who were then become their Supplicants. The generous *Indians* granted their Request, and allowed them Land to manure, and Seed to sow the Ground, upon the same Conditions and Tenure they enjoyed their own Farms: And there they settled first, and remain in and about that Country to this Day. They never marry into foreign Families, which makes them retain their native fair Complexion, little inferior to us *Europeans*, only their often Washing and Anointing, which is a Part of the Exercises of Religion, takes away the beautiful fresh Ruddiness that adorns ours. Their Rites of Marriage are performed like the other *Gentiles*, in Ostentation and Expence; but their Burials are quite different, for they enclose a small Piece of Ground, with a Wall about 4 Yards high, and place several Benches for the Corps to sit on, that the four Elements may each have a Share of the Matter their Bodies are composed of. The Sun or Fire exhales the putrid *Effluvias*.

The Water or Rain carries the putrified Flesh and the Bones to the Earth, that gives Burial to them, and the voracious Fowls carry what they can pick into the Air in their Maws. They watch the Corps all Day, till one of the Eyes is pickt out. If the Bird begins with the right Eye, they rejoyce and feast, but if with the left Eye, they mourn and lament for the ill Fortune of the Defunct's Soul, for they attribute future Happiness to the right Eye, and Misery to the left. They build these Charnel Places far from any Town or Village, lest the Stink should annoy them.

THEY are very industrious and diligent in their Vocation, and are bred to Trades and manuring Ground. They are good Carpenters or Ship-builders, exquisite in the Weaver's Trade and Embroidery, which may be seen in the rich Atlasses, *Bottadaars* and *Jemewaars* made by them, as well as fine *Baroach* and *Nunsaree Bastas* that come from their Manufactories. They work well in Ivory and Agate, and are excellent Cabinet-makers. They distil strong Waters, but that they do clandestinely, because that Trade is prohibited by the Government they live under; yet some of them get a good Livelyhood by it.

THE Fields about *Surat* are all plain, and the Ground very fertil towards the Country, but, towards the Sea, it is sandy and steril. They have excellent Beef, Mutton and Fowl daily exposed to Sale in the City, reasonably cheap.

one that comes in Boats put their Foot a-ſhore without a ſpecial Permiſſion; and all Boats or Veſſels muſt land at the Cuſtom-houſe, and the Boat and Men are narrowly ſearcht. The Cuſtoms on *Mahometans* Goods are two in the hundred, on *Chriſtians* three and three Quarters; but the *Chriſtians* are exempt from paying Poll-money, but the *Mahometans* are not, nor *Gentows*, who pay 5 *per Cent.* Cuſtoms on their Goods. The *Banyans* are Brokers even to *Mahometans*, who cannot well make Bargains without their Brokers.

THE *Mahometan* Women go always vail'd when they appear abroad. Their Garments differ but little from the Man's. Their Coats, which alſo ſerve both Sexes for Shirts, are cloſe bodied. The Mens are gathered in Plats below the Navel, to make them ſeem long waiſted, and the Womens are gathered a pretty Way above, to make their Waiſt ſeem ſhort. They both wear Breeches to the Ancle. The Men wear only Silver Rings on their Fingers, and generally but one for a Signet. The Women wear Gold Rings on their Fingers, and ſometimes one on their Thumbs, with a ſmall Looking-glaſs ſet in it; and often they wear Gold Rings in their Noſes and Ears. The *Gentiles* again permit their Women to appear bare-faced, and their Legs bare to the Knee. They wear Gold or Silver Rings, according to their Ability, one in their Noſe, and ſeveral ſmall ones in Holes bored round the Rim of the Ear, with one large and heavy in each Lappet. They wear alſo Rings on their Toes, and Shekels on their Legs, of the aforeſaid Metals, made hollow, and ſome Glaſs Beads looſe in them, that when they move the Leg they make a Noiſe like a rattle Snake. The Men wear Gold Rings in their Ears, and often three or four in a Cluſter, hanging at the Lappet. Some have a Pearl ſet in them. The *Mahometan* Men are known by their Garb, tho' the *Gentows* and theirs are of one Make, ſave only as they are all overlapt on the Breaſt. The *Mahometans* are tied on the left Side, which, among them, is the Side of Honour, and the *Gentiles* tie theirs on the right Side. The *Mahometan* Turbands are likewiſe of another Dreſs or Make than the *Heathens*; and the different Sects of the *Heathens* are known by the Figure of their Turbands.

WHEN the *Engliſh* firſt ſettled a Commerce in this Country, which was about the Beginning of the ſixteenth Century, they were held in great Eſteem; but the *Portugueze* pretending a Right to that Trade ſolely, diſturbed the *Engliſh* in theirs, murdering their People, and making Prize of all Ships and Veſſels they could overcome. One Seaſon the *Engliſh* had eight good large Ships riding at *Swally*, which is about ten Miles from *Ranier*, where the Preſident and his Council then reſided; and *Swally* was the Place where all Goods were unladed from the Shipping, and all Goods for Exportation were

were there ſhipp'd off. The *Portugueze* thinking it a fit Time to give a deadly Blow to the *Engliſh* Commerce, came with a Fleet of 6 large Ships, 10 ſmall, and 10 or 12 half Gallies, and anchored to the Northward of the *Engliſh*, in a narrow Chanel, not Muſket-ſhot wide, and a Tide generally of 6 or 7 Miles an Hour. The *Portugueze* landed near 3000 Men, and ſeized ſome Carts laden with the Company's Goods. The *Engliſh* could not bear the Inſults they daily received, held a Council, wherein it was reſolved to land 800 Men out of the Ships, and attack the *Portugueze*, while they were lulled in Security of their own Strength and Numbers, and if they were overpowered, that thoſe left on board the *Engliſh* ſhould try if they could cut a *Portugueze* Ship's Cables that lay near them, and her driving on board of another, might, with the Force of the Tide, put them all a-ground on the Shore, or a Sand Bank that they lay very near to. Accordingly, by Break of Day, the *Engliſh* were all landed, and every Ship's Crew led by their own Commander. As they had conjectured, ſo it fell out, the *Engliſh* were among the *Portugueze* before they could get in a Poſture of Defence, and put them in Confuſion. Thoſe on board had done as they were ordered, one being cut looſe, ſoon made all the reſt run a-ground, and moſt of them loſt, eſpecially the great Ships. The little *Engliſh* Army purſued the *Portugueze*, and killed many in their Flight; but at a

Point of Land, about three Miles from the Ships, the *Portugueze* made a Stand, and rallied; but the little victorious Army soon made them take a second Time to their Heels, and so the *English* got an intire Victory, with small Loss, for there were not twenty killed on the *English* Side, but above 1500 of the *Portugueze*. *In Anno* 1690. I was on the Field of Battle, and saw many human Sculls and Bones lying above Ground. And the Story of the Battle I had from an old *Parsee*, who was born at a Village called *Tamkin*, within two Miles of the Field, and could perfectly remember the Action.

CHAP. XV

Gives an Account of the famous Aurengzeb's *Birth, his Politicks and Actions in obtaining the Empire, and of his long and prosperous Reign.*

AND now, before I leave *Surat*, I will venture to relate *Aurengzeb*'s Origin, and some of his Actions.

Cha Jehan was one of the most polite Kings that ever ruled over that great Empire of *Mogulstan*. He was a great Patron to all skilful Persons in Arts and Sciences, and gave great Encouragement to Foreigners to come to his Court, treating them kindly and familiarly, and allowed them handsom Pensions to live on, and often sent for the most polite

lite of them, and discoursed them about the Customs, Laws, Commerce and Strength of the *European* Nations, and what he found valuable amongst them, he would fain have brought into his own Dominions. He was sorry to see the most beautiful Part of the Creation caged up in *Seraglios*, bred up in Ignorance, and kept from useful and pleasant Conversation, by the heavy Fetters of blind and unreasonable Custom. He turned his Thoughts to break those sordid Chains, and introduce the Ladies to a free Air, and reckoned his Court, which he then kept at *Agra* a great City, to be the most proper Part for the Stage to act it first upon.

THE first Step he took, was to order all the Ladies at Court to provide precious Stones to bring to a Market-place that he had erected, and there to shew their Wares publickly to all the Noblemen at Court, who were ordered to buy them at whatever Prices the Ladies put upon them; and the King himself was to be a Buyer, to put the greater Honour on the new erected Market. The Ladies obeyed, and took their Booths as they thought fit. On the Market Day the King and Noblemen came to Market, and bought the Jewels and other Trifles the Ladies had to dispose of.

THE King coming to the Booth of a very pretty Lady, askt what she had to sell She told him, she had one large fine rough Diamond still to dispose on. He desired to see it, and he found it to be a Piece of fine transparent

ſparent Sugar-candy, of a tolerable good Diamond Figure. He demanded to know what Price ſhe ſet on it, and ſhe told him with a pleaſant Air, that it was worth a Lack of Rupees, or 12500 *L. Sterl.* He ordered the Money to be paid, and, falling in Diſcourſe with her, found her Wit was as exquiſite as her Beauty, and ordered her to ſup with him that Night in his Palace. She promiſed to obey, and accordingly went, and ſtayed with him three Nights and Days, and then went back to her Husband, whoſe Name was *Jemal Chaun*, and was a Commander of 5000 Horſe. The Husband received her very coldly, and told her, that he would continue civil to her, but would never cohabit with her again, and would live with her in the ſame Manner as if ſhe was his Siſter. Upon which ſhe went back to the Palace, and deſired to be brought to the King, and, being conducted to him, ſhe fell at his Feet, and told what her Husband had ſaid. The King, in a Rage, gave Orders to carry the Husband to the Elephant Garden, and there to be executed by an Elephant, which is reckoned a ſhameful and terrible Death. The poor Man was ſoon apprehended, and had his Clothes torn off him, as the Cuſtom is when Criminals are condemned to that Death, and he was dragged from his Houſe, with his Hands tied before him. On his Way to the Garden, he was to paſs near the Palace, and he begged to have Leave to ſpeak to the King, and then he would die willingly, if his Majeſty

jeſty did not think fit he ſhould live. A Friend of his, who was an Officer of the Guards, ordered the Meſſengers of Death to ſtop a While, till he had acquainted the King with the Requeſt, which was accordingly done, and he was ordered to be carried into the Court of the Palace, that the King might hear what he had to ſay, and, being carried thither, his Majeſty demanded what he would have. He anſwered, that what he had ſaid to his Wife, was the greateſt Honour that he was capable to do his King, who, after he had honoured his Wife with his Embraces, thought himſelf unworthy ever after to cohabit with her. The King, pauſing a little, ordered him to be unbound, and brought to his own Room, where, aſſoon as he came, the King embraced him, and ordered a *Serpaw* or a royal Suit to be put upon him, and gave him the Command of 5000 Horſe more, but took his Wife into his own *Harran* or *Seraglio*, and, about nine Months after, the famous *Aurengzeb* came into the World. How long the Charter held for continuing thoſe Markets, I know not, but it ſeems *Cha Jehan* grew fonder of this Lady than of any he had before, tho' he had three Sons by them, the eldeſt of whoſe Names I have forgot. *Aurengzeb* was brought up and educated by his Mother, till he was about 12 Years of Age, and then he had Prieſts and Philoſophers to inſtruct him.

Cha Jehan finding his Empire too large, deſigned to divide it amongſt his Sons, and ſo ſo placed his eldeſt Son in the nothern Provinces of *Candahaar* and *Uzbeck*, to ſuperintend there, and make him acquainted with thoſe People and their Cuſtoms, that he deſigned ſhould be his Subjects. The ſecond Son *Morad Bucks* he ſent to *Decan*, to govern there. The third *Sultan Sujah* he ſent to *Bengal*, to govern that Country; and *Aurengzeb* he deſigned for *Guzerat*, being a ſmall Province in Compariſon of the others: But when *Aurengzeb* came to be about eighteen Years of Age, and had done with the School, he diſſembled his ambitious Thoughts, and declared that he deſired to live a private Life in the Province allotted him, and ſo took up the *Fakire* Habit and Way of Life, contemning the Honours and Riches of the World, and zealouſly kept the canonical Hours of Prayer, which, by the *Alcoran*, is five Times a Day. In this *Phariſaical* Way he ſpent eight or ten Years, till his Father began to be old and weak; and News being ſpread abroad that he was ſick, the eldeſt Son began to raiſe an Army in his Province, to march towards *Agra*, in order to ſeize the Crown on his Father's Demiſe. *Morad Bucks* knowing the cruel Cuſtom of his Country, which is either to die, or be ſent to an Hill near *Agra*, called *Goulour*, and there drink the *Pouſt*, (which is an Infuſion of Poppy Seeds in Water, that provokes Sleep) and ſpend his Days in a Lethargy; but, to avoid both, he alſo raiſed a good Army in his Province, and marched alſo towards *Agra*, and

Sul-

Sultan Sujah raiſed one in *Bengal*, but kept within his own Province. *Aurengzeb* continued in his Retirement and holy Exerciſes, and neither diſturbed his Father's Repoſe, as the reſt had done, nor was ſuſpected by his Brothers to have any Deſign to rule. *Aurengzeb* had a Siſter, called *Neur Mahaal*, that was continually about her Father *Cha Jehan*, and he had a great Eſteem for her, as ſhe had for *Aurengzeb*; and as ſhe was a Woman of a great Genius and Vivacity, ſhe fiſht out all the Deſigns of her Father and Brothers, and acquainted *Aurengzeb* with them by Letters, and promiſed her Aſſiſtance to ſet him on the Throne.

Cha Jehan ſent Letters to his Sons, who were in Arms, to disband their Forces, upon their Allegiance, but not one obeyed, alledging, that they kept in Arms for their own Security in caſe of his Death. The two eldeſt made daily Approaches towards *Agra*, and *Aurengzeb* raiſed a ſmall but good Army, pretending it was to keep the Peace of his own Province. However, as *Morad Bucks* was on his March towards *Agra*, he was obliged to paſs through ſome Part of *Aurengzeb*'s Territories, and they had an Interview, and agreed, that if the eldeſt Son would not be adviſed to retire back with his Army to his own Province, but continue diſobedient to their Father's Commands, then *Aurengzeb* would joyn *Morad Bucks*, and compel him by Force; but ſtill *Aurengzeb* preacht up Peace and Contempt of worldly ly Grandeur. They wrote preſſingly to their elder Brother, to honour their Father's Commands, but to no Purpoſe ; ſo *Aurengzeb* marched his Army always near *Morad Bucks*'s to meet their eldeſt Brother, and found him encampt on the Banks of the River *Gemna*, and, on the oppoſite Banks *Morad Bucks* encampt his Men. *Aurengzeb* went to wait on his elder Brother as a Mediator, but in reality to diſcover what Condition his Army was in. His Brother received him with all the Marks of Eſteem, and, after a long Conference, he invited *Aurengzeb* to joyn Forces with him, and that aſſoon as he came to the Crown, he would make him and his Heirs free Sovereigns of *Guzerat*. *Aurengzeb* anſwered, that as for his own Part, he had rather live a Subject than a Sovereign, whoſe Care about Government diſturbed the Mind, and rendred it unfit for ſweet Contemplation, and he only brought his Army there to joyn him who inclined moſt to Peace, which he found his Brother *Morad Bucks* averſe to, but that he would joyn neither till the laſt Extremity ; and, on his Return, he went to *Morad*, and told him, that his eldeſt Brother's Army was much inferior to theirs, and adviſed him to put all to the Fortune of a Battle, that he would ſtand at a little Diſtance neuter, till the Battle began, and then would fall on the Enemy's Flank and Rear with his Army, which accordingly he did, when his eldeſt Brother had no Suſpicion of ſuch Uſage. The Battle was ſhort,

but

but bloody, and the eldeſt Brother was killed, which the Remnant of his Army ſeeing, begged for Quarter, and had it, and liſted into the Conquerors Armies. The Victory was wholly imputed to *Aurengzeb*'s Conduct, by all the three Armies, which was a great Mortification to *Morad Bucks*, who expected that Honour. But *Aurengzeb* had another Game to play whilſt the Armies were ſo much at his Devotion, for his Brother *Morad Bucks* was violently inclined to the Love of Wine, tho' forbidden by their Laws. *Aurengzeb* got ſome of his own Creatures of the beſt Rank, to procure Wine and carouze with him, which they did, and he got beaſtly drunk, and vomited on the fine Carpets he lay on. While he was in that Pickle, *Aurengzeb* came to his Tent with his Guard, and demanded preſent Admittance, for there were News brought of the greateſt Importance, which he muſt, without Delay, communicate to his Brother, and ſtepping haſtily into the Tent, his Guards following him, he found his Brother in the Condition he wiſht for, and calling him ſeveral Times by his Name, he was not able to anſwer, wherefore *Aurengzeb*, out of an holy Zeal to Religion, vented many angry Words againſt the Beaſt his Brother, and then, in a ſanctified Choler, ordered one of his Guards to ſtrike off his Head, which was forthwith executed. The News of the Fratricide flew like wild Fire through the Armies, but *Aurengzeb*'s being in Arms ſoon calm'd thoſe that had a Mind to raiſe Troubles, and, in the Morning, made an Oration that pleaſed the Armies ſo well, that they ſwore Obedience to his Commands. The Clergy run his Praiſes as high as their Prophet's Paradiſe, commending his godly Piety and Zeal for poor diſtreſſed Religion, and, no Doubt, would have done the ſame for the Drunkard, had he been as politick as *Aurengzeb*, who is now ſaluted *Pautſhaw*, or Emperor, by the Army, notwithſtanding his Father was then alive.

Cha Jehan having loſt two of his Sons, expected that all his Troubles were now ended, ſent to *Aurengzeb* to come to him, and conſult about ſettling the Peace of his Country, which had been ſo long diſturbed by civil Wars, but *Aurengzeb* would not truſt himſelf within the Walls of a City, where he had not the Command in his own Hands, but wrote very ſubmiſſive Letters to his Father, and adviſed him to lay down the heavy Charge of Government on his Shoulders who was young, and much better able to manage it than a Man whoſe Age required Reſt, and gave Orders to build an high Wall round the Palace, and placed his own Creatures to guard the Palace, which ſo vext the old King, that he ordered all the Jewels of the Crown to be broken, and particularly his Throne, which he himſelf had cauſed to be made worth above a Million *Sterling*, but none durſt obey him. And *Neur Mahaal*, who had given her Brother *Aurengzeb* private Informations of her Father's Deſigns

ſigns all the Time of the Rupture, advertiſed him of the old Man's Deſign in that Affair, and cautioned him to take Care of what Meat and Drink he took, and to ſend an Army into *Bengal*, to reduce *Sultan Sujah*, who was invited by the old King, to come with his Army to *Agra*. *Aurengzeb* durſt not leave that Country where his Father was well beloved, for Fear of a Revolution in his Affairs, but ſent an Army under the Command of a truſty General, called *Emirjemal Chaun*, who, in three Years Time, chaſed *Sultan Sujah* out of the Dominions of *Bengal*, and *Cha Jehan* then dying, brought a ſerene Peace throughout the whole Empire. *Aurengzeb* remembring his Siſter's Services, made her Governeſs of the Palace, and retained her always near his Perſon, and would eat nothing but what came from her Hand.

BEING now ſettled in Peace, he invited his holy Brethren the *Fakires*, who are very numerous in *India*, to come to *Agra*, and receive a new Suit of Clothes, as a Teſtimony of his Kindneſs for them. Great Numbers came on the Invitation, and he pitched Tents in many Places round the City to entertain them, and he proclaimed, that on a certain Day the Diſtribution ſhould be made, and appointed Officers in every Tent to deliver the new Clothes, but to retain the old Rags in their Rooms, which Stratagem brought many Millions into his Treaſury, for thoſe pretended Saints having good Store of Diamonds and Gold ſewed up in their Rags, were

were forced to leave all behind them. He then bent his Thoughts on enlarging his Dominions, and quarrelled with the King of *Orixa* near *Bengal*, and with the King of *Visapore* near *Decan*, and, in ten Years, he annext their Dominions to his own large Empire. And so I leave him to take his Pleasure till the Year 1707. that he died in his Tent near *Agra*, and lies buried in a small Tomb of seven Foot long and three high, on the Side of an High-way that leads to that City.

He was a Prince every Way qualified for governing. None ever understood Politicks better than he. The Balance of distributive Justice he held in an exact *Æquilibrium*. He was brave and cunning in War, and merciful and magnanimous in Peace, temperate in his Diet and Recreations, and modest and grave in his Apparel, courteous in his Behaviour to his Subjects, and affable in his Discourse. He encouraged Virtue, and discountenanced Vice, and he studied the Laws of Humanity, and observed them as well as those of Religion, for in that Part he inclined to Superstition. He had five Sons, but three only made any Figure. The eldest was *Dara*, or vulgarly *Hazan Tarah*, the second *Shaw Allom*, the third *Furucksier*, the fourth *Eckbar*, and the fifth *Shaw Hazander*. The three first contended for the Crown after their Father's Death, but *Shaw Allom* carried it.

From *Surat* to *Damaan*, a Town belonging to the Crown of *Portugal*, and at 22 Leagues

gues Distance, are several Rivers and Villages, under the Superintendency of *Surat*. *Dumbass* is the first, but of small Consequence, either in Trade or Manufactory. *Nunsaree* is the second, that has a good Manufactory of Cotton Cloth, both coarse and fine. *Gundavee* is next, where good Quantities of Teak Timber are cut, and exported, being of excellent Use in building of Houses or Ships. *Seragoung* is a River of no other Consequence but limiting the *Mogul*'s Dominions on the Sea Side, as well as the *Portugueze* Territories. It is distant from *Damaan* about 4 Miles.

CHAP. XVI.

Treats of the Cities and Towns on the Sea-coast, belonging to the Crown of Portugal, *from* Damaan *to* Bombay.

DAMAAN was, in former Times, a Place of good Trade, but at present reduced to Poverty. It stands at the Mouth of a River on the Sea-shore, and is naturally very strong, by a deep Marsh that almost surrounds it. The Town is about half a Mile long, and near as broad, walled with a good Stone Wall, as the rest of the Buildings of the City are built of; and it has a large Cathedral to adorn it, that is conspicuous a long Way at Sea. There are two or three other Churches, and a Convent, a Monastery, a Nunnery, and an Hoſpital, and there is a Caſtle ſtands on the oppoſite Side of the River, chriſtned by the Name of St. *Salvadore*, and it is well ſecured by the Moraſs, as well as the Town. It has been for a long Time a great Eye-ſore to the Governors of *Surat*, who have often pickt Quarrels with the *Portugueze*, and laid Siege to *Damaan*, but without Succeſs.

FROM *Damaan* to *Baſſaim* is about 18 Leagues along the Sea-ſhore. There are ſeveral Rivers and Villages by the Way, *viz.* *Danaw*, *Tarrapore*, *Mahim*, *Kellem*, and the Iſland *Vaccas*, but they are all of ſmall Account in the Table of Trade.

Baſſaim is a fortified City belonging to the Crown of *Portugal*. It ſtands on a little Iſland, ſeparted from the Continent by a ſmall Rivulet. Its Walls are pretty high, and about two Miles in Circumference around the City, which has a little Citadel in the Middle of it. It contains three or four Churches, and ſome Convents and Monaſteries, with a College and Hoſpital.

IT is a Place of ſmall Trade, becauſe moſt of its Riches ly dead and buried in their Churches, or in the Hands of indolent lazy Country Gentlemen, who loiter away their Days in Eaſe, Luxury and Pride, without having the leaſt Senſe of the Poverty and Calamity of their Country. The Town is about half a League diſtant from the Iſland of *Salſet*, which Inlet ſerves it for an Harbour for ſmall Shipping, but there is not Water enough

enough to accommodate great Ships. The Governor is ſtiled, by the *Portugueze*, *General of the North*, having *Diu*, *Damaan* and *Chaul*, with all their Territories, ſubordinate to him, but the Church ſuperintends, which makes his Government both uneaſy and precarious.

Salſet is an Iſland about 25 Miles long, and, in ſome Places, 10 Miles broad. It is fruitful in Roots and Fruits, but not in Corn. It is ſtockt with Villages and Churches, but has no City on it, but an old one, called *Canra*, hewn out of the Side of a Rock, but by whom I never could learn. It is near a Mile in Length, and many antique Figures and Columns curiouſly carved in the Rock, and has ſeveral good Springs of Water to accommodate it. At preſent it is inhabited only with wild Beaſts, and Birds of Prey. The Iſland is almoſt cut in two by a narrow River that biſects it at a Town called *Verſua*, which lies on the Sea-ſhore, and has a little narrow Harbour, deep enough to receive Ships of the greateſt Burden, and is ſecured by a ſmall Fort ſtanding on the North Side, but the Town is on the South Side of the River. It drives a ſmall Trade in dry Fiſh, made here, and tranſported to the inland Countries and Villages, that want the Benefit of Fiſhing. The Fiſhers here catch their Fiſh in long Nets, faſtned to Stakes placed in the Sea, the outwardmoſt of which are driven in the Bottom on nine Fathoms Water; and they appear to Strangers like a Wood in the Sea. There are ſeveral Villages ſtanding between *Versua* and *Bombay*, on the Sea-ſhore, but *Bandara* is the moſt conſpicuous, which fronts *Mahim* on *Bombay*, about a Mile diſtant. The *Portugueze* have ſome great Guns planted at *Bandara*, but they have no Trade, becauſe the River belongs to the *Engliſh*; and all Cuſtoms of Goods, either imported or exported, are paid to the Cuſtom-houſe of *Mahim*. The Mouth of the River is peſter'd with Rocks, that forbid Entrance to any Veſſels of Burden.

In Anno 1694. the *Muskat Arabs* made a Deſcent on *Salſet*, and committed great Depredations in plundring and burning Villages and Churches, killing the Prieſts, and carried about 1400 Captives into irredeemable Slavery. And about the Year 1720. the Prieſts of *Salſet* diſturbed the *Engliſh* at *Mahim*, animating the People to Arms; but a Bomb or two thrown into the Church at *Bandara*, had no Reſpect to the Prieſthood, but ſacrilegiouſly killed one or two, beſides ſome Lay Brothers, which made them know that War was not their Trade, They were alſo troubleſom to the *Engliſh in Anno* 1722. but the *Engliſh* ſurpriſed a Parcel that were about repairing an old Fort, contrary to Articles of Agreement, and killed a Score or two, which made the reſt take to their Heels, and be quiet.

CHAP.

CHAP. XVII.

Gives a Description of Bombay, *with some historical Remarks on its Wars, Government and Trade, till* Anno 1687. *when the Foundation of a War was laid, which proved the Ruin of the then* English East-india *Company.*

B*OMBAY* comes next in Course, an Island belonging to the Crown of *England*. It was a Part of *Katharine* of *Portugal*'s Portion, when she was married to *Charles* II. of *Great Britain, in Anno* 1662. Its Ground is steril, and not to be improved. It has but little good Water on it, and the Air is somewhat unhealthful, which is chiefly imputed to their dunging their Cocoa-nut Trees with *Buckshoe*, a Sort of small Fishes which their Sea abounds in. They being laid to the Roots of the Trees, putrify, and cause a most unsavoury Smell; and in the Mornings there is generally seen a thick Fog among those Trees, that affects both the Brains and Lungs of *Europeans*, and breed Consumptions, Fevers, and Fluxes.

AFTER the Marriage, King *Charles* sent my Lord *Malberry*, with four or five Ships of War, to take Possession of it, and the King of *Portugal* sent a Vice-roy to deliver it, and all its Royalties, to the said Lord, and Sir *Abraham Shipman* was ordered to be Governor for King *Charles*. They arrived at *Bombay* in *September*, 1663. but the Church withſtood the Crown, and diſobeyed the Order: Nor would they acknowledge the Viceroy, unleſs he would come into their Meaſures, which, rather than loſe his new Dignity, he did. And the *Engliſh* Fleet was forced to go to *Swally* to land their Men, and get Refreſhments; but the Governor of *Surat*, in whoſe Diſtrict *Swally* is, grew jealous of the Numbers and Bravery of the *Engliſh*, and threatned the Factory eſtabliſhed in *Surat*, if they did not ſpeedily re-imbark, which, to avoid Suſpicion, they did, and the Governor allowed them the free Uſe of the Markets, ſo that they had no Want of Proviſions and Merchandize whilſt they ſtayed there. In *January* 1664. my Lord went back to *England*, carrying two Ships with him, and left Sir *Abraham* with the reſt, to paſs the weſterly Monſoons, in ſome Port on the Coaſt, but being unacquainted, choſe a deſolate Iſland, called *Aujadiva*, to winter at. It is ſo far from an Harbour, that it is even but a bad Road for Shipping in thoſe boiſtrous South-weſt Winds and turbulent Sea; however he landed all the Land-forces, and built Huts to defend them from the Weather. The Iſland is barren, but has ſome Springs of good Water. It is about a Mile long, and 300 Paces broad. Here they ſtayed from *April* to *October*, in which Time they buried above 200 of their Men.

When the Monſoons were over, the Squadron put to Sea, and put in to *Bombay*, to try if the Church had conſidered on the Obedience

bedience due to the King of *Portugal's* Orders, or if they had a Mind to draw the Arms of *England*, as well as their Sovereign's, upon them. Some of them had not forgot what Damages *Spain* and *Portugal* had sustained by the *English* Fleet in *Cromwel's* Time, advised the Church to obey the King, setting forth the Miseries they should be brought into in case of Noncompliance. At length their holy Zeal abated, and they were content to admit of a Treaty, but, before the Treaty was concluded, Sir *Abraham* died, and one Mr. *Humphrey Cook*, who was next in Commission, continued the Treaty, and articled, that the Inhabitants should enjoy their Lands and Religion under the King of *England*, but forgot to insert the Royalties appending on *Bombay*, which reacht as far as *Versua* on *Salset*, which Omission has been a Bone of Contention for both Parties ever since.

Mr. *Cook*, according to the Treaty, took Possession of the Island, in the King's Name, and forthwith began to fortify regularly, and, to save Charges of building an House for the Governor, built a Fort round an old square House, which served the *Portugueze* for a Place of Retreat, when they were disturbed by their Enemies, till Forces could be sent from other Places to relieve them.

After the Fort was lined out, and the Foundations laid, Sir *Gervas Lucas* arrived from *England* with two Ships, but Affairs being settled before he came, did not stay at

Bombay longer than *January* 1666. and left the Government of the Island in the Hands of Mr. *Cook* and his Council, the Presidency for the then Company, residing at *Surat*. Their Trade flourished, and increased wonderfully; but, after the Fort was finished, the King finding, that the Charge of keeping *Bombay* in his own Hands would not turn to account, the Revenues being so very inconsiderable, he made it over to the *East-india* Company in Fee Tail, which continues so till this Time.

In building the Fort where it is, Mr. *Cook* shewed his Want of Skill in Architecture, where a proper and convenient Situation ought to be well considered, for it is built on a Point of Rocks that jets into the Sea, where there are no Springs of fresh Water, and it stands within 800 Paces of an Hill, called *Dungeree*, that overlooks it, and an Enemy might much incommode it from that Hill, as we found by Experience *in Anno* 1689. when the *Mogul* sent an Army on *Bombay*. As for the Magnitude, Figure and Materials of the Fort, there is no Fault to be found in them, for it is a regular Tetragon, whose outward Polygon is about 500 Paces, and it is built of a good hard Stone, and it can mount above 100 Piece of Cannon; and that is all that is commendable in it: But had it been built about 500 Paces more to the Southward, on a more acute Point of Rocks, called *Mendham*'s Point, it had been much better on several Accounts. First, it had been much

much nearer the Road for protecting the Shipping there, it had been farther off *Dungeree* Hill, it would have had a Spring of pretty good Water, which served the Hospital that was afterwards built there, and the Shipping had been better secured that lay in the little Bay between the Point where the Fort now stands, and *Mendham*'s Point.

THEY went about building several other little Forts and Sconces in convenient Places, to hinder an Invasion, if any of their Neighbours should have attempted one. At *Mazagun* there was one, at *Souree* one, at *Sian* one, at *Mahim* one, and *Worlee* had one, and some great Guns mounted on each of them. Notwithstanding the Company was at so much Charge in building of Forts, they had no Thoughts of building a Church, for many Years after Sir *George Oxendon* began to build one, and charitable Collections were gathered for that Use; but when Sir *George* died, Piety grew sick, and the Building of Churches was grown unfashionable. Indeed it was a long While before the Island had People enough to fill a Chapel that was in the Fort, for as fast as Recruits came from *Britain*, they died in *Bombay*, which got the Island a bad Name.

THERE were reckoned above 5000 *L.* had been gathered towards building the Church, but Sir *John Child*, when he came to reign in *Bombay*, converted the Money to his own Use, and never more was heard of it. The Walls were built by his Predecessors

ſors to five Yards high, and ſo it continued till the Year 1715. that Mr. *Boone* came to the Chair, who ſet about building it, and, in five Years Time, finiſhed it by his own Benevolence, and other Gentlemen, who, by his Perſwaſions, were brought in to contribute. The Company alſo contributed ſomething towards that pious End.

About the Year 1674. Preſident *Aungier*, a Gentleman well qualified for Governing, came to the Chair, and, leaving *Surat* to the Management of Deputies, came to *Bombay*, and rectified many Things that were amiſs, and brought the Face of Juſtice to be unvailed, which before lay hid in a ſingle Perſon's Breaſt, who diſtributed her Favours according to the Governor's Direction. He erected a formal Court, where Pleas were brought in and debated; but that Method laſted but a few Years, when Sir *John Child* came to the Chair the Court was done. Mr. *Aungier* adviſed the Company to encloſe the Town from *Dungeree* to *Mendham*'s Point, for ſecuring the trading People from the Inſults of their troubleſom beggarly Neighbours on the Continent; but his Propoſals were rejected, and that neceſſary Piece of Work was reſerved for Mr. *Boone* alſo. And happy it was for the Inhabitants that the Town was ſecured by a Wall, otherwiſe *Connajee Augaric* would have haraſſed them with continual Inſults ſince his War with the *Engliſh* began.

The Name of Mr. *Aungier* is much revered by the ancient People of *Surat* and *Bombay*

Bombay to this Day. His Justice and Dexterity in managing Affairs, got him such Esteem, that the Natives of those Places made him the common Arbitrator of their Differences in Point of Traffick: Nor was it ever known that any Party receded ever from his Award.

THERE are no Dangers in going into *Bombay* Road, but one sunk Rock that lies about half a League from the Castle. It is dry at low Water, and has a Chanel within it deep enough for the greatest Ships to pass. I never heard of any Damage done by that Rock, but to a small Ship called the *Baden*, which, by Carelesness, run on it at Noonday, and was lost.

IN the Year 1673. the *Dutch East-india* Company having an Eye on *Bombay*, sent a Squadron of Ships, with a little Army, to try if they could take it in amongst their other Conquests of *India*, but, on their landing, met with so warm a Reception, that they were glad to get off with the Loss of 2 or 300 of their Men, and so left the *English* to the quiet Possession of it.

THE Governors proved tolerable good, till 1682. that Sir *John Child* spoilt it. The *India* Company knowing how to make use of King *Charles*'s Necessities, made him some Presents of Money, and he, in grateful Acknowledgments, granted them Power to rob their fellow Subjects in *India*; but they used that Power to their own Destruction, for Mr. *Child*'s Pride and Oppressions grew so intolerable, that even the Gentlemen in the

Com-

Company's Service had not the free Exercise of Trade, and much less private Merchants. And he, trampling on the established Laws of *England*, by Advice of his Namesake who governed the Company in *Europe*, by imprisoning and murdering their fellow Subjects, grew hateful to all.

In Anno 1684. he made his Brother in Law Mr. *Ward* his Deputy of *Bombay*, who designed to fish in troubled Waters. Mr. *Child* being honoured with the Title of Baronet, by the powerful Motive of the Company's Money to the King, he, at the same Time, got the Commission of General, which puft him up so, that he contemned all Laws human and divine. The military Gentlemen, who had made Contracts in *England* for their Salaries, tho' paid at 20 *per Cent.* Loss, yet to shew himself a good Oeconomist for his Master's Interests, sent his Deputy Orders to reduce their Pay to 30 *per Cent.* less than it was before, tho' it was so small, that they could hardly bring both Ends to bear at the Month's End. That hard Pill the Sons of *Mars* could not swallow, and so bent their Minds on a Revolution: And having come to some Knowledge of Mr. *Ward*'s tampering with the *Sevajee* to land on the Island, they detected some Letters of his to that Purpose, which gave them a Ground for a Revolt. The *Sevajee* indeed sent a Fleet of 80 Sail of small Vessels to land on the back Bay which faces the Ocean; but, on their trying to land some Forces, they were warmly repulsed,

pulsed, and lost many of their Men, which made them draw off again in Confusion, and Mr. *Ward*, being confronted with his own Letters, and having little to say in his own Defence, was made a Prisoner; and General *Child*'s Faction was sent to *Surat* to him. The Islanders, taking the Government of the Island into their own Hands, chose Captain *Kegwine* Major of the Military, to superintend military Affairs, and one Captain *Thorburn* to oversee the civil.

General *Child* soon dispatcht Letters to *England*, and gave an Account of the Rebellion, and King *Charles* dispatched a Frigat, called the *Phenix*, for *India*, to demand the Restitution of the Island, and put it again into the Company's Hands. They arrived at *Bombay*, in *September* 1685. and shewed the King's Orders, with a full Pardon to all who yielded Obedience, which unanimously the Islanders did; but, for their own Security, drew up some Articles to be signed by General *Child* and Captain *Tyrrel*, who commanded the *Phenix*, one of which Articles was, *That any Person that had a Mind to go for* England, *should have free Liberty, and a Passage on board the Company's Shipping*, which being agreed to and signed, Captain *Kegwine* took his Passage on board the first Ship; but *Thorburn* being a married Man, and having a small Estate, as well as a Family on the Island, could not so easily remove, but trusted to the Act of Grace, and the Treaty they had made.

AFTER

AFTER General *Child* had gotten the Reins of Government again into his Hands, he became more insupportable than ever. He erected a Court of Inquisition, and made an old *Greek*, one Captain *Garey*, Judge, who had condemned a Man to be hanged on a *Teusday*, and the Man suffered according to Sentence; but, on *Friday* after, the poor dead Fellow was ordered to be called before the Court, but he would not comply with the Orders.

CAPTAIN *Thorburn* was the first that felt the Weight of Mr. *Child*'s Displeasure. He got some Fellows to swear him out of his little Estate, who brought in forged Bonds for Sums borrowed from one *King*, whom he never had any Dealings with, and found Witnesses to attest them. All that *Thorburn* had, was too little to pay the Sums, for which his Estate was taken from him, and himself put in Prison, without the Permission of one Slave to attend or serve him in Prison. His own Wife was not permitted to visit him, which hard Usage brought him into a violent Fever, that soon put an End to his Life. About two Days before he died the Goaler acquainted his Lady of his Danger, and she, with two small Children, went to the General, and, on their Knees, begged that a Doctor might be permitted to visit her Husband, but he was inexorable, and would allow no such Favour, only granted her Leave to be in Prison with him till he died, and she stayed but one Day and a Part of a Night till he expired.

expired. When the Tragedy was over, she was going Home to her distrest Family, but found her Slaves and Children removed into a little Out-house of hers, and the Doors of her Dwelling-house shut against her. The Lady had two Sisters married on the Island, and she, hoping to find Relief from them, went to visit the eldest, but she met her at the Door and told her she could have no Admittance, her Husband being liable to Proscription, if he admitted her into his House; and she believed the other Sister's Husband durst not entertain her in his House. The poor Lady, full of Sorrow and Grief, being abandoned of all her Friends and Relations, went back to her distressed Family, and, having no visible Way of Support, had once some Thoughts of putting an End to her Miseries; but her Sisters, unknown to their Husbands, sent her some Relief by a trusty female Slave in the Night, and a Letter, (that they desired her to burn assoon as she had read) wherein they promised to be assisting in the Maintenance of her and her Children, till the Almighty should think proper to deliver her out of the Persecution.

THE poor Lady had both Beauty and Discretion enough to recommend her to the virtuous Part of Mankind; but none of the Gentlemen that wisht her well, durst make Addresses to her, only one, who had the Command of a Ship in the *Indian* Merchants Service, as he had no Dependence on the General, nor his Masters in *England*, thought

he

he could not well come within the Reach of their Perſecution, ſo he courted her, and married her, but that was thought a capital Crime, and the General acquainted his *Indian* Owners, that without they diſcharged him their Service, they ſhould alſo find the Weight of his Diſpleaſure; and accordingly, to avoid Conteſts with his Excellency, he was diſcharged: But Grief put an End to his Troubles, for he died within a Year after his Marriage, and left the poor Lady another Child to take Care of, but left her above 1000 *L. Sterl.* of Stock for her and her Family's Support.

As the *Phenix* was in her Way to *India*, ſhe called at the Iſland of *Johanna*, and there found an *Engliſh* Ship, called the *Briſtol*, ſtopping ſome Lakes in her Bottom Captain *Tyrrel*, by a diſpenſing Power from the King of *England*, ſeized her, and deſigned to have carried her to *Bombay*, in Company of a ſmall Veſſel that he had ſeized on the Coaſt of *Madagaſcar*. The *Briſtol* ſunk the third Day after they put to Sea, but the other came ſafe. The *Briſtol*'s Men were looked on as Pirates, and one Mr. *Mews* a Supercargo was arraigned before the General's Tribunal, where he himſelf ſat Lord chief Juſtice, and, after his uſual Manner of beſtowing opprobrious Names, he condemned Mr. *Mews* to loſe all that he had in the World, and 1000 Pounds beſide, and to ly in Priſon, at his own Charges, till the Fine was paid; but Mr. *Vaux*, who was Judge of the

the Island in petty Affairs, shewed him the Weakness of his Sentence, and perswaded him to set the poor Man at Liberty, and order him a Passage for *England*.

WHEN Mr. *Child* first got his Commission to plunder, there were two of his own Council at *Surat* that were great Eye-sores to him, *viz.* Messieurs *Petit* and *Boucher*. They were Gentlemen of good Interest in *England*, and had great Remittances of Monies on the Company's Shipping coming yearly to them, to buy up Diamonds and send Home. General *Child* let them know, that he expected Half of their Commissions as a Perquisite to his Post, but they could not be brought to think so: However they condescended, that if he would joyn his Commissions to theirs, which were much greater than his, they would be content to make an equal Dividend in the Commissions; but that Proposition he rejected, and was resolved to carry his Point by Fraud, and wrote to the Company in *England*, of those two Gentlemens ill Services relating to the Company's Affairs, tho' none knew of any, but Mr. *Child* himself. Those Gentlemens Friends in the Committee of the Company in *England*, acquainted them, by Letters over Land, of the Danger they were in, and gave them Warning to be on their Guard; and they accordingly took an House contiguous to the Factory, and, by Degrees, conveyed what they thought fit into their new Lodgings, but retained their old ones in the Factory. When the Shipping arrived, and the Company's Packet was opened, and read at the Council Table, Mr. *Petit* ſat in his Place as ſecond, and Mr. *Boucher* in his as fourth. When ſome few Paragraphs were read, one was to diſmiſs thoſe Gentlemen from the Company's Service, and were forthwith ordered to withdraw, which accordingly they did, and went to their new Lodgings without the Factory. Aſſoon as the Council broke up, Mr. *Child* ſent Orders to confine them in their Factory Rooms; but Word being brought that they were not in the Factory, but their Doors were lockt, he gave Orders to break them open, and ſecure all that was found in them for him, eſpecially their Papers and Books; but they found nothing but a Bed furniſhed, and ſome empty Trunks. When Mr. *Child* underſtood that their Effects and Papers were removed, he raved like a mad Man, but to no Purpoſe, ſo he perpetrated their Deſtruction by Fraud; but the proſcrib'd being well beloved by the Brokers, who were always of Mr. *Child*'s Cabinet Council, were timely advertiſed of his Plots, and prepared to counterplot him. He was the firſt that bribed the *Mogul*'s Governors to joyn in Villany with a Preſident; but 'tis now a very common Piece of Policy at *Surat*, and has been often made uſe of againſt the *Engliſh* Company, ſince Mr. *Child*'s Time: However, for a Sum of about 4000 *L. Sterl.* he got the Governor of the Town to ſtretch his Commiſſion,

in

in pretending to distribute Justice, which is only the *Cadjee*'s Place to do. He got the Governor to command the two Victims to meet at a Garden near the Town, and to deliver them up to the General, who was there with a Dozen of Grenadeers to receive them, and carry them on board of a Ship that lay ready to transport them to *Bombay*, and there to feed on the Bread of Affliction as long as they lived. He had suborn'd a Gentleman to draw up an Account, wherein the Delinquents were brought in Debtors to the Company 114000 Rupees, or, 14250 *L. Sterl.* and that Gentleman swore to the Account. The two Defendants being forewarned of the Plot, had given Bonds to their *Mahometan* and *Heathen* Friends, for above Double the Sum that the honest General demanded; and it is against their Law to force any Person out of the *Mogul*'s Dominions, who is indebted to his Subjects; but when Mr. *Harris* had sworn to the Account, (for that was the Gentleman's Name) the Governor ordered the two Gentlemen Defendants to be put in Irons, and to be delivered to Mr *Child*; but their Friends protested against their going, till they had satisfied their Creditors, and declared the Governor liable to make good all the Sums contained in their Bonds, if by Violence they were sent away. That Protest startled the General and Governor both, so the Gentlemen were delivered to their Friends, and the Governor was no Loser by the General's Honesty: However they could not live in Quiet, so Mr. *Petit* bought a Ship to go a Trading, whilst Mr. *Boucher* went to the *Mogul's* Court, or rather his Camp, to try if he could procure a *Phirmaund* or Charter to be under the *Mogul's* Protection; but the Company's Money had crept into the Secretary of State's Purse that retarded Mr. *Boucher's* Affair some time: But the General, being afraid of his Success, sent a *Banyan* from *Bombay* to poison Mr. *Boucher*. This *Banyan* being often about his Tent, got acquainted with his Cook, thinking him to be the properest Person to make use of in that Affair; and, after some Discourses about General *Child* and Mr. *Boucher's* Quarrel, he told the Cook, that he had a Commission from the General to settle a Salary on him during Life, and the Sum of 500 Rupees in hand, if he would poison his Master. The Cook seemed to like the Proposals, and bid the *Banyan* bring him the Poison and the 500 Rupees, and accordingly the next Day he did, and, on the Delivery of the Money, he gave him a Paper with some Powder of white Arsenick to mix with his Master's Rice, which is a common Dish there. The Cook gave him large Promises of performing what he would, and so left him, and went to his Master with the Bag of Money and the Paper of Arsenick, and told him, that he had made a Bargain with General *Child's* *Vakeel*, or Attorney, to poison him, and told him the Terms he had agreed on, and shewed the Money and Poison. Mr.

Boucher

Boucher commended the Cook's Fidelity, and told him, that he would give him 600 Rupees to be honest, and a Maintenance during Life. And Mr. *Boucher* being bred a Druggist in his Youth, presently knew the Poison, and carried it to the *Cautwal* or Sheriff, and shewed it. The *Cautwal* used his utmost Endeavours to catch the *Banyan*, but he could never be found there.

Mr. *Boucher* had been fourteen Months soliciting to procure his *Phirmaund*; but his repeted Petitions to the Secretary had no Effect: But he had an *English* Man, one *Swan*, for his Interpreter, who often took a large Dose of Arrack. *Aurengzeb* one Day had ordered his Camp to remove to another Place, and had got on Horse-back. *Swan* took hold of that Opportuity, and got pretty near the King, holding his Petition or *Rocca* above his Head, and cried with a loud Voice in the *Persian* Language, that his Master wanted Justice done him. The *Mogul* seeing him in an *European* Garb, ordered him to be brought to him, and askt the Cause of his Complaint. He answered, that his Master had been so long at Court about procuring a *Phirmaund* to become a Subject of his Majesty's, to be freed from the Oppressions of the *English* Company, who were grown intolerable by the Connivance of his Majesty's Governors of *Surat*, and therefore conjured his Majesty, as he should answer before God at the great Day, to do his Master Justice, and grant him a *Phirmaund*. The King was

 startled

ſtartled at the bold Expreſſions, ordered his Secretary to get one ready for the Seal againſt the next Day, which was accordingly done, aud Mr. *Boucher* had it delivered to him aſſoon as it was ſigned, and then took his Leave of the Court.

WHILE Mr. *Boucher* was at Court, Mr. *Petit* made ſome Voyages into the Gulf of *Perſia*, and going thither once, met with ſome *Sanganian* Pirates, who attackt him. He defended himſelf bravely, and beat them off; but his Gunner firing a Blunderbuſh out of one of the Gun-room Ports, blew the Ship up, and the *Sanganians* took up thoſe that were ſaved by ſwimming, among whom was Mr. *Petit* himſelf.

THE *Sanganians* carried their Priſoners to *Baet* on *Guzerat*, and laid a Ranſom on them, which Mr. *Petit* agreed on, and ſent Letters to his Friends at *Surat* to pay the Money: But General *Child* hearing of Mr. *Petit*'s Misfortune, and where he was, diſpatcht a *Banyan* to *Baet*, to perſwade the Pirates not to part with their Priſoner under 25000 *L. Sterl.* and ſo they, hearkning to the *Banyan*, would not ſtand to the ſtipulated Ranſom of 5000 *L.* Mr. *Petit* ſtayed about ſix Months their Priſoner, and then died through Grief, and the ill Treatment he had received by Mr. *Child*'s Perſwaſion; but the Pirates getting no Ranſom, curſt the General for his Counſel.

In Anno 1683. the *Dutch* diſpoſſeſt the *Engliſh* Company of their Factory of *Bantam*, *tain*, on the West End of *Java*; and the *English* having a Mind to regain it by Force of Arms, built several Ships between 60 and 70 Guns, so that *in Anno* 1685. they had a Fleet ready victualled, and mann'd with 7 or 8000 Men, to the Number of 23 Sail of Line of Battle Ships, which Expence, and the continual Craving of the Court, brought their Stock very low; yet since the Maw of the Court was not enough crammed, the King laid Embargoes on the Fleet from Time to Time, for nine Months, and then the *Dutch* Ambassador had Orders to present his Majesty with 100000 Pounds, if he would command the Company not to use Violence. He snapt at the Bait, and defeated the Design to all Intents and Purposes.

CHAP. XVIII.

Continues the Observations on the Affairs of Bombay, *with the Articles exhibited by Mr.* Child, *in order to embroil the Company's Affairs with the* Mogul *and his Subjects.*

THE Company having such a Number of great Ships on their Hands, were obliged to send them abroad; but having no Stock to employ them, ordered the General and Chiefs of their Factories in *India* to borrow what Sums they could on the Company's Credit, from the *Indian* Merchants, to lade their Ships Home, which accordingly they did, and what they could not lade Home, they were to employ by Freights in *India*. And I saw a Letter from the Governor of the Company in *England*, intimating, that when they had got as much Credit of the *Mogul's* Subjects as they could, then they would pick Quarrels with the Creditors, and put a general Stop to their Trade, which was accordingly done; for, in 1686 and 87. the *Surat* Merchants traded briskly by Sea to *Mocha*, *Persia* and *Bassora*, to the Westward, and to *Bengal*, *Atcheen*, *Malacca* and *Siam*, to the Eastward. The General granting Passes to all who required them, then, about the latter End of the Year 1687. he laid down a Complaint and Grievance before the Governor of *Surat*, and demanded Redress and Satisfaction. The Articles of his Grievances I saw in a printed Copy, and were as follows, in 35 Articles.

I. "LAST Year a Ship of *Molah Abdel* " *Gafoar's* coming from *Juddah*, in her Re- " turn met with two *Danish* Pirates, who " made a Prize of her. The News coming " to *Surat*, the said *Molah Abdel Gafoar*, by " Perswasions of *Meir Nazam*, and other " Merchants, made their Complaints to *Sa-* " *labat Caun* (then Governor) and other Of- " ficers of *Surat*, saying, the *English* belong- " ing to *Surat*, had taken his Ship, at the " same Time sending his Attorney to Court, " to complain to the King, who ordered the " Governor, &c. Officers of *Surat*, to en- " quire

" quire into it, and do Justice accordingly. " In this Affair, by Bribry, and disgracing me " to the King and his Subjects, as also the " *Dutch*, *French*, and other Nations, making " them believe it to be true, for which Dis- " grace I am not able to trade in these Parts; " but I hope the Disgrace will light on him, " that hereafter no such Scandal may be put " on me, or any other, we having traded " here these 80 or 90 Years, but never be- " fore accused as Robbers, but daily enrich- " ed the Port of *Surat*.

II. " THE Complaints of *Mulah Abdel Ga-* " *foar* have been much to my Prejudice, by " reason I could not clear my Money out of " the Custom-house, nor ship my Goods for " *Europe*, which were seized and hindred, " which hath made me leave the Port and " Trading, and retire to *Bombay*. I have by " me 30 or 40 Lack of Rupees in Money " and Goods in a Readiness; if you please " to send any Body, you may be certified of " the Truth. Consider the Loss I am at in " the Use of my Money, Damage of my " Goods, and detaining my Ships a Year. I " desire your Answer.

III. " *Mulah Abdel Gafoar*'s disgracing me, " makes People afraid to trust me, my Cre- " dit being lost by his false Reports, having " 12 Ships laden with Goods, which I de- " signed to have sent to *Surat*, there to have " provided Goods, and relade for *Europe*; " but his disgracing me is the Occasion of " the great Charges I am at, my Ships win-

" tering

" tering in these Parts, and my Goods lying " on my Hands, we Merchants trading for " Profit, which Hindrance hath not only " been a great Loss to the King in his Cu-" stoms, but to me, which I must answer to " my Masters.

IV. " Mr. *Petit* and Mr. *Boucher* being " indebted to the Company several Sums of " Money, I would have called them to ac-" count for the same; but they, like Trai-" tors, went to the Governor *Cortalab Caun* " for Protection. As for Mr. *Petit* he is " dead, and gone to the Devil. Mr. *Boucher* " still remains at *Surat*. I demand him, his " Wife, Child, or Children, Family, and all " *English* Men belonging to him, with their " Effects, that they be delivered to me, and " that he may not make his Escape from " *Surat*.

V " Formerly such Goods as we " brought from the *Malabar* Coast, *Mocha*, " and other Parts, which were for *Europe*, " and not to sell here, we had Liberty to " bring them ashore at *Swally*, to clean them, " and ship again, without paying Custom; " but the Governor *Cortalab Caun*, in his " Time, forced us to pay Custom for those " Goods. My Demand is, that what he took " more than the former Customs, may be " restored, and he do not the like again.

VI. " Of late Years we bring more Mo-" ney than formerly, which hath much en-" richt the Port, of which the Governor did " acquaint the King, who was pleased to take

" no

" no more than 2 *per Cent*. we paying no " more for many Years. Of late the Gover- " nor of *Surat* did write to the King, " to make us pay three and one half " *per Cent*. for Money as well as Goods, " which has been a great Prejudice to our " Trade. My Desire is, that we may pay " no more than formerly, and that the for- " mer Overplus may be repaid. Which " Exactings made *Salabat Caun* over-rate our " Goods in the Custom-house, to our great " Damage.

VII. " FORMERLY we never paid Cu- " stom for Apparel or Provisions, but of late " *Salabat Caun* forced us to pay Custom for " them. My Desire is that may be repaid, and, " for the future, no more Trouble on that " Account.

VIII. " WHEN our Goods came out of " the Country, if robbed by Thieves or o- " therwise on the Road, it is the King's Or- " der, that the Governors and Officers make " good all Damages, or else the King to sa- " tisfy us himself. Few Years since our " Goods coming from *Amadabant* and *Dur-* " *rimgum*, were robbed in the Way to *Su-* " *rat*. We have petitioned the Governor of " *Surat* for Satisfaction, but never obtained " any. My Desire is, that the King order " Satisfaction to be made for the Loss we " sustained, being great and considerable.

IX. " SEVERAL of the Natives are in- " debted to us, of whom we can get no Sa- " tisfaction, having several Times made Com- " plaints

" plaints to the Governors, where they re-
" ſide, for their Aſſiſtance, but, as yet, could
" have no Redreſs from them. Our Deſire
" is, that all Governors and their Officers
" may be aſſiſtant to us in recovering our
" Debts.

X. " We bring more Treaſure into the " Country than any other Nation, which is " carried to the Cuſtom-houſe, when clear- " ed from thence, we ſend it to the Mint " to be coined; but the Officers, for their " own Intereſt, delay the Coining, to the " Hindrance of the Diſpatching our Buſineſs, " for, if our Caſh was coined in Time, we " could have our Inveſtments out of the " Country, and lade our Ships according to " the Monſoons or Seaſon of the Year. Our " Requeſt is, that, for the future, the Coin- " ers may not delay the Coining, and that " our Treaſure may be coined apart, for " its more ſpeedy Performance.

XI. " At the Arival of our Ships, when " unladen, we carry our Goods to the Cu- " ſtom-houſe, where they are thrown up " and down very careleſly, where they are " broken, damaged and ſtolen. Our Requeſt " is, that we may have a Ware-houſe apart " by that of the *Dutch*, to put our Goods " in, that we may be no further Sufferers, " that, when we diſpoſe of our Goods, or " ſend them to our Factory, that the Cuſtomer " take Account of the King's Cuſtoms, clear- " ing them without farther Moleſtation.

XII. " For-

XII. "FORMERLY when we cleared our "Treasure, &c. Goods from the Custom-"house, we used to make up the Account "of our Customs at the latter End of the "Year, and then paid it. Of late Years the "Officers of the Custom-house daily and "monthly send to our Broker, demanding "the Custom, for which Reason we are for-"ced to fee the Officers not to affront our "Broker, which has been much to our Pre-"judice. Our Request is, that they demand "not the Customs till the End of the Year, "as formerly accustomary.

XIII. "WHEN *Gassadean Caun* was Go-"vernor of *Surat*, by Order of the King, "the City was walled, at which Time we "had a Garden near *Brampore* Gate, about "which we built 34 Shops, Stables for Hor-"ses, a Summer-house, and several other "convenient Places, all firm Buildings, which "cost to the Amount of 25000 Rupees, "when the Wall came near our Garden, "our Buildings were broke down, and our "Garden spoiled. We petitioned the Go-"vernor for Satisfaction, he promised to al-"low us the Charges out of the King's Trea-"sury; but we have not received any Satis-"faction. We demand Satisfaction for the "said Charges.

XIV. "FORMERLY when our Goods "came from other Parts to *Surat*, we paid "no more than due Custom, and shipped "them for *Europe*, or other Places, with-"out any farther Trouble. Of late Years the "Offi-

" Officers of thoſe Places, from whence our " Goods come, put us to much Trouble in " demanding the Governor's and Officers " of *Surat*'s Receits of us, and many Times " detain our Goods on that Account, by which " their Proceedings our Ships ſometimes re- " turn empty, and ſometimes are forced to " remain in the Country, which is a great Loſs " to the King in his Cuſtoms, as well as to us. " Our Requeſt is, that, for the future, ſuch " Receits may not be demanded of us, but that " we may have the ſame Liberty as formerly.

XV. " When our Goods are in a Rea- " dineſs, we ſend them to the accuſtomed " Place to be ſhopt, with a true Invoice of " the Contents of the Bales. Formerly they " uſed to make Choice of one or two Bales, " and if they found them according to In- " voice, then to ſhop and clear the reſt with- " out any farther Trouble. Of late the Cu- " ſtomer, *&c.* Officers, for their Intereſt, and " to delay Time, open moſt of our Goods, " which is not only a great Charge to us in " repacking our Goods, but alſo our Goods " are damaged. Our Deſire is, that they " may be ſhopt and ſhipt according to In- " voice, without any farther Trouble, as ac- " cuſtomary.

XVI. " Our Sloops and Boats coming " from *Swally* to the Cuſtom-houſe, the " *Meerbar* uſed to ſearch them, if empty, " cleared them, without any farther Trouble. " Of late Years the *Meerbar*, &c. Officers " will not clear them in three or four Days, " which

" which is a great Hindrance to us in the Dif-
" patch of our Bufinefs. Our Defire is, they
" may be fearcht and cleared as formerly,
" without Delay.

XVII. " SOMETIMES Merchants that buy
" our Goods, break, plead Poverty, that they
" have not wherewithal to pay us, apply-
" ing ourfelves to the Governor, *&c.* Offi-
" cers for Juftice, and their Affiftance, we
" can have no Redrefs. Our Defire is, either
" that the Governor, *&c.* Officers order Pay-
" ment to be made, or to fatisfy us out of
" the King's Cuftoms, that we may be no
" longer Sufferers by his Subjects.

XVIII. " SOMETIMES we fend our Brok-
" ers or Servants to the Governor, *&c.* Offi-
" cers, as our Affairs require, who cannot
" be admitted without bribing the Servants
" of faid Governor, *&c.* Officers. We defire
" it may be remedied for the future.

XIX. " OUR Horfes that come from *Per-*
" *fia*, *Boffora*, &c. at their Arrival we ufed
" to fend them to our Stables, without far-
" ther Delay. Of late Years at their landing
" are carried to the Governor, his Seal put
" about their Necks, and ourfelves not tru-
" fted to ufe or difpofe of them. Our De-
" fire is, that we may either ride them, or
" difpofe of them as formerly.

XX. " THE Governor, *&c.* Officers often
" fend to us for broad Cloth, Sword-blades,
" *&c.* in Civility we cannot deny them, but
" when we fend for the Money, they deny
" the Payment, and abufe our Servants, by
" which

" which we are Sufferers. Our Desire is, " that, for the future, if the Governor, *&c.* " Officers desire any Goods, they may pay " for them before they carry them away.

XXI. " Goods provided at *Agra*, *Amadabant*, &c. coming to *Baroach*, the Governor forces us to pay 18 *per Mill.* Custom, " which is contrary to the King's Order, for " we ought to pay but in one Place as the " *Moors* and *Banyans*. Our Desire is to be " cleared of that Custom, that at the Arrival of our Goods at *Surat*, they may be " sent for out abroad without farther Trouble, paying the King his due Custom. We " desire the same Goods shipt at *Baroach*, " *Cambay*, &c. that our Ships may not lose " their Passage to *Europe*.

XXII. " At the Arrival of our *European* " Ships, we send our Goods to the Custom-house, when cleared, carry them to the Factory, sometimes we have present Vend, " and sometimes we send them to other " Places, as we think convenient, and for " our Interest; in case we send our Goods to " any other Place, within the Term of six " Months, then to pay half Custom for the " said Goods; but, if kept a full Year, then " to pay full Custom. Sometimes we send " to *Swally* more Goods than will lade our " Ships, the Remainder we dare not keep " there, for Fear of Fire or Thieves. Our " Request is, that for all such Goods as have " paid Custom, we may freely bring them to " *Surat*, keep them there for our next Ship-

" ping

" ping, and ſhip them off without farther
" Trouble or Demands.

XXIII. " Our Servants, *Engliſh*, *Gentows*, " and others, many Times we ſend up the " Country, for the ſpeedier Diſpatching of " our Affairs. When we ſend to them for " our Accounts, being at a Diſtance, and out " of our Reach, like to Mr. *Petit* and Mr. " *Boucher*, they go to the Governors for " Protection, by which Means we cannot " call them to an Account, to our great Loſs, " and farther proceeding againſt them. Our " Requeſt is, that whatever *Engliſh* Man, em- " ployed in your Service, without our Leave " and Diſcharge, that they, with their Ef- " fects and Eſtates, be delivered to us, that " they may not be protected, but that we " may proceed againſt them, as we think con- " venient.

XXIV. " It is near 90 Years that we have " traded here. At our firſt Coming, the " King granted us a Piece of Ground for a " *Bunder* to repair our Ships and Veſſels. Of " late Years *Meer Naſſam* hath forced it from " us, and made it a Garden. We are deſti- " tute of a Place for repairing our Veſſels, " and other Conveniencies. Our Requeſt is, " that we may have the ſame Ground as for- " merly, or ſome other near the Water Side, " fitting our Occaſions.

XXV. " Formerly we uſed to pay for " each Bale of Indigo, two and an half Ru- " pees *per* Bale, without opening it. Of late " Years the Officers open it, valuing it at

" their Pleaſure, damaging the Goods, which " is a great Loſs and Charge to us in repack- " ing it. Our Deſire is, that, for the future, " it may not be opened, paying the Cuſtom " as formerly.

XXVI. " The Governor, &c. Officers buy " of us, for the King's Account, Iron, Guns, " Lead, giving us ſome Money in Hand. " When they are turned out, and others " come, when we demand the Remainder, " they delay the Payment of the Money, " ſaying the King did not want our Goods, " that we may take them again, ſometimes " after they have kept them one or two " Years. Our Requeſt is, that whatever they " buy of us for the King's Account, we may " be paid before they take them from us, " and whatever Goods we have that the King " has no Occaſion for, we may diſpoſe of " them at our Pleaſure.

XXVII. " As to the Iſland of *Bombay*, it " produceth no Corn. The *Mogul's* Fleet of- " ten winters there, which makes Proviſions " ſcarce and dear. We are in Want of Sup- " plies from *Surat*, and other the *Mogul's* " Ports. When we ſend to theſe Places, the " ſaid Governor and Officers will not let us " have any without giving them one and one " Fourth *per Cent*. Our Requeſt is, to be free " of this Tax, that we may have Liberty of " ſending what is neceſſary for Supply of the " King's People and ſaid Iſland.

XXVIII. " A Ship, with her Cargo, to the " Amount of 254000 Rupees, came out of

" *Eng-*

" *England* without our King's Licence, which
" came to *Surat*. Our King's Orders came
" to us to seize Ship and Cargo, which ac-
" cordingly we did; but *Salabat Caun* then
" being Governor, forced her from us, and
" delivered her to Mr. *Boucher*. Our Desire
" is, the said Ship may be re-delivered us,
" that Mr. *Boucher* and his Broker give us a
" just and true Account of the Remainder
" of the Cargo, and that the Governor
" take Care it be not squandred away by
" them.

XXIX " 'Tis the King's Grant, that Mer-
" chants pay but one Custom for their Goods,
" without farther Molestation, and, when
" they pay it, to take a Discharge. Of late
" Years, the Officers have forced us to pay
" double Custom, besides their Perquisites
" which they have demanded, which has been
" a great Hindrance to the timely Arrival of
" our Goods. We desire we may not be
" forced to pay more than accustomary.

XXX. " We formerly rented a Piece of
" Ground for Stables, on which we were at
" considerable Charges in building and Re-
" parations. *Meer Nassam*, by buying it, de-
" prived us of it. We desire he may satisfy
" us the said Charges.

XXXI. " Some Years since we lost an
" Anchor at the River's Mouth, which *Mir-
" za Mossum*'s People took up. We have of-
" ten demanded it, offering to defray the
" Charges he was at, but cannot get it. Our
" Request is, that his Son *Mirza Mahomud*

" *Araff* deliver the ſame, we paying the " Charges they were at.

XXXII. " At the Arrival of our Ships, " they ſend the Boat up with News. At the " Cuſtom-houſe they ſtop her a whole Day " before they will let our People come a- " ſhore with Letters, which is a great Impe- " diment to our Affairs. Our Requeſt is, " that they may not be hindred for the fu- " ture, but ſuffered to land aſſoon as they " come to the Cuſtom-houſe.

XXXIII. " As concerning my *Bengal*, we " hear ſeveral Ships have been taken and " burnt, in which Affair we are not concer- " ned, neither do we know whether Peace " be concluded there or not. Our Requeſt " is, that the King iſſue out his Orders, that " no Perſon queſtion us, or make Demands " on us on that Account.

XXXIV. " Some Years ago the *Sedee*, " with the King's Fleet, wintered at *Bombay*, " in which Time ſome of his People murde- " red two of our *Engliſh* Men, which made " our Men reſolutely reſolve to revenge their " Death, but, with great Perſwaſions were " pacified, being promiſed Satisfaction. We " acquainted the Governor of it, who orde- " red the Murderers to be impriſoned; but, " three Days after, they were cleared by " the *Sedee*. Our Requeſt is, they may be de- " livered, that we may proſecute them, and " that Juſtice may be done.

XXXV. " When we are minded to take " our Pleaſure out of the City, altho' we re-

" turn

" turn before the usual Time of shutting the " Gates, the Porters shut them against us, " demanding Money before they will let us " enter the City. Our Request is, that Or- " der be given by the Governor, that we be " no more affronted by those People.

THESE Grievances were the Foundation on which General *Child* built a War with the *Mogul*, without ever sending them to Court to know the King's Pleasure, but, without declaring War, seized his Subjects Ships wherever they were found, altho' they had the Sanction of his own Passes. If the fourth Article be *Christian* the *Mahometans* and *Heathens* abhor it. The seventeenth and twenty third are unjust, as well as the twenty eighth; and the thirty and thirty first were but weak Arguments to help to support his Complaints and raise a War, that cost his Masters above 400000 Pounds before they could lay it, besides the Loss of their Credit with the *Mogul* and his Subjects, which, to this Time, is not quite recovered. Or by what Rule in Policy could Sir *Josiah* or Sir *John Child* think to rob, murder and destroy the *Mogul*'s Subjects in one Part of his Dominions, and the Company to enjoy a free Trade in the other Parts? or how they could expect that he would stand neuter, let Politicians answer them, and I'll proceed.

THE General having such a Number of great Ships on his Hands, and little Employment for them, sent them to *Mocha*, *Persia* and *Bengal*, where the *Suraters* had sent theirs under the Protection of his Passes.

 Cap-

Captain *Andrews* in the *Charles* II. went to *Mocha*, and ſet up the King of *England*'s Flag on his Factory, and there he ſeized two *Engliſh* Ships, one from *England*, called the *Streights Merchant*, commanded by Captain *Bear*, and another belonging to Mr. *Samuel White* at *Siam*. She was commanded by one Captain *Wren*, whom they killed in his Cabbin, becauſe he would not deliver his Ship up voluntarily. There was but little of their Cargoes on board of the Ships, ſo they might as well have let them alone: However ſuch Doings diſpleaſed the Governor and Merchants of *Mocha*, and they had a Deſign to force Captain *Andrews* to reſtore the Ships, but he ſuſpecting as much, fled on board, and left his Colours flying on his Factory.

He ſoon after left *Mocha*, and carried his two Prizes with him, and Mr. *Clive*, Supercargo of the *Streights Merchant*, got Bills for his Stock, payable at *Grand Cairo*, except about 60 Bales of Coffee that he carried with him to *England*, where it ſold very well, and the Company were obliged by the Law to make good all the Ship's Cargo *pro rata*, as thoſe 60 Bales ſold for, which amounted to 32000 Pounds. The *Briſtol*'s Cargo was alſo made good to her Owners, with the Ship that was taken at *Johanna* by the *Phenix*, which came to 60000 Pounds. And the *Little Betty*, that was alſo taken by the *Phenix* in her Way to *India*, coſt them 12000 Pounds, tho' ſhe and her Cargo were ſold at *Bombay* for leſs than 600 Pounds. The Owner of that Veſ-

ſel

sel was one Mr. *Hastewell* a Quaker, and a substantial Merchant in *London*, who arrested Captain *Tyrrel* going off the Exchange. The Captain proferred King *James* for Bail, but the Quaker would not accept of him, but was content to accept of Sir *Joseph Herne*, who became Bail.

THE *Charles*, *Cesar*, and *Royal James* and *Mary* way-laid the *Surat* Shipping, and brought in fourteen Sail to *Bombay*, where I saw them lying *in Anno* 1688. and yet no War with the *Mogul*, only with the Inhabitants of *Surat*, whom he threatned to humble.

IN *October* 1688. he went to *Surat* Road, in the *Royal James* and *Mary*, with three or four other Ships of Countenance, to try if he could bully the Governor, and frighten the Merchants into a Compliance of losing their Estates, but was disappointed in both. He staid there till the Beginning of *January* 1689. and then left *Surat* in an Huff, and brought all the *English* Ships along with him, except the Ship *Adventure*, whom the *Phenix* had forced over the Bar, when she was lying at the River's Mouth, taking in a Cargo for *England*, under the Protection of Mr. *Boucher*'s *Phirmaund*, which was the Grievance complained of in the 28 Article: However, her Supercargo dying, the Ship's Bottom was eaten up with Worms in the River, and Part of the Cargo remained many Years in Mr. *Boucher*'s Possession.

ON the General's Passage to *Bombay*, he met with a Fleet of Vessels that were carrying Corn to an Army of the *Mogul*'s that lay at *Dunder-rajah-pore*, about 14 Leagues to the Southward of *Bombay*. That Fleet he alſo ſeized, and carried to *Bombay*, tho' againſt the Opinion of moſt of his Council. Before this Seizure he askt the Opinion of ſome Sea-officers, and one Captain *Hilder*, being the eldeſt, adviſed him not to meddle with the Corn Fleet, becauſe it would ſtraiten the Army, and force them to look abroad for Proviſions, where it might beſt be procured, and perhaps might affect *Bombay*, which was in a great Meaſure beholden to their Neighbours for Suſtenance and Fire-wood. The General took him up with ſcurrilous Language, calling him Coward and Fool, and bragg'd, that if *Sedee Yacoup* (which was the *Mogul*'s General's Name) ſhould dare to come with his Forces on *Bombay*, he would blow him off again with the Wind of his Bum.

COWARDS are generally ſtout when Dangers are at a Diſtance, and ſo was our General, who had never ſeen a Sword drawn in Anger, and conſequently very ill acquainted with War; and when it came to his Door, none was ever ſo confounded and dejected as he was, as appeared by his Conduct in that War that he ſo fooliſhly brought on himſelf and his Country.

CHAP.

CHAP. XIX.

Gives an Account of the War of Bombay, *between the* Mogul *and the* English East-india *Company, with* Aurengzeb's *Letters of Advice to the Governor of* Bombay, *on granting them a Peace and new Indulgences in Trade.*

WHEN the News came to *Sedee Yacoup*, that his Fleet, with his Provisions of Corn and Cloth, were seized and carried to *Bombay*, he sent a civil Letter to our General to discharge his Fleet, protesting, that as he had not meddled in the Affairs between him and the *Suraters*, he would continue neuter, unless he was forced to do otherwise: But our General gave him an insolent Answer, and the Fleet was unladed at *Bombay*.

Sedee Yacoup sent again to desire the Delivery of his Fleet in fair Terms, otherwise he would be obliged to come with his Army, and quarter on *Bombay*, where his Provisions were detained, and that if his Fleet was not set at Liberty before the 11 of *February*, which was near at hand, he would certainly be on *Bombay* the 14. but still receiving uncivil Answers, he performed his Promise to a Tittle, for that very Night he landed at a Place called *Souree* (about four Miles distant from the main Fort) with 20000 Men at his Back.

OUR General's Security had made him neglect providing for receiving such Guests, trusting

ſting to the Reputation of his Forces, who were greater then than ever they had been before, or ever were ſince that Time, and he had ſmall Ships enow, had they been placed in proper Places, that might certainly have hindred his Landing, and forced him Home again; but all thoſe neceſſary Preparations were neglected, and the *Sedee* landed at Mid-night, and the Redoubt where he landed, fired a great Gun to give the Alarm, and ſo deſerted their Poſt, and the *Sedee* took Poſſeſſion of it. At One in the Morning the Caſtle fired three Guns to give the general Alarm, which brought ſuch Fear on thoſe that lived ſecurely in their Houſes without the Caſtle, that the poor Ladies, both white and black, run half-naked to the Fort, and only carried their Children with them; but they were all obliged to wait without the Wall, till Day-light relieved them.

NEXT Morning the *Sedee* marched to *Mazagun*, a ſmall Fort of 14 Guns, and about a random Shot diſtant from the Caſtle. On the Enemy's Approach, that Fort, tho' ſituated on a Point of Rocks, where the Sea defended three Quarters of it, was alſo deſerted in ſuch Precipitancy, that eight or ten Cheſts of Treaſure, which generally contain 1000 Pounds each, and four Cheſts of new Arms, were left behind, tho' the Seamen that were ſent in Boats to bring them off, proferred to carry them along with them; but the commanding Officer thought them not fit to be truſted with Money and Arms, and

and so they were left for a Present to *Sedee Yacoup*, with fourteen Cannon, two Mortars, with some Powder, Shot and Shells: But why that Treasure, and those Arms and Ammunition were deposited in *Mazagun*, few could account for, and the Reasons why they were left to the Enemy were as wonderful; but it was plain, that the old Way of Fishing in troubled Waters was known at *Bombay*, and the Officer was never called to account for his Oversight.

Sedee Yacoup finding no Opposition, sent a Party of Men towards *Mahim*, to plunder the poor Peasants, and to take that Fort, which, he thought, might be deserted as the rest had been, and was not in the least out in his Conjecture, for the Garison had embark'd in Boats, and came by Sea to *Bombay*, before they saw an Enemy. The *Sedee* taking Possession of *Mazagun*, hoisted his Flag there, and made it his head Quarters.

THE following Day some of the Enemy appeared on *Mazagun* Hills, which grieved our General's righteous Soul to see Infidels come so near him in an hostile Manner. He called a Minion of his own, one Captain *Pean*, who was no better Soldier than himself, and ordered him to take two Companies, each containing about seventy Men, and march to those Hills, and drive the Enemy out of his Sight. He ordered one *Mouro*, who had been a Soldier at *Tangier*, to be his Lieutenant. In *Tangier* he had received a Wound in his Heel, that spoiled his Running, and accordingly they marched in good Order within Shot of the Enemy, who ſhewed their Heads above the Surface of the Hill, but did not offer to advance or expoſe their Bodies. Several Gentlemen Volunteers took their Arms, and accompanied the little Army.

THE Lieutenant adviſed the Captain to march up the Hill in Platoons, to ſeparate the Enemy's Forces. The Captain took it as an Affront to be adviſed, told his Lieutenant, that, when he had the Command in his own Hands, he might uſe it as he thought fit, but, as it was intruſted to him, he would uſe it according to his own Mind, and ſo ordered his Men to ſpread as much as they could, and when they ſaw the Enemy open in the Plain, to diſcharge all at once amongſt them, which, he ſaid, would terrify them. *Monro* oppoſed his Scheme, and told him of the Danger he would bring himſelf and them into, if the Enemy ſhould attack them whilſt their Arms were reloading; but nothing could diſſwade him from his Project, and ſo commanded his Men to fire as he had directed. The *Sedee*'s being ten to one in Numbers, and better Runners than our Men, and better acquainted with cloſs Fighting with Sword and Target, took hold of the Opportunity, and advanced with all their Speed, which the Captain perceiving, betook himſelf to his Heels, and was the foremoſt Man to the *Portugueze* Church, where he took Courage to look behind him, to ſee what was become of his Men. Poor *Monro* thinking to ſtop the Enemy's

Enemy's Carreer by a Part of the Wing that he commanded, found himſelf deſerted by all, but 13 or 14 ſtout Fellows, who were ſoon ſurrounded by the Enemy, and cut to Pieces.

Pean had not ſtopt at the *Portugueze* Church, had he not found a Party of 100 Men that lay there ready to ſupport or receive him, as his Caſe ſhould require. He was a Fellow as well made for running as any I ever ſaw, and was ſo much in the General's Favour, that he had not ſo much as a Reprimand for his Cowardice and Misbehaviour. This Relation I had from a Gentleman Volunteer, who kept always near the Captain while he could keep Pace with him.

WHEN the General left *Surat*, there were ſeveral Gentlemen in it, ſome in the Company's Service, and ſome private Perſons, who were all impriſoned, and put in Irons, except Mr. *Boucher* and his Dependents, who were protected by his *Phirmaund*. Thoſe impriſoned were ſcurvily uſed, being obliged to paſs thro' the Streets with Irons about their Necks, for Spectacles to pleaſe the Mob. Captain *Johnſon* and Captain *Yeaman*, tho' particular Merchants, were obliged to act their Parts in the Tragi-comedy, and continue Priſoners, where Captain *Johnſon* died, but Captain *Yeaman* got his Liberty at the End of the War, which was about the Beginning of *June* 1690.

I will now return back to the Year 1686. when Sir *John Weyburn* was ſent from *England*, with a Commiſſion of Judge Admiral from

from the King, and he had likewise another Commission from the Governor of the Company (which they made him believe was also from the King) to condemn and hang 13 of the Inhabitants of St. *Helena*, where, in a Tumult caused by the Oppressions of the Governor of that Island, one *Johnson* the Second was killed. Sir *John Weyburn* took his Passage to *India* on board the Ship *London*, and, in his Way, called at St. *Helena*, and hanged up the 13 proscribed Persons, without Form of Process, for which the Company paid dear afterwards, and so had Sir *John*, had he lived; but he finding the illegal Proceedings of Mr. *Child* to be insupportable, and meeting with many Affronts (from that Man without Manners) died at *Bombay* about two Months before the *Sedee* came on it. He was much lamented by all honest Men that knew him. He was Captain of the *Happy Return* who accompanied the *Glocester* when she was bringing the Duke of *York* to *Scotland*, and lost by the Way. It was Captain *Weyburn* that sent his Barge to wait on the Duke, and brought him safe on board of the *Happy Return*, who carried him forward to *Scotland*, for which good Service he was knighted. He was ever after a great Favourite of King *James*, who seeing he could not be brought into his Measures, put that Employ on him, to dismiss him with Honour.

And now the *Sedee* being Master of the whole Island, except the Castle and about half

half a Mile to the Southward of the Caſtle, he raiſed Batteries on *Dungeree* Hill, which overlookt the Fort Wall, and diſturbed the Gariſon very much; then he put four great Guns in the Cuſtom-houſe, commonly called the *India-houſe*, and raiſed a Battery at the *Moody*'s Houſe, within 200 Paces of the Fort, and another in the Lady's Houſe that he had been ſo unkind to, ſo that it was dangerous to go out or in at the Caſtle Gate, till we got up an half Moon before it. All Men were then preſt into the Company's Service, and I amongſt the reſt. We paſt the Months from *April* to *September* very ill, for Proviſions grew ſcarce by the Addition of 3000 *Sevajees* that were employed as Auxiliaries in the military Service of the Company. When the Winter Months were over, at *September* we went to Sea with our ſmall Ships, to cruize on the *Mogul*'s Subjects, and had pretty good Succeſs. I was employed in that Service, and had the Command of a ſmall Privateer of 7 or 8 Tuns, with twenty fighting Men, and ſixteen Rowers. In three or four Months I brought nine Prizes into *Bombay*, laden moſt with Proviſions and Clothes for the Enemy's Army, which was now increaſed to 40000. but we were not allowed any Plunder, but were rather plundred our ſelves, for when we brought our Prizes in, our Cheſts were ſeverely ſearcht, and if we had ſaved any of our Pay, it was ſeized for the Company's Uſe, as Money we had found in the Prizes, which made us careleſs in purſuing the Ene-

my

my at Sea. Except when Hunger pincht we never lookt out for Prizes, by which Indifference of ours many of the Enemy escaped that we could have taken.

THE ill Success we had ashore with the Enemy, made our General sick, and, in *December*, he dispatcht two Factors to the *Mogul*'s Court, with a *Surat* Merchant, called *Meer Mezamie*. He was our Friend, and had some Interest at Court. They went under the Name of the *English* Ambassadors. Mr. *George Weldon* was first in Commission, and *Abraham Navaar* a *Jew* was second. In fifteen Days they arrived at Court, being then at *Jehanabant*. They were received but coldly; but, about the Middle of *April*, by the special Assistance of Presents to the Officers at Court, they were admitted to Audience, but were brought to *Aurengzeb*'s Presence after a new Mode for Ambassadors, their Hands being tied by a Sash before them, and were obliged to prostrate. The King gave them a severe Reprimand, and then askt their Demands. They first made a Confession of their Faults, and desired Pardon, then that their *Phirmaund* which was forfeited, should be renewed, and that the *Sedee* and his Army should be ordered off *Bombay*. Their Submission he accepted of, and pardoned their Faults, on Condition that Mr. *Child* should leave *India* in nine Months, and never come back again, the *Phirmaund* to be renewed, on Condition that Satisfaction should be given his Subjects on account of Debts

Debts contracted, Robberies committed, and Losses and Damages made good, and, on Security given for the due Performances of these Premisses, the *Sedee* and his Army should be ordered off the Island. In *January* General *Child* died, which much facilitated their Affairs, but it was kept secret at Court, till they knew how the King would order the Affair about him. In *March Meer Mezamie* died also, and, it was supposed, was poisoned by some Enemies, contracted by his good Services to the *English*. When he was given over by Physicians, our Ambassadors sent to know what he had done with 50000 Rupees, he had received for secret Services. He answered, that he was sorry that ever he had meddled in their Affairs, for he had served them even with his Life, and yet they were not contented, for what Use that Sum was put to, he durst not divulge.

When our Affairs were in so bad Circumstances at the *Mogul*'s Court, the *Dutch* Company had one Mr. *Baroon* their Ambassador there, who designed to impose on *Aurengzeb*, who, he thought, was ignorant of *European* Affairs. The News of the Revolution in *Britain* being arrived in *India*, when he had an Audience of *Aurengzeb*, he began to magnify the Power and Grandeur of his Country, and vilify the *English*. The *Mogul* seemed to be pleased with his Discourse, to encourage him to go on. He told, that the *English* were but contemptible in Comparison of his Sovereigns, for they were forced to send the *English* a King to rule over them, and that if his Majesty would exclude the *English* from the Trade of his Dominions, the *Hollanders* would carry it to a much greater Height, and enrich his Treasury, and the *English* would not know where to get Bread. The *Mogul* gravely answered, That if his Masters were so much superior to the *English* in Power and Riches, they might easily drive them out of *India*, and engross all the Trade of his Countries to themselves, and commanded him to tell his Masters, that he expected it from them. Then the Ambassador excused himself, and told, that he could act nothing in that Affair till he received Orders from *Holland*. *Aurengzeb* then reprimanded him, and shewed him wherein he had lied, for, says he, about seventeen Years ago, the King of *France* conquered most of your Country in a few Days, and that it was the *English*, and not the Power of *Holland*, that repelled him, and that if *England* did not hold the Balance of Power, either the Emperor or the King of *France* could conquer it in one Campain.

THE Ambassador knew not how to answer to those Truths: But, being sent to solicite some Indulgence in their Trade, he could obtain none, and so left the Court dissatisfied.

AFTER our Ambassadors had obtained Pardon, they began to be respected, and had Liberty to take their Diversion abroad, till a a new *Phirmaund* was drawing up, which, according to the Method of the eastern Courts, took up some Time: However Orders were sent to the *Sedee* to forbear Hostilities, and the *English* had the same Orders, so that frequent Visits past between the *Sedee*'s People and ours. And, during the War, about 60 *Europeans* of several Nations, had deserted from us, and took Pay of the *Sedee*. The Reason they gave for their Desertion, was ill Usage they had received from some *Irish* Officers; yet most of them returned after the War, on Promise of Pardon.

THE *Phirmaund* being ready, and the required Security given, *Sedee Yacoup* left *Bombay* the 8 of *June*, 1690. but he also left a Pestilence behind him, which, in four Months Time, destroyed more Men than the War had done, and, for Joy, made a malicious Bonfire of his head Quarters *Mazagun* Fort.

NOW we may see the *Mogul*'s Stile in his new *Phirmaund* to be sent to *Surat*, as it stands translated by the Company's Interpreters, which runs thus in the printed Copy annext to Sir *John Child*'s 35 Articles of Grievances.

THE Occasion of your writing to me, was your being in Fault of all these Troubles, that you have repented of what you have done, that you made several Complaints against former Governors, all which I have here from several of my Umbras, *and the several Abuses received from them, and their Officers, all which you should have acquainted me with, before you proceeded so violently. Having acknowledged your Error, and desired Pardon, I do not only grant your Request, pardoning what is past, but granting you a* Phirmaund *according to your Desire, and have ordered* Assit Caun *to forward it to the Governor of* Surat, *with such Particulars as he will acquaint you with.*

At the Arrival of my Phirmaund, *receive it with great Respect, acknowledging the great Glory you have got in obtaining the same, that you may trade as formerly at your Pleasure, and as accustomary. That you deliver the Merchants, that have complained against you, their Ships with their Effects. That, for the future, you do not commit the like Error, in doing as you have done, and proceed according to my Will and Pleasure, and be not forgetful of the same.*

If you receive any Affronts from my Governors, or their Officers, or any of my Subjects, be not negligent in acquainting me of the same. I have ordered Assit Caun *to write accordingly.*

What you write concerning former Governors, protecting Mr. Boucher, *that you have several Demands of him, that you cannot call him to an Account, desiring that he may be delivered to you. My Order is, that you prove your Demands according to Law, that Justice may be done accordingly.*

Dated the 31 Year of *Aurengzeb*'s Reign.

It seems the King was not ignorant of the hard Usage his Subjects had met with, nor was he desirous to use Severity in punishing Offences and Affronts; but, like an indulgent Prince, only told them of their Faults, and prudently admonished them not to be guilty of falling into such like Errors, and, in a majestick Stile, advised them to receive his Favours and Graces with great Respect, and that they ought to make the Law the Standard of Justice, and, in all his Words and Actions, used a *Christian* Moderation.

General *Child* being dead, Mr. *John Vaux* succeeded him in the Government of *Bombay*; but Mr. *Bartholomew Harris*, who had been Prisoner at *Surat* (all the Time of the Rupture) had the Seigniority in the Company's Service; but it being not the Custom, for one that had been the *Mogul*'s Prisoner (for any Crimes judged to be capital) to receive publick Marks of Esteem from the State, without a singular Amnesty from the King, Mr. *Vaux* was obliged to go to *Surat* and receive the *Phirmaund* and the King's *Serpaw* or Present, which, on such Occasions, is generally a fine Horse, and a Suit of Clothes from Head to Foot, made of rich Atlasses or *Zeerbastas*. Those are Sattins or Taffataes full of Gold or Silver Flowers wrought in them. The Horse must never after be sold, on no Account whatsoever. They have also a fine Turband, embroidered Shoes, and a Dagger of Value, stuck into a fine *Cummerband* or Sash; and, being equipt in that

Habit, the *Phirmaund* is presented (by the *Goosberdaar* or *Hosbalhouckain*, or, in *English*, the King's Messenger,) and the Governor of the Province or City makes a short Speech adapted to the Occasion, setting forth the great Honour conferred upon him by the greatest King in the World, with an Admonition to make future Actions deserve the Merit of such Favours.

After the aforesaid Manner Mr. *Vaux* received the *Phirmaund* in a gilded Box, and, according to Custom, put it on his Turband for a little While, and, by an Interpreter, returned the Governor's Compliment, acknowledging the King's Favours, and the Governor's Civilities; and then the Governor conducted him from the Garden (where the Ceremony was performed) into the City, through a great Concourse of People, who welcomed him with Shouts of Joy as he past thro' the Streets to the *English* Factory.

After Mr. *Vaux* had staid in the City about a Week, he sent to acquaint the Governor of the Necessity he lay under to return back to his Government of *Bombay*; but the Governor sent him Word, that none but he could be trusted by the King to see the Performance of the Contract accomplished, and begged, that he would not think of leaving the City, lest the King should take it amiss, and repent him of the Favours he had shewed to the *East-india* Company; and so Mr. *Vaux* was detained an Hostage for his Masters future good Behaviour.

Mr.

Mr. *Harris*, according to that Company's ordinary Custom, demanded the Presidency from Mr. *Vaux*, who, to save Contention, gave it to him, tho' his Mind was so debilitated, that he was but few Degrees wiser than an Ideot, and, in two Years Time, Mr. *Vaux* was suspended the Company's Service, and to remain their Hostage at his own Charges, and so he continued till the Year 1697. that he, by Accident, was drowned in *Surat* River, by a Pinnace's oversetting, in which he and his Lady had been taking a Pleasure on the Water.

This Mr. *Vaux* had been Book-keeper to Sir *Josiah Child* in *England*, and, for his good Services and Behaviour, was preferred by his Master to a Supercargo's Post in a Ship to *China*, which Trade, in those Times, was the most profitable of any within the Limits of the Company's Charter. *In Anno* 1684. he was sent thither on board a Ship called the *Carolina*, commanded by one Captain *Harding*; but, Mr. *Vaux* and *Harding* disagreeing in their Passage to *China*, Mr. *Vaux* laded the Ship, and sent her back to *England*, while he himself went Passenger on board a *Surat* Ship for *Bombay*, where he was entertained in the Company's Service as a Factor, and wrote to Sir *Josiah Child* the Reasons he had for leaving the *Carolina*, and his Resolution of staying in *India*. Sir *Josiah* continued his Esteem for Mr. *Vaux*, and procured him several profitable Posts at one and the same Time in the Company's Service, and, amongst the rest, constituted him Judge in civil Affairs, which brought him both a good Salary and Perquisites. After he was installed in that Office, Sir *Josiah* wrote him a Letter of Admonition and Reminiscence, wherein, after many Postulates, put him in Mind of the many Favours he had done him, and that now, having the Power of condemning the Company's Enemies, or such as should be deemed so, particularly those who should dare to question the Company's Power over all the *British* Subjects in *India*, and that he expected his Orders, from Time to Time, should be observed and obeyed as statute Laws.

Mr. *Vaux* gratefully acknowledged Sir *Josiah*'s Favours in his Answer to that Letter, and promised, that, as he had put him into that Post of Honour and Profit, he would strive to acquit himself with all the Integrity and Justice he was capable of, and that the Laws of his Country should be the Rule he designed to walk by.

In Answer to that Letter, Sir *Josiah* seemed to be angry, and wrote roundly to Mr. *Vaux*, that he expected his Orders were to be his Rules, and not the Laws of *England*, which were an Heap of Nonsense, compiled by a few ignorant Country Gentlemen, who hardly knew how to make Laws for the good Government of their own private Families, much less for the Regulating of Companies and foreign Commerce.

I am the more particular in this Account, because I saw and copied both those Letters *in Anno* 1696. while Mr. *Vaux* and I were Prisoners at *Surat*, on Account of Captain *Evory*'s robbing the *Mogul*'s great Ship, called the *Gunsway*.

HAVING given an Account of some Part of Sir *John Child*'s Reign, I must also remark a few Slips in the Government of some of his Successors, and of the Ways that they took to get into the Chair of *Bombay*.

I remark'd before, that Mr. *Harris* was a very weak and indolent Person, very unfit to govern a Colony and the Factories subordinate to *Bombay*, and, by that Means, a cunning designing Fellow, one Mr. *Samuel Annesley* had the Reins of the Government wholly in his Management, who shewed, that he had malicious Wit and Avarice enough to embroil both his Masters and the private Merchants Affairs in *Surat* in *Harris*'s Time, and, on *Harris*'s Death, got into the Presidency, or rather Tyranny.

THE *Mogul*'s Subjects have a good many fine large Ships that trade all over *India*. The Owners of those Ships had a very great Regard for the Courage, Conduct, and Art of Navigation of the *English*, above any other *European* Nation in *India*; and, for those Qualifications, the *Indian* Owners procured *English* Officers to go in their Ships, and allowed them very handsom Salaries and Indulgences. The Captains had from 10 to 15 *L. per* Month. Mates from 6 to 9 *L.* and the

the Gunners and Boatswains had also good Salaries, besides the Privilege of carrying some Goods and Merchandizes, Freight free.

MR. *Annesley* thought those Salaries and Indulgences were too great for Seamen, so he went about to reduce them to about one Half, and the other Moiety he lookt on as his own due by virtue of his Post.

SOME through Fear or Necessity complied, others again, who despised both his Power and Tyranny, would, by no Means, come into his Measures, and those he lookt on as Rebels, and persecuted them to the utmost of his Power, bribing the *Mogul*'s Governor to plague us; so some were ruined by his Villany, whilst others bade him open Defiance: And we were not wanting on our Side to expose him and his Masters to the *Mogul*'s Subjects, which, in the End, was the Loss of both their Esteem and Credit among the trading People of that Country. The poorer Sort, whose Maintenance depended on their Labour and Industry, losing their Employs in the *Moorish* Merchants Service, were obliged to fall on new Schemes to support themselves, not very well suited to the Company's Interest, for some went and joyned themselves with the Pirates.

THE Company in *England* receiving Accounts from every one that came from *India*, of *Harris* and *Annesley*'s Maladministrations, sent out Sir *John Gayer* to take Care of their Affairs. He arrived *in Anno* 1694. with the lofty Title of General of all *India*. He conti-

continued *Anneſley* in the Company's Service till the Year 1700. but diveſted him of all Power of doing more Miſchief; but, in the End, he diſmiſt him the Company's Service.

SIR *John Gayer* was a Man not vitious in his Temper, yet he had ſome Slips in his Government that proved prejudicial to his Character, tho', in Matters of common Commerce, he acted pretty regularly, till a young Laſs of 3000 *L*. Portion made him diſpenſe with the common Methods of Matrimony. This young Gentlewoman was a Daughter of Mr. *Ward*'s before mentioned. She had no Relations alive, and unadviſedly married one Mr. *Solomon Loyd* a Factor, and the Marriage was clandeſtine, which was poſitively againſt the ſtatute Law of *Bombay*, where no Marriage is binding but when the Governor's Conſent is tackt to it. This Law Sir *John* had got by Heart, and unmarried the poor Factor after Conſummation, and married her to his own Son; but the ſecond Marriage was attended with ill Conſequences, for, whilſt her Husband was at *China*, one *Coleman* was ordered to teach her to write good *Engliſh*, but, neglecting thoſe Orders, he taught her ſomething elſe, and was diſcovered in the Practiſing, by a watchful Mother in Law. The poor School-maſter was ſent, in Irons, on board of a Ship for *England*. And the poor Husband's Head aked as long as he lived.

ANOTHER Piece of ill Conduct was in forcing the *Mocha* Frigat's Men on board, againſt

gainſt their Wills, to proceed on a Voyage to *China*, notwithſtanding their juſt Complaints againſt *Edgecomb* their Captain, whom the Mutineers ſhot in his Cabbin, and then turned Pirates, and infeſted the Streights of *Malacca*, robbing and plundring all Ships that they could overcome. Captain *Hide*, in the *Dorrel*, met her there in her Paſſage to *China*, and had a ſharp Engagement with her, but got clear with the Loſs of 16 Men killed, and ſome wounded, which diſabled the *Dorrel* ſo, that ſhe proceeded no farther than *Malacca*.

AND another Fault of Sir *John*'s was in ſuffering himſelf and his Lady to be taken Priſoners at *Swally*, by the Governor of *Surat*'s Order, when he might either have avoided that Diſgrace by Force or Flight; but it was generally believed, that that was only a Piece of Policy to get to *Surat*, in order to employ his Money, which he could do much better there than at *Bombay*.

SIR *Nicholas Waite* ſupplanted Sir *John* in the Government of *Bombay*, and in the Preſidency. He was a Man of very looſe Morals; and his bare-fac'd Injuſtices and Prevarications irritated the Inhabitants and Soldiery of *Bombay*, that they ſeized him, and ſent him Priſoner for *England*. Tho' his Reign was ſhort, it was very pernicious to his Maſters, as well as to particular Merchants under his Juriſdiction. But, to return from this Digreſſion,

Bom-

Bombay was governed by a Deputy, ſince the Preſident was obliged to ſtay at *Surat*. And of ſeven or eight hundred *Engliſh* that inhabited before the War, there were not above ſixty left by the Sword and Plague, and *Bombay*, that was one of the pleaſanteſt Places in *India*, was brought to be one of the moſt diſmal Deſerts; but the Spirit of Injuſtice ſtill reſided in it, for thoſe who had ventured thro' the War and Plague in Defence of the Iſland, had not the Liberty of returning Home to their own Country, nor to raiſe their Fortune by private Trade, but all were continued preſt Men in the Right Honourable Company's Service, without the Hope of Preferment, which made ſome Diſcontents.

AND, even in the Time of War, when Strangers ſhould have been encouraged to bring Proviſions on the Iſland, the Company's Taxes of 5 *per Cent.* were exacted with great Severity, for I have ſeen the *Portugueze* Subjects bring twenty or thirty Poultry to the Market, and have had five of the beſt taken for the Cuſtom of the reſt.

CHAP

CHAP. XX.

Gives an Account of what is remarkable on ſome Iſlands, and of the Sea-coaſt, as far as Goa.

TWO Leagues from the Caſtle is a ſmall Iſland belonging to the Company, called *Butcher*'s Iſland, but of no Uſe, beſides hauling Ships aſhore to clean, and graze a few Cattle. And, a League from thence, is another larger, called *Elephanto*, belonging to the *Portugueze*, and ſerves only to feed ſome Cattle. I believe it took its Name from an Elephant carved out of a great black Stone, about ſeven Foot in Height. It is ſo like a living Elephant, that, at two hundred Yards Diſtance, a ſharp Eye might be deceived by its Similitude. A little Way from that ſtands an Horſe, cut out of a Stone, but not ſo proportionable and well-ſhaped as the Elephant.

THERE is a pretty high Mountain ſtands in the Middle of the Iſland, ſhapt like a blunt Pyramid, and, about the Half of the Way to the Top, is a large Cave, that has two large Inlets, which ſerve both for Paſſage into it and Lights. The Mountain above it reſts on large Pillars, hewn out of a ſolid Rock, and the Pillars curiouſly carved. Some have the Figures of Men, about eight Foot high, in ſeveral Poſtures, but exceedingly well proportioned and cut. There is one that has a Giant with four Heads joyned, and

The Effegie of the God Gunnies

in Chap. 20.

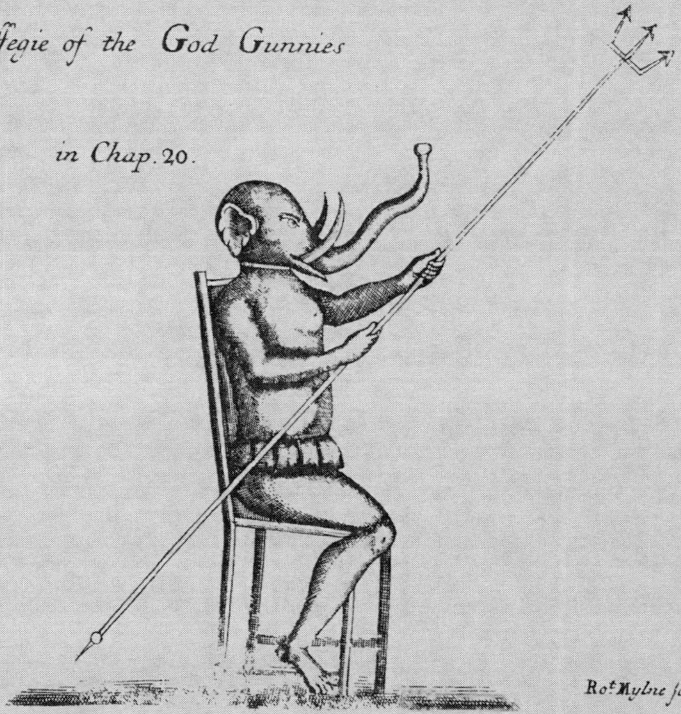

Rot Mylne sc.

and their Faces looking from each other. He is in a ſitting Poſture, with his Legs and Feet under his Body. His right Hand is above twenty Inches long. There are ſeveral dark Rooms hewn out of the Rock, and a fine Spring of ſweet Water comes out of one Room, and runs thro' the Cave out at one of the Inlets. I fired a Fuzee into one of the Rooms, but I never heard Cannon nor Thunder make ſuch a dreadful Noiſe, which continued about half a Minute; and the Mountain ſeemed to ſhake. Aſſoon as the Noiſe was over, a large Serpent appeared, which made us take to our Heels, and got out of the Cave at one Door, and he, in great Haſte, went out at the other. I judged him about 15 Foot long, and 2 Foot about. And theſe were all that I ſaw worth Obſervation on that Iſland. I askt the Inhabitants of the Iſland, who were all *Gentows*, or *Gentiles*, about twenty in Number, if they had any Account, by Hiſtory or Tradition, who made the Cave, or the *Quadrupeds* carved in Stone; but they could give no Account. About a League from *Elephanto*, is an Iſland called *Salvageo*. It affords nothing but Fire-wood, with which it ſupplies *Bombay*. And, about half a League from it, is the Iſland of *Carronjaa*, belonging to the *Portugueze*. It affords no Trade, but Eatables for *Bombay*, from whence it lies Eaſt about two Leagues. Between it and the main Land, is the Mouth of *Pen* River. And four Leagues South of *Bombay*, are two ſmall Iſlands, *Vudra* and *Cun-*

Cundra. The firſt has a Fortreſs belonging to the *Sedee*, and the other is fortified by the *Sevajee*, and is now in the Hands of *Connajee Angarie*. The *Engliſh* have made ſeveral Attempts to take it, but never could, tho' *in Anno* 1719. it had certainly been taken, had not a *Portugueze* Traìtor, who lay on one Quarter of it with ſome Veſſels of War to hinder Relief coming to it, betrayed his Truſt, and let ſome Boats paſs by in the Night with Proviſions and Ammunition, which the Iſland was in great Want of. The *Engliſh* landed, and were obliged to retire by ſome Loſs they received.

About four Miles to the South-eaſt of *Cundra*, is *Culabee*, a Fort built on a Rock a little Way from the main Land; and, at high Water, it is an Iſland, belonging to the *Sevajee*. And, 2 Leagues to the South of *Culabee*, is *Chaul*, a Town belonging to the *Portugueze*, whoſe River affords an Harbour for ſmall Veſſels. The Town is fortified, and ſo is an Iſland on the South Side of the Harbour, called *Chaul Moar*, which may be known 5 or 6 Leagues off at Sea, by a white Church built on it. *Chaul*, in former Times, was a noted Place for Trade, particularly for fine embroidered Quilts; but now it is miſerably poor.

Dande Rajapore lies ſeven Leagues to the Southward of *Chaul*, a Town belonging to the *Sedee*, who generally lies there with a Fleet of the *Mogul*'s Veſſels and Ships of War, and an Army of 30 or 40000 Men. This Place affords

affords a good Harbour for his Fleet, and the Country about feeds good Numbers of black Cattle, from whence *Bombay* is mostly supplied, when they keep in good Terms with the *Sedee*, otherwise he makes them feed on Fish, which that Island is plentifully stored with; but now worse than before the *Sedee*'s War. There is a Rock fortified by the *Sevajee*, that lies within a League of the Mouth of *Dande Rajapore* River, to the Northward, and another as far to the Southward, called the *Whale*, that shews his Back at low Water.

COASTING to the Southward from *Dande Rajapore*, are several small Rivers and fishing Towns. *Zeferdon* is the best, and two little Islands called *Horney Coat*, fortified and kept by the *Sevajee*. It lies 5 Leagues to the Northward of *Dabul*, which stands at the Mouth of a large River, and, of old, was a Place of Trade, and where the *English* once had a Factory.

THERE is an excellent Harbour for Shipping 8 Leagues to the Southward of *Dabul*, called *Sangufeer*; but the Country about being inhabited by *Raparees*, it is not frequented: Nor is *Rajapore*, about 7 Leagues to the Southward of *Sangufeer*, tho' it has the Conveniency of one of the best Harbours in the World, and had formerly both an *English* and *French* Factory settled there; and the Place where General *Child* had his Education, from ten Years old to eighteen, under his Uncle Mr. *Goodshaw*, who was Chief there, and having betrayed ſome of his Uncle's Secrets, in making uſe of the Company's Caſh in his own private Trade, his Uncle was caſhier'd, and, before the Nephew was come to four and twenty, he had the Honour to fill his Chair.

ABOUT the Year 1685. when *Aurengzeb*'s Army was in *Decan*, in order to bring *Sevajee Rajah* to Submiſſion, but could never do it, a Son of *Aurengzeb*, called *Sheek Eckbar*, had contracted a Friendſhip with the *Rajah*. His Father having Notice of it, diſſembled his Reſentment, till he had, by fair Promiſes, entic'd the *Sevajee* to come to his Camp on the publick Faith, but had a Deſign to have him cut off in his Return from the Camp. *Sheek Eckbar* forewarned him of his Danger, while he was in the Camp, which made the *Rajah* depart in the Night, without taking a formal Leave, which *Aurengzeb* imputed to his Son's Advice to the *Rajah*, and, to requite his Son, he had a Mind to make his Life atone for the *Rajah*'s, but deſigned it to be taken from him by Stratagem; wherefore, pretending more Kindneſs than ordinary to his Son, he ſent him a fine Horſe, richly furniſhed, and a Veſt, which was very rich and beautiful, but was poiſoned by a perfumed Powder. His Son, with great Acknowledgments, received the Preſent, but, being too well acquainted with his Father's Subtilty, put not the Veſt on, but deferred it to another Time, that he might put it on with more Solemnity; however he orde-

ordered it to be put on a Slave, who died in a Day or two after he put it on. On which *Sheek Eckbar* fled to *Rajahpore*, and took Shipping, with a few Attendants, for *Muskat*, where he was kindly received by two *English* Gentlemen, Messieurs *Bendal* and *Stephens*, and they provided a Vessel to carry him to *Persia*, where he had a royal Welcome, and was soon after married to that King's Sister, whom *Meriweys* dethroned, and beheaded at *Isphahan*.

When the *English* had a Factory at *Rajahpore*, that Country produced the finest Beteellas and Muslins in *India*; but now all Arts and Sciences are discouraged, and the Port not frequented. There are fine artificial Cisterns for Water there, and a natural hot Bath, within three Yards of a very cold one; and both are reckoned very medicinal.

Ghiria is another Harbour, about 2 Leagues to the Southward of *Rajahpore*. That is the common Place of Residence for *Connajee Angarie*, which is well fortified by a strong large Castle, washt by the Sea. Whether *Ghiria* is also called *Vizendruck*, or whether it lies about seven Leagues more southerly, I am not certain; but that Place, to the Southward, determines the Limits of his Government that Way.

About 12 Leagues to the Southward of *Ghiria*, is an Island about 2 Miles in Circumference, and fortified with a Stone Wall round it, called *Malwan*. It lies about a Mile from the main Land, and is governed by an independent *Rajah*, who is alſo a Freebooter, and keeps three or four Grabs at Sea to rob all whom they can maſter. And that is all I know of him.

Vingurla lies about 4 Leagues to the Southward of *Malwan*, and was formerly a Place of Trade; and the *Dutch* Company had a Factory there for Cloth, both fine and coarſe. But, *in Anno* 1696. a *Rajah*, called *Kempaſon*, overrun that Country, and ſubdued it, and, under Pretence of viſiting the *Dutch* chief Factor, took an Opportunity of the *Dutch* being in Security, ſeized their Factory, and plundred it, but killed no Body. The trading People in the Country, in and about the Town, having no Security for their Perſons and Eſtates, fled to the *Portugueze* Dominions of *Goa*, that lies within 6 Leagues of *Vingurla*. The *Rajah* finding the Country deſerted by the Natives, wrote to the Viceroy of *Goa* to ſend them back, but, on his Noncompliance, entred the *Portugneze* Territories, and plundred and burnt all he could lay Hands on, not ſparing the Churches and Images, for which Sacrilege the *Portugueze* gave him the Name of *Kema Sancto*, or, Saint *Burner*; and they raiſed a Force ſufficient to drive him and his Freebooters out of their Dominions, but, for many Years, continued in his Robberies, when Opportunity preſented, which kept the poor Country Peaſants continually alarmed; and, for all the *Portugueze* Haughtineſs and Pride, they were at

laſt

last forced to buy a Peace, and allow him a yearly Pension to keep him quiet.

He is a Soldier of Fortune, and will serve those *Rajahs* who hire him best, so that if he assists one at one Time, if another gives him better Hire, he tacks about, and serves on the other Side. His Army consists of 7 or 8000 Men, and he had 2 Grabs a Pirating at Sea, but, in a Dispute about a Prize which *Connajee Angarie* laid Claim to, they went to War, and *Connajee* being much superior to him in Power, first took his Grabs and burnt them, and then landed at *Vingurla*, and burnt and destroyed the Villages near the Town. And I know not if ever they made Peace since.

Two Leagues to the Northward of *Vingurla* River there is a Parcel of Rocks that stretches about 2 Leagues into the Sea. The outermost lies in 17 Fathoms of Depth. They seem to have been *Vulcanoes*.

The Religion of all the Countries, from *Dande Rajapore*, to the Dominions of *Goa*, is *Paganism* ; but they are not tied up to divine or moral Rules. And so I leave them, and take a View of *Goa*.

CHAP. XXI.

Gives an Account of Goa *its Situation, Trade, Religion and Churches, with the Fortifications about it, the Limits of the* Portugueze *Dominions there, as far South as* Cabo de Rama.

GOA, the Metropolis of *India*, under the Dominion of the Crown of *Portugal*, ſtands on an Iſland about 12 Miles long, and 6 broad. The City is built on the North Side of it, on a Champain Ground, and has the Conveniency of a fine ſalt Water River, capable to receive Ships of the largeſt Size, where they ly within a Mile of the Town. The Banks of the River are beautified with noble Structures of Churches, Caſtles and Gentlemens Houſes; but, in the City, the Air is reckoned unwholſom, which is one Cauſe why at preſent it is not well inhabited. The Vice-roy's Palace is a noble Edifice, ſtanding within Piſtol Shot of the River, over one of the Gates of the City, which leads to a ſpacious noble Street, about half a Mile long, and terminates at a beautiful Church, called *Miſericordia*. The City contains many noble Churches, Convents and Cloiſters, with a ſtately large Hoſpital, all well endow'd, and well kept. The Market-place ſtands near the *Miſericordia* Church, and takes up about an Acre ſquare, where moſt Things of the Product of that Country are to be ſold; and, in the Shops about it, may be had what

what *Europe*, *China*, *Bengal*, and other Countries of less Note furnish them with. Every Church has a Set of Bells, that one or other of them are continually ringing, and, being all christned, and dedicated to some Saint, they have a specifick Power to drive away all Manner of evil Spirits, except Poverty in the Laity, and Pride in the Clergy; but, to those that are not used to nocturnal Noises, they are very troublesom in the Nights. The Vice-roy generally resides at the Powder-house, about two Miles below the City, on the River Side, the Springs of Water there being reckoned the best on the Island, which is a Liquor very much esteemed by the *Portugueze*, except when they can get Wine or Spirits Cost free, and then they'll drink to Excess.

THE Religion, established by Law, is the *Romish*, and here are the most zealous Bigots of it; and the Laws of the Church (but not of their Country) are rigorously observed, and there is a severe Inquisition Court to punish any whom the Inquisitors have the least Suspicion of, which aws both Clergy and Laity to such a Complacency, that I question if there is such a Pack of notorious Hypocrites in the World; and yet their *Indian Converts*, who go by the general Name of *Cannarians*, retain so much of their ancient *heathnish* Superstition, that they abstain from eating Cows Flesh, because of the Veneration paid to that Beast, above others, by the *Gentows*, whose Offspring they are.

THERE are many *Gentows* dwell in the City, who cannot be brought to change their idolatrous Superſtition for the Religion of *Rome*, but they are tolerated, becauſe they are generally more induſtrious than the *Chriſtians*, eſpecially in mechanical Employments and Agriculture; but the mercantil Part of them are very ſubject to the Inſults of the *Reynolds*, or *European Fidalgoes*, who will often buy their Goods, and never pay for them, which Cuſtom has alſo crept into ſome Countries better poliſhed than the *Portugueze*, only with ſome Reſtrictions, that they dare not uſe Force in taking what they have Occaſion for, as the *Portugueze* do, nor inflict corporal Puniſhments on their Creditors, when they ask for their Money, ſo that it is dangerous for the poor induſtrious Merchant, either to refuſe their Goods, or ask for their Money when it is due, for Fear of a Baſtinado in either Caſe, and ſometimes worſe Conſequences, which Abuſes make the Circulation of Trade very faint and weak.

THE Clergy at *Goa* are very numerous and illiterate, and are a very great Burden on the State. Their Churches are richly furniſhed with fine Decorations and Images, and, as I ſaid before, richly endow'd to maintain the Luxury of a great Number of idle Drones.

THEIR Houſes are large, and their Outſides magnificent; but within (like their Owners Heads) they are but poorly furniſht, and their Tables very mean. Green Fruits and Roots, in in their Seasons, with a little Bread and Rice go far in their Diet; and candied and preserved Fruits are their *Regalio* in all Seasons. They have Hogs and Fowl plenty, but use them sparingly; and the Church feeds most on Fish, but not miraculously, for the poor Fishers dare sell none till the Priesthood is first served, so that the Laity mostly eat stale or stinking Fish. And the Soldiery, Fishers, Peasants and Handicrafts feed on a little Rice boyled in Water, with a little Bit of salt Fish, or *Atchaar*, which is pickled Fruits or Roots, and drink fair Water, when they can get it. This fine spare Diet never loads them with superabundant Flesh on their Bones, and, without the Church, it is rare to find a corpulent Man among them. They are generally very weak and feeble, but whether that proceeds from their Diet, or from their too great Inclinations to Venery, or from both, I am not Physician enough to determine.

THEIR Soldiers Pay is very small and ill paid. They have but six *Xerapheens per* Month, and two Suits of Calico, stript or chequered, in a Year. Their two Suits may amount to forty *Xerapheens*; and a *Xerapheen* is worth about sixteen Pence half Peny *Ster*. Out of their six *Xerapheens* in Money that they are to receive, their Captain, who is Barrack-master and Victualler to his Company, detains five, and the other one is paid in small Money to discharge the Accounts of the Shoemaker, Taylor, Barber, Washerman and

and Tobacconist, so that Frugality is no great Virtue among them, tho' Theft is, and really they are very dextrous in that Art, as well as in Murder, for if they are detected in committing such innocent Crimes, the very next Church is a Sanctuary for them, and neither divine nor human Laws can affect them after they get in there.

THIS Nation was famous in the fifteenth Century for their Navigation and Discoveries into the *East Indies*, where, by Friendship or Force, they made Settlements all over its Sea-coasts. Their Settlements were thick set between *Mozambique* and *Japon*; and, as a Monument of their Grandeur then, their Language goes current along most of the Sea-coast at this Time. Their insolent Pride and War with the *Dutch* have brought them to the Poverty and Contempt they are in, as I shall remark in their proper Places.

THE *Muskat* War, (that has lasted since the *Arabs* took that City from them) tho' the longest, has done them least Harm, for it obliges them to keep an *Armada* of five or six Ships, besides small Frigats and Grabs of War, which gives Bread to great Numbers of People, who otherwise would be much more burdensom to the State, by crowding into Churches. The *Arabs* and they have had many Encounters, but no great Damage done on either Side. I was Witness to one Engagement near *Surat* Bar, but it was not bloody.

THEY

THEY alſo have had ſeveral Wars aſhore, but the moſt dangerous to the City of *Goa*, was that with *Sevajee Rajah*, who got Footing on the Iſland about the Year 1685. He raiſed ſome Batteries againſt the Town, which would have annoyed it very much, had not a *Portugueze Heroine*, in a Sally, got into a Redoubt of the Enemy's, and cut them to Pieces, which ſtruck ſuch a Terror into *Sevajee*'s Army, that they quitted their Poſts and fled. The Lady was alive *in Anno* 1705. and received the Pay of a Captain all her Days after that noble Exploit. She was called *Donna Maria*. She came to *India* in Man's Apparel, in Queſt of a Gentleman that had promiſed her Marriage, and then deſerted her, and went, in Quality of Captain, to *India*; but ſhe found him, and challenged him at Sword and Piſtol, but he rather choſe to make the Quarrel up amicably by Marriage.

I have ſtood on a little Hill near the City, and have counted about eighty Churches, Convents and Monaſteries within View; and I was informed, that, in the City and its Diſtricts, which ſtretch about 40 Miles along the Sea-coaſt, and 15 Miles within Land, there are no fewer than 30000 Church Vermin, who live idlely and luxuriouſly on the Labour and Sweat of the miſerable Laity, ſo that every Body that has Sons and Subſtance, ſtrives to buy Places for them in the Church, becauſe neither military nor civil Preferments can be expected from the State, or if by Merit

rit they chance to raiſe themſelves, yet the Tyranny and Oppreſſions of the domineering Clergy is inſupportable; for Inſtance, I knew a Gentleman that bought a Parcel of freſh Fiſh, and a Prieſt coming ſoon after to the Fiſhers, and finding that none was left for the Church, he demanded the Gentleman's Bargain, who excuſed himſelf, by telling the Prieſt, that he had ſome Friends to dine with him, and could not ſpare them. The Prieſt gave him a Reprimand in ſcurrilous Language, and the Gentleman uſing ſome tart Language to the Prieſt, that offended him, he let fly the ſharp Dart of Excommunication, that pierced him ſo deep, that it coſt him above 7 *L. Sterl.* to take it out again, and beg his Pardon on his Knees before the Archbiſhop, before he could be abſolved.

In a fine ſtately Church dedicated to St. *Paul* the Apoſtle, lies the Body of St. *Francis Xavier* a *Portugueze* Apoſtle, and a *Jeſuit* by Trade, who died in his Miſſion to *Japon* in the fifteenth Century; and, about fifty Years after, as a *Portugueze* Ship was going to, or coming from *China*, being near an Iſland on that Coaſt, called after St. *Juan*, ſome Gentlemen and Prieſts went aſhore for Diverſion, and accidentally found the Saint's Body uncorrupted, and carried it Paſſenger to *Goa*, and there, with much Veneration and eccleſiaſtical Ceremony, it was depoſited in an Iſle of St. *Paul*'s Church, where it lies ſtill, and looks as freſh as a new ſcalded Pig, but with the Loſs of one Arm; for

for, when the Rumour of the Miracle reached *Rome*, the sovereign Pontiff ordered his right Arm to be sent, that he might find out if there was any Imposture in it or no, or perhaps make him fadge in a *China Bonzee* into his Calendar, under the Name of a *Christian* Saint. Accordingly his Arm was fairly cut off by the Shoulder, and sent to *Rome* to stand its Trial. When his Holiness had viewed it, he called for Pen, Ink and Paper to be brought on a Table, and the Arm set near them. After a little Conjuration, in full View of the sacred College, who were there present, and no Body else, the Saint's Hand took hold of the Pen, and dipt it in Ink, and fairly wrote *Xavier*.

I take it to be a pretty Piece of Wax-work that serves to gull the People of their Money, for many visit it with great Veneration, and leave something at its Shrine for the Maintenance of Candles and Olive Oyl, that continually burn before it: And a Priest attends weekly to shave his Head and Beard; but none but that Priest has the Honour to come within the Iron Rails that are placed about the Corps, four or five Yards distant from it. Now if any should question the Truth of *Xavier*'s Story at *Goa*, they would be branded with the odious Name of an obstinate incredulous Heretick, and perhaps fall in the Hands of a convincing Inquisition.

But, if any incredulous Heretick should be squeamish, and cannot swallow the Story of *Xavier* without chewing it, I will tell them

of

of another that doubtleſs will go glibly down. At a certain Time, but God knows when, a Ship of *Portugal* coming to *India*, got the Length of *Cabo de bona Eſperanza*, and then met with ſuch a violent Storm, that drove the Ship ſo violently before it, that it was paſt the Pilot's Skill to keep her to Rights in her Courſe; and who ſhould come to their Aſſiſtance in that critical Juncture, but *Senhor Diabolo*, who took the Helm, and managed it very dextrouſly: And the Virgin *Mary*, to ſhew her Kindneſs, and Skill in Navigation, ſtood a whole Night on the Forecaſtle, directing the Devil how he ſhould ſteer, and behold, to the great Admiration of all concerned, the Ship was high and dry in the Morning, in a Valley on the South Side of the River of *Goa*, about half a Mile within the Land. The Ship ſailed very well, for that one Night ſhe ran, according to a moderate Computation, 1500 Leagues. And, in Commemoration of this Miracle, there is a fine Church built where the Ship anchored ſo ſafely, and the Structure is juſt the Length, Breadth and Height of the Ship. The Church I have often ſeen as I paſt up and down the River. And this Story is ſo firmly believed at *Goa*, that it is dangerous to make any Doubt of it.

Of all the Churches in or about *Goa* none is honoured with Glaſs-windows, but one in the City dedicated to St. *Alexander*, for the reſt are all ſerved with clear Oyſter-ſhell Lights, that are far inferior to Lights of

Glaſs.

Glaſs. And all their ſtately Houſes are furniſhed with Oyſter-ſhel Lights.

THE Country about *Goa* is ſteril in Corn, but it produces ſome excellent Fruits. The *Goa Mango* is reckoned the largeſt and moſt delicious to the Taſte of any in the World, and, I may add, the wholſomeſt and beſt taſted of any Fruit in the World. Their *Jambo Malacca* is very beautiful and pleaſant, and they have very good Pine Apples and Melons.

THE little Trade they have, is moſtly from their Arrack, which is diſtilled from *Toddy* of the Cocoa-nut Tree, which grows in great Abundance in the Territories of *Goa*. The *Engliſh* are their beſt Cuſtomers, for they buy great Quantities yearly for Punch. It is ſold by the *Candy*, or two Casks, about 45 Gallons each, for 25 *Xerapheens per* Cask; but I have bought it for 20. when there was no great Demand for it. They alſo make a great Deal of Salt in Ponds made in low Grounds, where they may convey the Water at ſpring Tides. It may be bought for a Crown the Tun, and ſometimes cheaper.

THE River's Mouth is guarded, and the Entrance defended by ſeveral Forts and Batteries, well planted with large Cannon on both Sides. On the Iſland is the black Fort, which ſtands within half a Musket-ſhot of the Bar, which is ſhut up by the South-ſouth-weſt Monſoons, from *April* to *September*, when is St. *Anthony*'s New-moon, as they call being the firſt New-moon in *September*. The Freſhes coming down from the Mountains,

tains, carry off the Sands, which choke the Mouths of the Rivers along all the Coaſts of *India*. And, without the black Fort, is a Battery built cloſe to the Sea on a little Promontory, called *Nos Senhor de Cabo*, about a Mile without the black Fort. And, juſt over that Battery, on a little Hill about 40 Yards high, is a fine Monaſtery, always kept as white as Snow, and may be ſeen a good Diſtance off at Sea. The Monaſtery has a large pleaſant Garden towards the Land, and an Orchard of excellent Fruit Trees. And, on the Oppoſite of *Nos Senhor de Cabo*, is a Fort built on the Face of a little Hill, which commands that Side of the River. And, without that, is the *Aguada*, fortified with a Fort on its Top, and ſeveral Batteries at the Foot of its high Grounds, which are alſo about 40 Yards high. In the Caſtle is placed a large Lantern for a Light-houſe, to ſhew Shipping the Way into the Road about the Beginning of *September*, when thick Clouds obſcure the Land, that it cannot be well known at Sea. All Boats that are bound to the City, are obliged to call at *Aguada*, to give an Account from whence they came, and what their Buſineſs is; and if any preſume to paſs without calling there, they are ſure of a Shot fired from a Battery at them, to put them in Mind of their Duty. Two Leagues to the South of *Aguada* are the *Marmagun* Iſlands, being five in Number, and run a League into the Sea. The two innermoſt are fortified, to command the Entrance of the

River

River of St. *Lorenzo*, which is a Branch of *Goa* River, parting about five Leagues from their Mouths, and compose the Island called *Goa* Island.

This Country belonged formerly to the Kings of *Visapore*; but in the fifteenth Century, when *Albukerk* settled the *Portugueze* Colonies in *India*, he purchased the Islands of *Goa* and *Salset*, which lie contiguous to *Goa*, from the King, who did them many singular Services, which afterwards were repaid by Ingratitude.

About the Year 1660. when the *Dutch* had a War in *America* and *India*, with the *Portugueze*, the *Dutch* sent a Squadron, to try if they could add *Goa* to the rest of their *Indian* Conquests, but found its Avenues so well fortified, that it was thought impracticable to land. Their Ships were forced to ly at a good Distance from *Aguada* and *Nos Senhor de Cabo*, and so continued riding at Anchor triumphantly, without Action, except a little Diversion they had with a *Portugueze Bravo*, who, with a small Ship of forty Guns, would needs pass thro' the *Dutch* Fleet, as they lay at Anchor; but they soon made him sensible of rash Folly, by sinking his Ship, and either killing or drowning him and all his Crew.

When the *Portugueze* and the *Sevajee* had War, I think that *Conde de Villa Verde* was then Vice-roy, there were so few Soldiers, and so many Priests, that he was obliged to take Recruits for his Army, out of the

Church; but the King of *Portugal* was forced to recal him for that great Offence.

BETWEEN *Goa* and *Salset* there is a little River that is another Branch of the River of *Goa*, which disembogues about a League to the South of *Marmagun*, at a Village called *Bangricoal*, and affords a little Harbour for small Vessels, from which Place the Island of *Salset* stretches five Leagues along the Sea-shore, in a fine level Plain, planted with Cocoa-nut Trees and Churches. The Product of this Island is as that of *Goa*, Arrack and Salt. The Churches and Monasteries are Seminaries for black *Romish* Priests, and the Country, besides them, produces good Store of Hogs and Poultry. At *Cabo de Rama*, which is contiguous to *Salset*, are the Limits of the Dominions of the *Portugueze* on that Part of *India*.

CHAP. XXII.

Gives an Account of the Sundah Rajah'*s Dominions, the Product, Religion and Customs of his Country, with Observations on his War with the* English East-india *Company*, in Anno 1718.

C*ABO de Rama*, or, as the *English* call it, Cape *Ramus*, begins the Limits of the *Sunda Rajah*'s Country, to the Northward, and has a Castle on the Cape to secure his Frontier; but there is no River or Harbour for

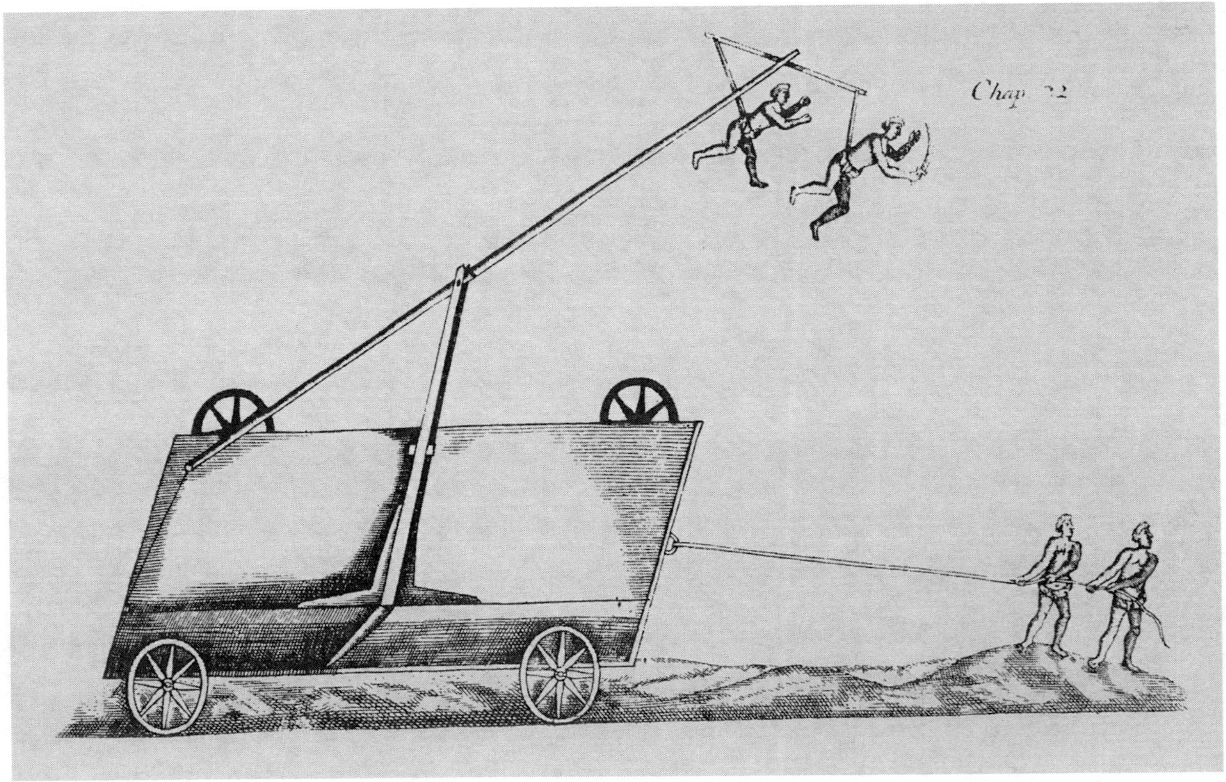
Chap. 22

for Shipping, till we come to *Sevaſeer*, and that is but a bad one, tho' it has the Cover of a large Caſtle with few Guns in it. But,

Carwar, which lies ſeven Leagues to the Southward of Cape *Ramus*, has the Advantages of a good Harbour, on the South Side of a Bay, and a River capable to receive Ships of 300 Tuns. The *Engliſh* have a Factory here, fortified with two Baſtions, and ſome ſmall Cannon for its Defence. The *Rajah* is tributary to the *Mogul* at preſent, but formerly was a Part of *Viſapore*'s Dominions, before *Aurengzeb* conquered that Country. This *Rajah*'s Dominions reach from Cape *Ramus* to *Merzee*, about fifteen Leagues along the Sea-coaſt, and ſixty or ſeventy Leagues within Land.

About the Year 1660. *Aurengzeb* came into *Viſapore* with an Army of 3 or 400000 Men, and ſoon conquered the open Country, but the Metropolis, called the City of *Viſapore*, took him ſeven or eight Years to reduce it, for being built on a flat Mountain of difficult Acceſs, and Room enough to ſow Corn on it, obliged *Aurengzeb* to ſurround it with his Army, and make a Blockade, but at laſt it yielded, and *Aurengzeb* put the King in Chains of Silver, and carried him in Triumph along with his victorious Army, near the Space of thirty Years, and then he died an inglorious Captive. He was reckoned a good ſimple peaceable Prince while he reigned, but was in no Way related to the God *Mars*.

The *Sundah Rajah*'s Country is mountainous, and lies on both Sides of the Mountains of *Gatti*. The Vallies abound in Corn and Pepper, the beſt in *India*; and the Woods, on the Mountains, with many Sorts of wild Beaſts, as Tigers, Wolves, Monkies, wild Hog, Deer, Elks, and wild Cattle of a prodigious large Size. I have ſeen a wild Bull killed there, whoſe four Quarters weighed above a Tun Weight, beſides the Hide, Head and Guts. I meaſured his Horns, which were not long in Proportion to their Thickneſs, being twenty three Inches in Circumference about the Roots, and his Marrow-bones ſo large, that I took the Marrow out with an ordinary Silver-ſpoon. The Fleſh was not ſo ſavoury as that of ſmall tame Cattle, nor would it take Salt kindly, but grew hard, dry and black when ſalted.

This Country is ſo famous for hunting, that two Gentlemen of Diſtinction, *viz.* Mr. *Lembourg* of the Houſe of *Lembourg* in *Germany*, and Mr. *Goring*, a Son of my Lord *Goring*'s in *England*, went *incognito* in one of the *Eaſt-india* Company's Ships, for *India*. They left Letters directed for their Relations, in the Hands of a Friend of theirs, to be delivered two or three Months after their Departure, ſo that Letters of Credit followed them by the next Year's Shipping, with Orders from the *Eaſt-india* Company to the Chiefs of the Factories, where ever they ſhould happen to come, to treat them according to their Quality. They ſpent three Years at

Car-

Carwar, viz. from *Anno* 1678. to 1681. then, being tired with that Sort of Pleasure, they both took Passage on board a Company's Ship for *England*, but Mr. *Goring* died four Days after the Ship's Departure from *Carwar*, and lies buried on the Island St. *Mary*, about four Leagues from the Shore, off *Batacola*, and Mr. *Lembourg* returned safe to *England*.

THERE are three Species of Tigers in *Carwar* Woods. The smallest is the fiercest. It is not above two Foot high when it walks. It is very cunning, and delights much in human Flesh. The second Sort is about three Foot high, and hunts Deer and wild Hog, and a little Creature, called a Pissay. Its Body has the Shape of a Deer's, but its Head like a Swine; and, as a Boar has two long Tusks growing upward from the nether Jaw, so it has two long small sharp Teeth which grow downward from the upper Jaw, and reach as low as the under Part of the lower Jaw. They are very harmless and fearful, and feed on Grass and Herbs. They are hardly so big as a full grown Cat, and their Flesh is black, and tastes like an Hare's. The largest Size of the Tigers is above three Foot and an half high, when they walk. They are less rapacious than the others, seldom greedy of human Flesh, and sooner frightned. A poor Peasant in this Country had a Buffalo bemired in a Bog, and while he went to his Neighbours for Assistance, came a large Tiger that saved them the Trouble, for he pulled it out by his own Dexterity and

Strength, and, when he had done, threw him over his Shoulder, as a Fox does a Goose, and was carrying it, with its Feet upwards, to his Den, but, when he saw the People, he let it fall, and went away; but he had killed the Buffalo, and had suckt his Blood. 'Tis a small Buffalo that weighs not above 500 *lb.* Weight, and some weigh 1200.

I once was in the Woods with my Fuzee, to try if I could kill a Deer, but a small Rain happened to fall that damped my Powder, which was only wrapt up in Paper; and, my Gun being useless, I was making towards the Plain where our Factory stands, and falling on a Foot-path from the Mountains towards the Plain, I kept in that Road, and had not gone far, till I espied a Tiger of the largest Size standing in the same Path, with his Face towards me. Assoon as he saw me, he squatted his Belly to the Ground, and wagged his Tail, and crawled slowly towards me. I thought it would be in vain to flee, so I stept leisurely forward, till I came within ten Yards of him, I then clubbed my Fuzee, and made what Noise I could to frighten him, and he, out of Civility, rusht in amongst a Thicket of Bushes, and left me the Road, which I did not think fit to accept of, but got in among the Bushes on the opposite Side to him (I dare say) much more frightned than he was. And, before I got to the Plain, I saw a wild Bull and a Cow grazing. The Bull grew angry, and snorted, but the Cow only gazed on me; but I soon got out of

their

their Sight, and got ſafe to the Factory; but never went into the Woods again, but with a numerous Company.

THE Chief of the *Engliſh* Factory is held in very great Eſteem in this Country, and when he goes a hunting, is generally accompanied with moſt Part of the People of Diſtinction in the Vicinage, who bring their Vaſſals and Servants with them, armed with fire Arms and other Weapons, both miſſive and defenſive, with Trumpets, Hautboys and Drums. The fire Men place themſelves at convenient Diſtances, along the Skirts of an Hill or a Wood, except ſome that are ſent in to guard thoſe who are ſent with their loud Muſick to rouze the Game. The Drums, Trumpets and Hautboys ſpread themſelves ſometimes for a Mile or two, and, on a Signal given, ſtrike up at once, and march towards the Skirt where the fire Men are placed. The wild Inhabitants being aſtoniſhed with the unuſual Noiſe, betake themſelves to their Heels, and fall in the Ambuſcade, and many of them are killed and wounded in their Flight. I ſaw, in one of theſe Huntings, above a Dozen of Deer killed, two wild Cows with their Calves, who would not leave their dead Parents, tho' they had done ſucking; alſo four or five Sows, who had above a Dozen of Pigs following them, and were all killed, with ſome Piſſays; and all in leſs than two Hours Space. The Hunters made good Cheer of what they lik'd beſt, and what remained was ſent to the Factory;

and the Chief ſoon following after, was conducted Home by the whole Company, and, at the Factory Gate, made him a Compliment, and departed. At this Time, which was *in Anno* 1692. the Factory had about a Score of good Dogs for Game, of *Engliſh* Brood, and the Company allowed each of them about 2 *lb.* of boyl'd Rice daily, but now they are better Husbands of their Money, and have diſcharged all their Dogs and other Superfluities, except one good old Cuſtom of treating Strangers that come there from *Europe*, with pretty black female Dancers, who are very active in their Dancing, and free in their Converſation, where Shame is quite out of Faſhion.

THE Woods produce great Quantities of good Teak Timber, uſeful in building both Ships and Houſes. It is more durable than Oak. And there is good Poon Maſts, ſtronger, but heavier than Fir. There is a Shrub grows in the Woods, that has a Leaf bigger than that of the Fig-tree; and the Dew that falls on that Leaf being carefully gathered, and ſet in the Sun a Day or two, becomes the pleaſanteſt and ſtrongeſt Acid that ever I taſted.

BEFORE *Aurengzeb* conquered *Viſapore*, this Country produced the fineſt Betteellas or Muſlins in *India*. The *Engliſh* Company had a great Cloth Trade here, and employed about 50000 People in that Manufactory; but the *Mogul*'s licentious Soldiers fell into this Province, and ruined all Manner of Trade, plun-

plundring the induſtrious Inhabitants of all they could lay Hands on, and cut the Company's Cloth from the Loom, and uſed the Weavers ſo rudely, that they left their own Country, to look for Protection in Countries farther to the Southward, where War had not ſet up her bloody Banners.

WHEN the *Mogul*'s General had taken Poſſeſſion of that Province in his Maſter's Name, he invited the Gentlemen of the *Engliſh* Factory to an Entertainment in his Tent, under Pretence of ſettling the Company's Commerce, and, while they were at Dinner, he ſent a Party of Men, who plundred and burnt their Houſe, which made the Company build and fortify what they now have; but he who built it where it is, had no great Foreſight in chooſing his Ground, for it ought to have been built in a Place of free Communication with the Sea, but now it ſtands a League from it. And, *in Anno* 1718. the *Rajah* ſhewed them their Error, and built Batteries at the Mouth of the River, ſo that the Factory is nothing at preſent but a gentile Priſon, which by dear bought Experience, we found in a War we had with him, by the Indiſcretion of one *Taylor* who was Chief, who pretended to be Lord of the Mannor, in appropriating a Wrack to his own Uſe, that was caſt away above four Miles from the Factory. The *Rajah* could not bear to be ſo bare-fac'dly affronted in his own Dominions, by Tenants that would hear no Reaſon. He beſieged the Factory for 2 Months before

before the Season would admit of Forces coming to assist them by Sea; and when they arrived, the Seas run so high on the Shore, that there was great Difficulty of landing in the Teeth of an Enemy, who had ten Times our Numbers, so that the first Attempt of landing was unsuccessful, by our Mens Neglect and Disobedience to the Orders they had received, and about fourscore of our bravest Fellows were cut off, and some taken Prisoners: But, about six Weeks after, we had some Revenge on the Enemy in an Engagement on the Side of an Hill among thick Bushes. The Enemy being above our Men, began their Fire at Break of Day, to beat our Men from a Spring of fresh Water close to the Sea; but our small Vessels lying near the Shore to cover about 400 Men, that lay to guard the Water, fired with so good Success, that, in an Hour's Time, they were obliged to run, and leave near 200 dead in the Woods; and our Men pursuing them in their Flight, did some Execution on them.

We were in daily Expectation of more Forces, and did not offer the Enemy Battle, because of their Numbers and our Want of Experience; but we harassed the Enemies in the Nights, in burning Villages, for there was little to plunder; and at Sea we took some Vessels laden with Salt going to the Enemy, and three Ships of the *Rajah*'s coming from *Arabia* with Horses, to the Number of 140. which created us much Trouble to find Provender and Water for them: However,

ever, when our Reinforcement came, we could muster, in our Fleet, of Seamen and Soldiers, 2250 Men. The Enemy raised some Batteries on the Strand to hinder our landing; and we took two of the Prizes, and made them Shot-proof above Water, and laid them ashore at high Water to batter their Batteries, and keep the Enemy at a Distance with their great Shot, till our Men were landed and drawn up. Each of our floting Batteries were covered with a Frigat of 20 or 24 Guns. When all was ready, we landed 1250 Men, without the least Hindrance from the Enemy, for they were preparing to flee to the Woods; but our fresh Water land Officers were so long a drawing up their Men in a confounded hollow Square, that the Enemy took Courage, and, with Horse and Foot, came running towards our Men, firing, and wounding some as they marched in their Ranks, which our Commandant seeing, pulled off his red Coat, and vanished. Some other as valiant Captains as he, took Example, and left their Posts, and then the Soldiers followed, and threw down their Arms. We lost in this Skirmish about 250, but our floting Batteries would not permit the Enemy to pursue far, nor durst they stay to gather up our scattered Arms, so about 80 Sailers went on the Field of Battle, and brought on board of the Commodore about 200 Stand of Arms, most of them loaded: However the Enemy had some Loss too, for we found eleven Horses dead, and saw many Fires along

long the Foot of the Hills to burn their dead Men in.

THE *Rajah* had, by this Time, 7000 Men engaged in this War, which Expence he began to be tired of, and the Loſs of his Ships and Horſes was ſome Mortification to him, beſides the *Saw Rajah* had made an Inroad into his Northern Borders, which made him incline very much towards a Peace, and accordingly he ſent a *Brahman* on board the Commodore of the Fleet, to negotiate about a Peace. The Commodore heard him, and adviſed him to make his Overtures to Mr. *Taylor*; but he ſaid, that the *Rajah* would by no Means conſent to treat with him, complaining, that he was not only the Occaſion of that War, but even, before the War, had done ſome Detriment to him and his Subjects, for receiving the Company's Pepper above 100 Miles from the Factory. He made the Servants that went to receive the Pepper, take certain Quantities to ſell out by Retail in his Villages, to the utter Ruin of many poor Inhabitants, that had no other Way to get their Livelihood, but by huckſtering, and becauſe the Company's Agreement with his Forefathers and himſelf, gave them a free Trade in all his Dominions, he paſt all over, but was forced to relieve the poor *Botickeers* or Shop-keepers, who before could pay him Taxes; however we being tired of War as well as he, by the Mediation of a *Seid*, who was a Friend to both Parties, in ten Days after the firſt Overture was made, Peace was

pro

proclaimed on easy Terms for both Parties.

There is one Trick that the Priests yearly put upon the People in this Country, that would puzzle the best Merry-andrews in *Europe* to imitate, and that is, about the latter End of *May*, or the Beginning of *June*, there is a Feast celebrated to the infernal Gods, with a Divination or Conjuration to know the Fate of the ensuing Crop of Corn The Ceremony I saw here, and at other Places on the Coast of *Canara*. The Priests having perswaded some Fools to bear a Part in the Farce, proclaim the Feast to be on such a Day, at a certain Grove, where several thousands of People assemble, and in the Middle of the Grove is placed a black Stone of 3 or 400 Weight, without any designed Shape, but some Places bedaub'd with red Lead mixt in Oyl, to serve for a Mouth, Eyes and Ears, and a little earthen Pot of Fire placed before the Stone, and a Girl about ten Years of Age to attend it.

Some Priests, all naked, except a Bit of Cloth to hide their Privities, run and dance round the Stone and Fire for half an Hour, like mad Men, making strange Distortions in their Phizes, and now and then bellowing like Calves. And this was the first Scene. Those Priests had erected a Scaffold on two Axle-trees, that had Trucks fitted for them like the Carriage of Ship Guns. In the Middle of the Scaffold (which might be about 15 Foot long, and as broad) was erected a Piece of of Wood about 15 Foot high, with a Notch cut in the upper End, like the Cheeks of a Ship's Pump, with Holes bored for a Bolt to paſs through, as Pump Cheeks have. A Tree hewn for their Purpoſe, about 40 Foot long, was laid about the Middle in the Notch, and a Bolt paſſing through the Cheeks and that Tree, like a Pump-brake. At one End of the Tree were placed two croſs Pieces, one at the very End, and the other about 4 Foot within it. Each of thoſe croſs Pieces were about 4 Foot long, and, at the other End, had a Rope faſtned to it. And this was the Vehicle for the Actors to hang on for a Mile or two.

The Actors preſenting themſelves to the Prieſts, being four in Number, dreſt as the Prieſts were; only on their Heads, Crowns were made round their Temples, of Sugar-cane Leaves, open at the Top, like ducal Crowns. The Prieſts brought two Tenter-hooks, ſuch as the Butchers in *Britain* hang their Meat on, for each Actor, and, after ſome ridiculous Ceremony, hookt them on each Side of the Back-bone, a little above the Kidnies. Thoſe Hooks had Cords faſt to them, ſo they went dancing round the Stone, and the Prieſt holding their Strings faſt, and, after two Minutes Dancing, they came tamely to the End of the Tree, where the croſs Pieces were faſtned, and one was tied up to each End of the croſs Pieces, and the Mob was ready to hale down the other End, and faſtned it to the End of the Scaffold,

fold, and the foolish Fellows were hung up by the Back, above ten Yards from the Ground. The Populace broke some old Cocoa-nuts on the Scaffold, and some hundreds of them got hold of the Ropes fastned to the Scaffold, and haled it over plowed Ground, above a Mile, to another Grove; and the Girl with the Pot of Fire on her Head, walking all the Way before. When they came to the End of their Journey, they were let down, and going into the Grove, where was placed another black Stone Pagod, the Girl set her Fire before it, and run stark mad for a Minute or two, and then fell in a Swoon, and in that she lay sweating and foming at the Mouth prodigiously. When she grew mad, the Men fell flat on the Ground before the Image, and then arose after she fell in her Trance. She continued immoveable about a Quarter of an Hour, and then awoke, and seemed to be very sick. The Priests interrogated her about what she had seen and heard from the terrestrial Gods, and she gave them a satisfactory Answer, on which they all bowed to the Image, and put their Hand on a Cow that was there ready, dedicated to the Image; and so all departed satisfied.

ON sight of the new Moon in *August* they have another Piece of Superstition, in a Feast dedicated to the Sea, for the prosperous Navigation of the ensuing Season. They have the Effigies of the God *Gunnies*, which is a Man's Body, with an Elephant's Head, clapt cleverly on his Shoulders, and carried in Procession

ceſſion to a River's Side, and thrown into the River, upon which, all Rivers who have Bars are opened for Navigation.

THIS *Gunnies* was Son to *Ram* another God, who had a great War many Years with a certain Sort of gigantick Devils, that inſulted the Land, and carried away all the Virgins they could lay their Paws on; at Length *Ram* overcame them in a bloody Battle, for which Succeſs, he ſwore, he would make a Sacrifice of the firſt living Creature he ſhould meet in his own Dominions,to the great God of Heaven; and poor *Gunnies* was the firſt Object that preſented himſelf; for being a good loving Son, came on Purpoſe to meet and welcome his Father from his Fatigues in War: You may judge what a Pack of Troubles *Ram* was in, but there was no Remedy, but *Gunnies* muſt die; and, with great Regret, he was about to have his Head ſtruck off, when a clever Fellow of a *Brahman* Doctor came, and told *Ram*, that by his Art he could ſave *Gunnies*'s Life, if his Advice might be followed, which *Ram* promiſed to do, on which the Doctor ordered a young Elephant to be brought; and when the Father whipt off his Son's Head, the Doctor very skilfully cut off the Elephant's at one Stroke, and nimbly ſet it on *Gunnies*'s Shoulders, to the great Admiration of all the Beholders; and from that Day to this, *Gunnies* has wore an Elephant's Head.

THERE are a Set of *Brahmans* in this Country called *Buts*, they ſtudy Aſtrology, and

and are in great Repute for their exemplary innocent Lives, and Skill in prophesying. In the Year 1684. one *Moam But* told some Things very surprising, when Mr. *Walsel* was Chief for the *English* at *Carwar*.

In the Space of three Years no *English* Ship from *Europe* had called there, and the Gentlemen longing for one, and *Moam But* coming to visit the Chief, Mr. *Walsel* askt him if he could tell when a Ship from *Europe* would call there. He answered, he could tell, and musing a little While, told, that on that same Day forty Days, which happened to fall out on a *Sunday*, one would arrive, and that she was, at that Time, at Anchor at an Island on this Side of the Cape of *Good-hope*, taking in Refreshments. The Chief told him, if he prophesied true, he would present him with as much scarlet Cloth as would make him a Coat. The *But* answered, that he thank'd him, but that neither of them would live to see her arrive, and therefore advised Mr. *Walsel* to set his House in Order; and that, to prove some Part of the Prophecy true, the *But* himself should die ten Days after the Day he prophesied, and that Mr. *Walsel* should die so many Days after. Accordingly the *But* died, which put the other's Mind out of Order, till the Day of his Death came, and that Morning Mr. *Walsel* said, he believed the Conjurer was out in his Reckoning, for he never was in better Health in his Days; but, after Dinner, he had an apoplectick Fit, that carried him off. And the Ship's Pinnace came ashore at the Factory Gate that Noon that the *But* told she should arrive. The Ship was the *Mexico Merchant*, commanded by Captain *Roger Paxton*, whom I well knew.

THE pretty nimble female Dancers at *Carwar* are not so by Choice; but all Trades and Occupations being listed into Tribes, none can marry out of their own Tribe; and, as it fortuned, the Originals of this Tribe were Ladies that could not be confined to one Husband, and so would not marry. Their Posterity are not suffered to marry, because there are no Men in their Tribe allowed. When the Lasses bring forth Children, the Males are brought up Soldiers, and the Females are learned to dance, and what they earn by dancing goes to the *Rajah*, except a small Share for the Girl's Maintenance. What they get by their Kindness to Strangers is all their own; and I have seen some have very fine Clothes and Jewels acquired by their Trade.

THE *Portugueze* have an Island called *Anjediva* (before mentioned) about 2 Miles from *Batcoal*. They fortified it, for fear that *Muskat Arabs* or the *Sevajees* should have settled on it; if they had, they might have incommoded the *Goa* Fleet that goes yearly to *Canara* for Corn.

AT the Mouth of *Carwar* River, are two fortified Islands, called *Shipe* and *Gur*. One is fortified by Walls built round it, and some Guns mounted on it. The other is steril and dry,

dry, and not worth walling. They both belong to the *Rajah* of *Sundah*. There are some Islands ly athwart the Mouth of the Bay, that make the Harbour of *Carwar*, but none inhabited. The Bay has two large Entrances for Shipping. That to the North is clear from Danger; but the South Chanel has a sharp Rock like a Pyramid in the Middle of it, that several large Ships have struck on, for there is too much Water on it for small Ships to be frightned by it, having at least 15 Foot Water on its Top.

There are several more little Harbours in this *Rajah*'s Dominions to the Southward of *Carwar*, *viz.* *Ankla*, *Cuddermuddy* and *Merzee*, whose River terminates the *Sundah*'s Territories, and brings us on to a better Country, *viz.* *Canara*.

CHAP. XXIII.

Gives a Description of Canara, *shewing its Fertility, Product, Government, Religion, Customs, and Temper of its Inhabitants.*

ONOAR is its northermost Port, and has the Benefit of a River, capable to receive Ships of 2 or 300 Tuns. It has a Castle on a low Hill, about a Mile within the Bar, built, of old, by the *Portugueze*, when they were Lords Paramount of all the Sea-coasts of *India*; but the *Rajah* of *Canara* was so affronted by them, that he laid

Seige to the Castle, but was three Years in reducing it; and so long he blockt it up, till Hunger forced a Surrender.

THE Religion, by Law established, here, as well as in *Sundah*, is the *Pagan*. And there is a Pagod or Temple, called *Ramtrut*, that is visited yearly by great Numbers of Pilgrims. Close by the Temple there is a fine Cistern or Tank, of a square oblong Figure. It is continually furnished with good Water, that gushes out of the Face of a Rock, as big as a Man's Thigh. There are about 50 Steps cut out of the same Rock, that lead from the Surface of the Earth down to the *Tank*; and at the Foot of the Stairs is a little Summer-house built. The *Tank* is about three Fathoms deep in the Middle, and is stored with Plenty of pretty brown Fish, with a white Stroke from their Head to Tail, on each Side of the Back-bone. And when any musical Instrument is played on by the Sides of the *Tank*, they come in such Numbers towards the Musick, that they may be taken up in Baskets; but none dare meddle with them, because they are consecrated to the Pagod.

SOMETIMES they carry the Image of the Pagod in Procession. In Figure he is more like a Monkey than a Man. They put him into a Coach in Form of a Tower, with a pyramidal Top about 15 Foot high, where eight or ten Priests are set to bear the Image Company, and to sing his Praises. The Coach has four Wheels, and a Rope of a good

good Thickneſs made faſt to it, and drawn through the Streets, by Strength of Hand, with a great Mob attending his Godſhip, wherever he is drawn.

In *Canara* there are ſeveral Cuſtoms peculiar to itſelf, and many of them are ſpread abroad to remote Countries. Here it was, that the Cuſtom of Wives burning on the ſame Pile with their deceaſt Husbands had its Beginning. It is reported, that before the *Brahmans* invented this Law, Poiſon was ſo well known and practiſed, that the leaſt Quarrel that happened between a married Couple, coſt the Husband his Life, and this Law put a great Stop to it; and now Cuſtom ſo far prevails, that if any fainted-hearted Lady has not Courage enough to accompany her Spouſe to the other World, ſhe is forthwith ſhaved and degraded, and obliged to ſerve all her Husband's Family in all Kinds of Drudgery.

I have ſeen ſeverals burned ſeveral Ways. In this Country they dig a Pit about 10 Foot long, and 6 broad, and fill it with Logs of Wood. One great Piece is ſet at the Brim of the Pit, ready to fall down on pulling a Bit of String. When all is ready, there is good Store of Oyl or Butter thrown on the Wood, and then the Husband's Corps is placed about the Middle of the Pile, and Fire ſet to it, which blazes in an Inſtant. Then the Spouſe took her Leave of all Friends and Acquaintances, and Drums, Trumpets and Hautboys being playing cheerfully, ſhe walked three or four Times round the Pile,

 which,

which, by this Time, was all in a great Blaze, and then leaps in on the Corps. Assoon as ever she leapt in, a Priest drew the String, and down fell the great Log of Wood, at least 500 Pound Weight, over her Body, and all consumed together.

In other Parts they do not use Pits, but a Pile is built, and the Corps laid on it, and Fire put to it; and the Victim dancing round it for a little Time, to the Noise of loud Musick, leaps in; and, if she hesitates, the Priests thrust her in with long Poles, making such an hideous Noise, that she cannot be heard; and, all the While she is a burning, the Priests dance round the Fire. Others again take somnifick Medicines, and stand by the Pile till they fall on it while asleep. I heard a Story of a Lady that had received Addresses from a Gentleman, who afterwards deserted her, and her Relations obliged her to marry another, who died shortly after the Marriage, and who, according to Custom, was laid on the Pile; and, as the Fire was well kindled, and she going to act the Tragedy on herself, she espied her former Admirer, and beckned to him to come to her. When he came, she took him in her Arms, as if she had a Mind to embrace him; but, being stronger than he, she carried him into the Flames in her Arms, where they both consumed, with the Corps of her Husband: Yet I have known some faint-hearted Girls that had not the Courage to accompany their Spouses into an unknown World, but rather

live

live in this, tho' under the Badge and Umbrage of Ignominy and Shame.

THIS Country of *Canara* is generally governed by a Lady, who keeps her Court at a Town called *Baydour*, two Days Journey from the Sea. She may marry whom she pleases; but her Husband never gets the Title of *Rajah*, tho' if she has Sons, the eldest of them does; but neither Husband nor Son have any Thing to do with the Management of the Government, while she lives: Nor are the Queens obliged to burn with their Husbands. The Subjects of this Country observe the Laws so well, that Robbery or Murder are hardly heard of among them And a Stranger may pass through the Country without being askt where he is going, or what Business he has.

NO Man is permitted in this Country to ride on Horses, Mules or Elephants, but Officers of State, or Troopers, tho' we are allowed to ride on Oxen or Buffaloes: Nor none are permitted to have Umbrellas carried over them by Servants, but must carry them themselves if the Sun or Rain offend them; but in all Things else there is Liberty and Property.

THE next Sea-port, to the Southward of *Onoar*, is *Batacola*, which has the *Vestigia* of a very large City, standing on a little River, about four Miles from the Sea. There is nothing of it left now worth noticing, but ten or eleven small Pagods or Temples covered with Copper and Stone. The Country produces good Quantities of Pepper; and the *English* Company had a Factory there: But, about the Year 1670. an *English* Ship coming there to lade, had a fine *English* Bull-dog, which the Chief of the Factory begged of the Captain.

After the Ship was gone, the Factory, which consisted of eighteen Persons, were going a hunting, and carried the Bull-dog with them; and, passing through the Town, the Dog seized a Cow devoted to a Pagod, and killed her. Upon which the Priests raised a Mob, who murdered the whole Factory; but some Natives, that were Friends to the *English*, made a large Grave, and buried them all in it. The Chief of *Carwar* sent a Stone to be put on the Grave, with an Inscription, *That this is the Burial-place of* John Best, *with seventeen other* English *Men, who were sacrificed to the Fury of a mad Priesthood, and an enraged Mob.* The *English* never resettled there since; but often buy Pepper there. The Island St. *Mary* lies West-north-west from the Mouth of the River of *Batacola*, about four Leagues distant, being the Burial-place of Mr. *Goring* before observed. There are some more Islands lying close to the Shore, but are beset with Rocks under Water. And what Ships pass between St. *Mary* and them, ought not to venture above two Miles within that Island; but there is no Danger within a Quarter of a Mile of it, but what is visible.

THE next Town, to the Southward of *Batacola*, is *Barceloar*, ſtanding on the Banks of a broad River, about four Miles from the Sea. The Country abounds in Rice, having in many Places two Crops in a Year, by the Advantage they have of ſome Lakes at the Feet of the Mountains of *Gatti*, whoſe Waters being confined by Sluces, are let out at convenient Times to water their Rice Fields. The *Dutch* have a Factory here, only to buy up Rice for their Gariſons on the *Malabar* Coaſt. It ſtands about a Mile from the River's Mouth, that has a Bar of 13 or 14 Foot Water on it at ſpring Tides, and has a Caſtle on its North Side for its Guard, that none may go in or out without Leave.

THE *Portugueze* alſo get Supplies of Rice for *Goa*, and they have ſix or eight Ships belonging to *Barceloar*, that carry their Cargoes of Rice to *Muskat*, and bring back in Returns, Horſes, Dates, Pearl, and other Merchandize of the Product of *Arabia*. To the Southward of this Place, on a plain Road that leads to *Mangulore*, are planted four Rows of Trees, on the Sides of a Walk about eight or ten Miles long, which being very large, and having ſpreading Branches ever green all the Summer, ſerve for Umbrellas to Paſſengers that travel that Road. And, on ſeveral Places, there are Huts built, where ſome old People ſtay in the Day-time, with Jars of fine clear Water for the Paſſengers to drink *gratis*, at the Charge of the State. *Bac-*

canoar

canoar and *Molkey* ly between *Barceloar* and *Mangulore*, both having the Benefit of Rivers to export the large Quantities of Rice that their Fields produce.

Mangulore is the greateſt Mart for Trade in all the *Canara* Dominions. It has the Conveniency of one River produced by three that come into it by different Ways, *viz.* from the North, South and Eaſt, all proceeding from the great Rains and Dews that fall from the Mountains of *Gatti*, which ly 25 or 30 Leagues up in the Country, and are the inland Bounds of the *Canara* Dominions. Thoſe three Rivers joyn about a Mile from the Sea, and, at *Mangulore*, diſembogue at one Mouth into the common Receptory of Rivers.

The *Portugueze* have a Factory for Rice here, and a pretty large Church, becauſe great Numbers of black *Chriſtians* reſide there. The Prieſts, as well as their Congregations, are the very Scum of *Chriſtianity*. The Clergy are ſo ſhameleſs, that they will bargain with a Stranger to pimp for him. And the Laity look on Whoring, Thieving and Murder as no Sin, if any Gain can be got by them.

The Fields here bear two Crops of Corn yearly in the Plains; and the higher Grounds produce Pepper, Bettlenut, Sandal-wood, Iron and Steel, which make *Mangulore* a Place of pretty good Trade. The Town is poorly built, along the Sides of the Rivers, and has no Defence againſt an Enemy, but

two

two ſmall Forts, one on each Side of the River's Mouth. The *Rajah* or *Rana* keeps generally about 15000 Soldiers on their *Malabar* Frontiers, to repel the Inſolence of the *Malabars*, and another Army towards the *Sevajee* Borders, to cover them from the Inroads of thoſe *Harpies*; for the *Malabars* and *Sevajees* being poor in reſpect of the *Canarines*, watch Opportunities to borrow the Superfluities of their rich Neighbours. Such Practices have been uſed, in former Times, amongſt us in *Britain*, and, no Doubt, would ſtill be ſo, if good wholſom Laws, backt with good Forces to ſee them put in Execution, did not reſtrain us.

ALONG the *Malabar* Frontiers, the *Canarines* have Forts built of Earth, wherein are kept about 2 or 300 Soldiers ready, on all Occaſions, to encounter any ſmall Party of the *Malabars* that clandeſtinely come in to thieve or rob; but the *Muskat Arabs*, *in Anno* 1695. came with a Fleet, and plundred the Sea-coaſt of *Canara*, and burnt *Barceloar* and *Mangulore*, and carried away a great Booty. And *Conajee Angarie*, *in Anno* 1720. came along the Coaſt, and inſulted it; but, on landing ſome Men, found ſuch Reſiſtance, that made him embark again, without doing much Miſchief to the Country.

THERE is only one ſmall Sea-port more in *Canara*, called *Manguzeer*, about five Leagues to the Southward of *Mangulore*, and three from *Decully*, a large Fort built on an Iſland cloſe to the Land. And three Leagues

gues farther South is a ſmall River that divides the *Canara* and *Malabar* Territories.

CHAP. XXIV.

Treats of the Malabars *their Forces and Families, Religion, Laws and Cuſtoms, Product of their Country, and their Commerce; with ſome miſcellaneous Obſervations on their Cuſtoms and Wars.*

MALABAR is a pretty large Country, divided into many Principalities, and I have a Liſt of them as they were given in to the ingenious and curious *Heer Van Rede* Commiſſary General for Affairs of the *Dutch East-india* Company *in Anno* 1694. who died off *Bombay* in his Voyage towards *Surat*.

THE Province of *Tipopoſoriwan* can raiſe Forces by its Clans, *viz.*

	Men.
Terivancoar - -	100000
Attinga - -	30000
Eledaſoriwan - -	50000
Peritalie - - -	3000
Seigenatie - -	30000
Tcirewey - -	15000
Odenadie Carree	
Coilcolong - -	50000

Pana

	Men.
Pana Pollie - -	15000
Martin Gallie - -	15000
Carimbalie - -	15000
Teiom Balanore Koilie -	3000
Reubanie Aregalie - -	3000
Chitawa Canaar.	
Tellicherry Baakie - } *Elependre May Porombo* } -	3000
Dedamaadie Peneretta } *Moeterte Manka Polie* }	15000
Perombara Cormaar.	
Arregatte Calgampolie } *Mamalie Madonie* } -	15000
Bambellendada.	
Kilpolie Chitway -	75000
Martingalie Coer -	37000
Tekellenore - -	37000
Doenjatte Penmaal -	3000
Cottenadie.	
Zembaga Cherry -	30000
Tesegidin Genatie.	
Elertecore - -	10000
Moutere Coree -	10000
Ambada Coree - -	10000
Rapolin.	
Elengoly Serewan -	5000

Con.

	Men.
Courour Nadie.	
Courour Monta Coil -	15000
Billiatte Serewan -	15000
Badecancore.	
Manna Tellam	30000
Moda Callie - -	3000
Bov Pilcore - -	15000
Kilmalle Core -	15000
Perimba Daponadie.	
Martingaly Tavil -	3000
Moute Tavil -	3000
Palombe Tavil - -	3000
Teilor Tavil - -	3000
Ela Tavil - -	3000
Teſieragatta Nadie.	
Teiragalle Caymaal -	15000
Padanarie erte Caymaal -	8000
Pindereretol Nade.	
Pindereretel Nambi Deri -	15000
Coil Pade - -	1000
Mangela Nade.	
Belatte Tavil -	10000
Cara tà Tavil - -	15000
Nambouries, or, Prieſts.	
Bay Pinade -	6000
Aaron Ade - -	2000
Merinade Nambouri	3000

Nan-

	Men.
Nanderetti Nade.	
Coro Seir Caymal -	30000
Coriès Caymal - - -	5000
Siangrande Caymal -	5000
Panna Maketts Caymal -	3000
Tollapoli Nade.	
Amacotta Nambedi -	15000
Manacotta Nambedi -	15000
Cacatte Nambedi -	15000
Tistul Nambedi - -	15000
Terratekin Nair -	15000
Nambiar, or, Priests of the second Order	
Relolaste Nambiar - -	3000
Relo Canadarie -	30000
Erenaden Caree.	
Cannal Canædrie - -	40000
Rete Coil - -	5000
Paro Pachoil - -	3000
Ropo Coil - -	2000
Tomera Serinade.	
Aya Nade - -	20000
Payanade - -	15000
Iregale Nade a Priest of the first Order } -	3000
Candette Nayer - -	10000
Omnitrie - -	10000
Palangier Nayer -	3000

Man-

	Men
Mangalacka - -	3000
Dana Seir Ilerda -	10000
Ramenatte Coric -	15000
Polletti Nade.	
Calliſtree Odiroſe Coilan } *Palle Coilan Ziereck Coilan* }	23000
Ballanore Burgary -	30000
Tellicherry Mota Naire -	15000
Zitre Caymal Mar -	30000
Alarte Tere Caymal -	30000
Alarte Nade Adovodic -	15000
Paravia Coil - -	60000
Bayella Nade.	
Mangalette Naire -	1000
Manetane Naire - -	1000
Callepatte Naire -	1000
Teyka Patte Naire -	1000
Motrel Naire - -	3000
In all	1262000

Fit to carry Arms.

THERE are ſeveral other Principalities in this Country, that I do not find mentioned in this Liſt, as *Cannanore* and *Tannore*, whoſe Government are in the Hands of *Mahometans*, or *Malabar Moors*. The Kingdoms of *Couchin* and *Porcat* are not put down in the Liſt, nor *Paarow*, which are potent Principalities; and the *Samorin*, or or Empire of *Calecut*, one of the most potent of them all, has no Place in this List. But,

THE Country, tho' large and populous, is not fruitful in Corn, for there is Abundance of Rice imported from *Canara*; but, being low and sandy all along the Sea-coast, except a few rising Grounds, which are the most steril, yet it nourishes vast Numbers of Cocoa-nut and *Arecka* Trees, whose Fruit brings them great Gains from other Countries. The higher Grounds produce Pepper and *Cardamums*, the best in the World; and their Woods Teak Timber and Angelique for building, Sandal-wood, or Saunders, white and yellow *Cassia Lignum*, or wild Cinnamon, and *Cassia Fistula*, *Nux vomica*, and *Cocolus India*. Drugs grow plentifully in their Woods, which are also well stored with wild Game, both for Pleasure and Use. Their Mountains produce Iron and Steel, but not so good as we have in *Europe*. And their Sea is stored with many Species of excellent Fishes.

WHEN the *Portugueze* came first into *India*, the *Samorin* of *Calecut* was Lord Paramount of *Malabar*; and, in his Dotage, when he was well advanced in Years, he would needs be a *Mahometan*, and, to shew his Zeal, would go in Pilgrimage to *Mecca*, to visit the Tomb. Before he took his Voyage, which was by Sea, he made a Will, and having four Nephews, bequeathed each of them a Part of his Empire. To the eldest he bequeathed *Callistree*, whose Sea-coast reaches from *Decully* to *Ticorie*, about 24

Leagues. To the ſecond, whom he loved beſt, the Title of *Samorin*, and a Sea-coaſt from *Ticorie* to *Chitawa*, about the ſame Diſtance. To the third *Attinga*, which reached from *Chitawa* to Cape *Comerin*, about 50 Leagues, becauſe that Part of the Country is confined between the Sea and the Mountains of *Gatti*, and is divided by Rivers from thoſe Mountains, into more than 1000 Iſlands between *Chitawa* and *Quoiloan*. The youngeſt had *Coil*, which reached from Cape *Comerin* to the River of *Nayapatam*, about 50 Leagues more.

THE old Zealot dying in his Voyage, made great Diſturbances in the State among the Brothers; and, after a long and bloody War, they concluded on the Partitions of the foregoing Liſt. Many of the Tribes continue Tributaries to the Provinces mentioned in the old King's Will; but many more are independent. And ſo I'll return to *Decully*, and proceed in my Obſervations along the Shore.

BETWEEN *Decully* and Mount *Delly* there is no Harbour, tho' a fine deep River keeps its Courſe to the Southward, along the Shore, for about 8 Leagues, never, in all that Tract, going above a Bow-ſhot from the Sea. It diſembogues itſelf by the Foot of Mount *Delly*, over Rocks and Sands, in a Chanel of half a League broad. The Inhabitants are a wild ſuperſtitious uncivilized People. There is alſo a ſmall River that runs cloſe by the Foot of Mount *Delly*, on the

the South Side. And 3 Leagues South from Mount *Delly* is a ſpacious deep River, called *Balliapatam*, where the *Engliſh* Company had once a Factory for Pepper; and the aforementioned Mr. *Boucher* was the laſt Chief for their Affairs there.

Cannanore was formerly a Town belonging to the Crown of *Portugal*, with a very ſtrong Fort to guard it, built on a Point of Land ſo commodiouſly, that the Sea fortified above four Fifths of it, and had the Conveniency of a ſmall Bay for an Harbour, that could ſhelter ſmall Ships from the Fury of the South-weſt Monſoons. The *Dutch* came with a Fleet about the Year 1660. and landed a ſmall Army, and were joyned by a great Number of the Natives, who were weary of the Tyranny of the *Portugueze*. The very firſt Day that they opened their Trenches a *Portugueze Fidalgo* was killed on a Baſtion, by a Shot from the *Dutch*, which ſo frightned the Governor of the Fort, that, in the Night, he made his Eſcape, and left the Gariſon to capitulate for themſelves, which they did next Day, to ſave the Effuſion of *Chriſtian* Blood by heretical Cannon.

The *Dutch* continue ſtill Maſters of the Fort, and added a large Curtain, with two royal Baſtions fronting the Land Avenues. They demoliſhed the Town, and, with its Stones, built thoſe Defences. Their Trade is very ſmall, ſo that their Gariſon conſiſts of about forty Soldiers and a Captain, who is Governor of the Fort: But there is a pretty large Town built in the Bottom of the Bay, that is independent of the *Dutch*, and that Town, with ſome circumjacent Country, is under the Government of *Adda Rajah*, a *Mahometan Malabar* Prince, who, upon Occaſion, can bring near 20000 Men into the Field. His Government is not abſolute, nor is it hereditary; and, inſtead of giving him the Truſt of the Treaſury which comes by Taxes and Merchandize, they have Cheſts made on Purpoſe, with Holes made in their Lids, and their Coin being all Gold, whatever is received by the Treaſurer, is put into thoſe Cheſts by theſe Holes; and each Cheſt has four Locks, and their Keys are put in the Hands of the *Rajah*, the Commiſſioner of Trade, the chief Judge and the Treaſurer; and, when there is Occaſion for Money, none can be taken out without all theſe four be preſent, or their Deputies.

In Anno 1668. the Prince came into the *Dutch* Fort to pay a Compliment to the Captain. He had brought about 50 Attendants with him. While the Prince was complimenting the Captain, the *Malabars* took the Opportunity of the *Dutch* Security, and killed the Sentinel at the Gate; but the *Dutch* Soldiers being all in their Barracks, and their Arms ready, made a ſeaſonable Sally, and drove the *Malabars* out, with the Loſs of twenty of their Number; and the *Dutch* ſhut their Gate. The Fort is large, and the Governor's Lodgings at a good Diſtance from the Gate, ſo that the Fray was over before not half conquered yet by the *Spaniards*, tho they are possest of all the Sea-coast, as the *Dutch* are of *Zealoan*; and the Natives lose no Opportunity of cutting off their Lords the *Spaniards*, when they can do it without Danger. They have fortified their Mountains and Vallies so well with thick Hedges of *Bambows*, that the *Spaniards* cannot easily molest them, tho' they have secret Ways to sally out and disturb their Enemy.

THE chief City in *Luconia* is *Manhila* or *Manilla*, the Residence of the *Spanish* Vice-roy, and the Port where all the Galleons that come yearly from *New-spain*, resort to. The Harbour is spacious, commodious and safe. They admit of Trade from *India* and *China*, but not with any *European* Nation. The *Mahometans* are tolerated in their Religion, but not the *Pagans*, so that all *Chinese* that go there for Commerce, get a little Brass Image hung about their Neck, with a String of Beads in their Hands, and learning to cross themselves, cry *Jesu sancta Malia* (for they cannot pronounce *Maria*, because the Letter *R* is excluded the *Chinese* Alphabet) I say, when they have got all those fore-named Qualifications, they are good *Spanish Christians*.

AND when they have featherd their Nest by cheating the *Spaniard*, and taken their Leave of *Manilla* or *Manhila*, at their passing by a Mountain dedicated to the *Virgin Mary*, they throw their Beads over board, and thank the *Virgin* for her Kindness to them.

In Anno 1719. there happened a Mutiny in *Manilla*, wherein the Vice-roy loſt his Life, and he had a Son that might have ſaved his, but was obſtinate, and would needs follow his Father. It was occaſioned by Oppreſſion and Avarice, for the Vice-roy having a Mind to fill his Coffers at any Rate, ſet up a Tribunal, wherein the richeſt Merchants in the City were impeacht for high Crimes and Miſdemeanours, by ſuborned Informers. Evidences were not wanting to prove Things that never were done by the innocent Merchants, and on thoſe falſe Informations and Evidences their Perſons were impriſoned, and their Eſtates ſeized. Thoſe that had not been proſecuted ſeeing their Danger, carried their Goods and Money into the Churches and Convents for Security, and fled into the Country themſelves, till the Times ſhould amend; but thoſe Places of Sanctuary were violated, and when the Merchants were ſummoned, and did not appear, their Eſtates were confiſcated, and brought out of the Churches and Convents by Force.

THE Arch-biſhop, and his Army of Prieſts, went to him, and laid the Peoples Grievances and his own Oppreſſions and Crimes before him; but he treated them rudely, which ſoon put the whole City in an Uprore. A cunning and bold Prieſt of the *Auguſtin* Order ſeeing the People's Diſpoſition to Mutiny, took a large Crucifix on his Shoulder, and invited all who were true *Catholick Chri-*

ſtians

stians to follow *Jesus Christ's* Banner, and afford Succour and Assistance to *Christ's* persecuted Flock.

The Citizens came thronging after the Priest and Crucifix, well armed, and they marched directly to the Vice-roy's Palace. His Guards all deserted him on Sight of the Priest and Crucifix, and he and a few of his Domesticks fired some small Arms, and killed some, and wounded others, which so enraged the Multitude, that they rusht furiously up Stairs, and shot him dead. His Son was Governor of a Castle a little Way from the City, and he hearing that his Father was in Danger, came with his Garison to rescue him, but being killed before the Assistance came, the Citizens complimented him, and desired him to return to his Post, for they had nothing to lay to his Charge, but he refused, and swore he would be avenged on his Father's Murderers, and beginning to use Violence on those next to him, his Men deserted him, and he soon fell a Sacrifice to his own Folly. There were above a Million and an half of *Spanish* Dollars found in his Treasury, out of which those whom he had unjustly robbed were reimbursed.

It is about 120 Leagues from South to North, and the South End is about 100 Leagues in Breadth. It breeds good, hardy, small Horses, and, if it were in the Hands of some industrious Nation, it is able to furnish good Materials to build a good Commerce with; but the *Spaniards* are rich, lazy and proud, and rather difcourage than improve Trade, or to engage the Natives to be civil and induftrious.

THE next Ifland of Note is *Formofa*, but there are feveral fmall Iflands between it and *Luconia*, which belong to *China*, tho' of no great Account, and becaufe they are flat and low, they are called the *Bafhee* Iflands.

Formofa is a noble Ifland, and produces many valuable Commodities, as well for the Suftenance of Mankind as for Pleafure and Luxury. It affords Plenty of Gold, raw Silk, fine white Sugar, Sugar-candy, and Copper finer than in *China*, but coarfer than in *Japon*, and feveral Drugs, as *Gallingal*, *China* Root, &c. Before the *Tartars* fubdued it, it had Kings of its own, but tributary to *China*. The Natives differ much from the neighbouring People of *China* and *Luconia*, both in Phifiognomy and Make. They are of a low Stature, with a large Head and Fore-head, hollow-eyed, and the Cheekbone very high, a large Mouth, and a fhort flat Chin, with little or no Beard on it, long-jaw'd, and a fmall long Neck, their Body fhort and fquare, their Arms and Legs long, fmall and ill-fhaped, their Feet long, and broad at the Toes, and generally they are baker-kneed. The *Englifh* and *Dutch* had their Factories there, but about the Year 1678. when all *Fokien* had fubmitted to the *Tartars*, they were ordered to withdraw their Factories from *Teywon*, a fmall Ifland clofe to the great one, on which their Facto-

ries

ries ſtood. The *Engliſh* obeyed, and removed over to *Amoy*, but the *Dutch* received Supplies from *Batavia*, and endured a long Siege, but were at laſt forced to ſubmit, tho' they ſold their Factory, and many of their Mens Lives pretty dear, for the *Tartars* loſt above 5000 Men in reducing it. It is now wholly under the *Tartars*, and the *Chungtock* of *Fokien* has the Superintendency of it.

WHEN it was tributary to *China*, about the Year 1650. there was a ſtrange Diſtemper raged on the Iſland for three Years together, for moſt of the Virgins between twelve and eighteen Years of Age, had a Trick of hanging themſelves, in ſo much that very few Maidens were left on the Iſland, nor could any Remedy be found to prevent it, before an old *China* Man found one out, and addreſt himſelf to the King, deſiring him to make a Trial of hanging (all thoſe that hanged themſelves privately) up by one Leg on the Sides of High-ways, for Paſſengers to gaze on. The King took his Counſel, and hanged up ſome ſo, and in one Month's Time the Maidens refrained from hanging, and have continued good Girls ever ſince.

THE Religion of *Teywon* (for that is the Name that the *Chineſe* call the Iſland of *Formoſa* by) is purely *Pagan*. They all worſhip the Sun and Moon, and the Stars their Children. Some worſhip the firſt living Thing they ſee in the Morning, except a Lizard.

BETWEEN *Teywon* and the Coaſt of *Fokien*, ly the *Piſcadores* Iſlands, ſo called from the

the great Quantities of Fiſh caught about them. There are many Shallows ly a good Diſtance off them, on which an *Engliſh* Ship from *Surat*, called the *Joſiah*, was ſhipwrackt *in Anno* 1697. but all the Men were ſaved; and on the Report of a *Jeſuite* Miſſionary who was Paſſenger, that he had ſome Things on board for the Emperor, one Mr. *Reynolds* the firſt Supercargo, was forced to take a Journey to *Peking*, who cleared himſelf, but brought Scandal on holy Mother Church, for forging Things ſo palpably falſe, for the good Father's Trunk was ſaved, and opened by proper Officers, and not one Thing that he had reported to be in it, was found.

Many other Iſlands ly along the Coaſt of *China*, but of no great Note, till we come to the Iſland *Chuſan*, which lies off the Mouth of *Limpoa*. It firſt became famous in the *Tartar* Wars, for many *Chineſe* of Note repaired thither with their Families, who thought to have found a quiet Retreat there, but they were miſtaken, for by *Coxinga* from *Amoy*, and the *Tartars* continually warring thereabout, they were haraſſed between them, and at length a Gariſon of *Tartars* ſettled on it, and gave it their Laws.

In Anno 1700. the new *Eaſt-india* Company of *England*, ſettled a Factory on *Chuſan*, by Mr. *Allan Catchpole* before mentioned, but by the Oppreſſion of the *Tartar* Officers, and the Company's Neglect of ſending Money ſufficient to carry on their Trade, Mr. *Catchpole* removed the Factory again in the

Be-

Beginning of the Year 1703. and carried it to *Pullo-condore*, as is before obſerved.

FROM the North End of *Formoſa*, to the South End of *Japon*, the Diſtance is about 220 Leagues, and in the Fair-way are ſeveral Iſlands of no great Account in Commerce. They are moſt of them very high, and on one of them is a very great *Vulcano*, which continually ſends forth a prodigious Flame that may be ſeen in the Night above 30 Leagues Diſtance from it.

Bungo is a Province of *Japon*, and was honoured with the Name of a Kingdom, but about the Year 1655. it loſt its Title and moſt of its Inhabitants, for being too zealous in promoting *Chriſtianity* by barbarous Ways. The *Portugueze* found this Iſland and *Japon* to be eaſily brought over to their Notions of *Chriſtianity*, and that the Country abounded in Gold and Silver, drove a very great and advantagious Trade there, for above one Century of Years. Nor were their Prieſts idle in making Converts, for in the Space of 100 Years, they proſelyted 180000 Families, when at the ſame Time, the Emperor gave great Encouragement to the Prieſts to go on in their Apoſtleſhip, every one having free Liberty to embrace *Chriſtianity*, and had not the giddy-headed *Chriſtian* Prieſts, been too zealouſly hot and haſty, it was believed that the Emperor himſelf would have become *Chriſtian*, but a civil War breaking out in *Japon*, and the Emperor's Forces much diminiſhed, the *Chriſtian* Prieſts thought it a pro-

proper Time for them to ſettle their Religion on the ſame Foundation that *Mahomet* did his, by eſtabliſhing it in Blood.

THEIR Thoughts run on nothing leſs than extirpating the Heathen out of the Land, and formed a Conſpiracy of raiſing an Army of 50000 *Chriſtians* to murder their Countrymen, that ſo the whole Iſland might be illuminated by *Chriſtianity*, ſuch as it was there But the Emperor having Intelligence of their holy Deſign, thought fit to prevent them, and coming to an Agreement with his rebellious *Pagan* Subjects, diſcovered the common Danger they all lay under from the *Chriſtians*, and they, to ſecure themſelves, joyned their Forces with the Emperor's, but lay ſilent till they ſaw where the *Chriſtians* would begin their Tragedy, and it was not long before they began the Maſſacre, near a large City called *Oſſacca*. The Emperor's Army marched ſpeedily thither to chaſtiſe their Inſolence, and a very bloody Battle enſued, wherein the *Chriſtians* had the better. The Emperor ſoon levied a greater Army, and engaged the *Chriſtians* a ſecond Time with Succeſs, and quite routed them, and never gave them Time to form themſelves into another Army after, but followed his Blow, ſparing neither Man, Woman, or Child that had been baptized, and the *Pagan Bouzies* or Prieſts, were very good Informers, ſo that in two Years, above 300000 Perſons periſhed by the violent Zeal of bigotted Prieſts, and an Edict was publiſhed, that whatever *Chriſtian* ſhould

ſhould, for the future, be found within the Dominions of *Japon*, ſhould be put to Death without Mercy.

MANY new Inventions were found out to torture the *Chriſtians*, and the Prieſts were the firſt that made Trial of the Exquiſiteneſs of their Pain. The poor Women and Virgins were torn Limb from Limb, by being tied to Stakes placed in the Ground, under the Branches of large Trees bended down, and their Limbs being faſtned to the Stakes and Branches, by the Elaſticity of the Branches they were torn to Pieces. Children were thrown down Precipices, and daſht to Pieces, and Infants were drowned, and ſo *Romiſh Chriſtianity* ended in *Japon*, with a very diſmal and tragical Cataſtrophe.

THE *Engliſh* and *Dutch* at that Time had their Factories on a ſmall Iſland called *Firando*, that lay cloſe to the Shore of the Iſland *Bungo*, and drove a very advantagious Trade, but *in Anno* 1664. when the *Engliſh* Shipping arrived, our never failing Friends taking the Advantage of our being *Chriſtians*, and coming thither contrary to the Edict, were in Hopes to have a ſecond Part of *Amboina* acted at *Japon*. They gave Information that the *Engliſh* were *Chriſtians*, and not only ſo, but that our King had married the King of *Portugal*'s Siſter, and had a Mind to introduce the *Portugueze* ſecretly into *Japon*, and how dangerous that might be to their State, they knew by dear bought Experience, and as an undeniable Truth of our being *Chriſtians*

ſtians, they might ſee in the very Colours that our Ships wore, the Sign of the Croſs. Their Information had ſome of the deſired Effects, tho' not the cruel Part. The Emperor being acquainted with the *Dutch* Information, ordered the *Engliſh* to be civilly treated, their Cargoes to be taken off their Hands as before, and a new *Japon* Cargo to be provided for them, in lieu of what they brought, and at the uſual Time to diſpatch them, with ſtrict Orders for the *Engliſh* never to return again upon Pain of Death, by which fair Dealings the *Dutch* got the ſole *Japon* Trade into their own Hands, except what is carried on by the *Chineſe*. This Account I had from Captain *John Baer*, who was in the laſt *Engliſh* Ship that traded to *Japon*.

THE *Dutch* and *Chineſe* are both limited in the Numbers of their Shipping that trade to *Japon*, the *Dutch* from one to four yearly, and the *Chineſe* from Ten to Twenty. Aſſoon as their Ships arrive, all their Crews are ſent aſhore to Houſes provided for them, and the *Japoneſe* take Poſſeſſion of the Ship, and all that ſhe has aboard of her; they unhinge the Rudder, and ſend all the great Guns and Ammunition aſhore. Each Cargo is unladed and ſent to the Factory appointed for its Factors, and there opened and repackt before proper Officers. The Goods are ſent away without any Enquiry what they coſt, or what they are content to take for them, and the Officers take a Memorandum of what Commodities they deſire in barter, and theſe

are

are provided and delivered on board their Ships by the Middle of *October*, and about the Beginning of *November* they deliver their Rudder, Guns, and Ammunition, and are dispatched in Form, to be gone without Delay.

THE *Dutch* Factory is now settled at *Nangesaak*, on a little Island close to the Shore, and are there confined, without a special Permission from Court, either when they have a Desire to go on the main Island, or to remove from their Factory to *Batavia*.

I heard of a mortifying Accident that happened to the *Dutch* Affairs in *Japon*, when Mr. *Charron* a *French* Man, had the Directorship of their Factory. He had been several Times at *Jeddo* and *Meaco*, two great Cities where the Emperor keeps his Court, sometimes at one or other of those Places, as his Fancy or Affairs lead him. The Emperor took a Liking to Mr. *Charron*, and often sent for him to hear the Accounts he could give of *Europe*. *Charron* presuming on his Favours from the Emperor, begged Permission to build an House on the little Island where their Factory stood, on his Masters Account, which Request the Emperor granted.

ACCORDINGLY the Foundation was laid very large for an House; however the Building went cheerfully on, till it grew into an handsom Fortification of a regular Tetragon. The *Japonese* being ignorant of the Art of Fortification, had not the least Suspicion of Deceit, but suffered them to finish it.

WHEN

WHEN it was finiſhed, Mr. *Charron* adviſed his Maſters at *Bathvia*, of the Progreſs he had made, and deſired by the next Shipping to have ſome Cannon ſent him in Casks filled with Rubbiſh, ſuch as Oaccam or Cotton, the Casks to be well bound with Iron Hoops, and the Heads ſecurely fixt in, with ſome Casks of the ſame Make, filled with Spices, which Advice was accordingly followed.

WHEN the Shipping arrived, the Lading was landed according to Cuſtom, but in rolling the Casks, one of thoſe that contained a Braſs Gun, had the Misfortune to have one of its Heads fall out, and the Cheat was by that Accident diſcovered. This put a Stop to all Commerce till the Emperor's Pleaſure was known about this ſtrange Affair.

THE Emperor forbad to interrupt the Trade, but ordered their new built Houſe to be razed to the Ground, and to ſend Mr. *Charron* to Court, that he might expoſtulate the Matter with him. The Orders were ſpeedily obeyed, and *Charron* went to Court, and when brought before the Emperor, was much dejected in his Looks to what he uſed to be formerly.

THE Emperor interrogated him on the diſcovered Cheat, and finding he had no Anſwer ſufficient to vindicate himſelf, the King upbraided him with abuſing his Kindneſs, and ordered a Barber to be brought, who pulled poor *Charron*'s Beard out Hair by Hair, and then a Fool's Coat and Cap were put on him, and

and he carried through the Streets of *Jeddo*, for a ridiculous Spectacle, and was sent back to his Factory with Orders to go off with the first Ships that were ready to sail for *Batavia*.

THE *Japonese* are strict Observers of moral Rules, and particularly in Commerce, in so much, that a Merchant of Reputation, in his Payments puts up 5, 10, or any decimal Number of *Cupangs*, which is a broad, oblong, thin Piece of Gold (of twenty Shillings Value there) into a Silk Bag, and putting his Seal on the Bag, passes current for what the Seal mentions, for several Generations, without so much as once looking what is in the Bag; and Gold is so plentiful and cheap, that a *Cupang* of twenty Shillings in *Japon*, passes current at *Batavia* for thirty two Shillings, and when the Lion is stampt on it by the Company, it passes for forty Shillings *Sterl.*

THEIR *Purcellein*, or *Japon* earthen Ware, is finer than *China* Ware, but much thicker and heavier, and the Colours brighter, and it sells much dearer, either in *India* or *Europe*, than what is made in *China*, but their Tea is not half so good. Their lackt or japon'd Ware is, without any Doubt, the best in the World. The best Sort will hold boyling Water without Detriment to it, and is so hard, that I have made a full Pass with a Rapier against a Cabinet, and there was not the least Shadow of a Mark to be seen after the Pass. They abound in Silks both wrought and raw, much stronger than what *China* produces.

Japon, with the neighbouring Islands under its Dominions, is about the Magnitude of *Great Britain*. It is in Length from North-east to South-west, near 300 Leagues, and the Mean of its Breadth about 160 Miles. It is well peopled, and produces all Things necessary for human Sustenance, in great Plenty. They are exact Observers of Justice, and rigorous in their punishing Crimes.

A Man of Distinction, if convicted of a capital Crime, the Emperor sends him a Letter, that on such a Day, and such an Hour, he must be his own Executioner on Penalty of exquisite Torments, if he survives the appointed Hour. So the common Custom is, that the Delinquent sends for his nearest and best Friends to a sumptuous Feast on the Day set him, and after the Feast is over, he shews them the Emperor's Letter, and while they are reading it, he takes a Dagger that he has about him for the Purpose, and with it he stabs himself below the Navel, and rips himself up to the Breast-bone.

THE inferior Sort has not that Honour, but are forc'd to be contented with hanging, beheading, or throwing over an high Precipice, and for small Faults, whipping and stigmatizing are common Punishments.

THEIR Houses are for the most Part built of Wood, but the Emperor's Palaces are of Marble, and covered with gilded Copper. Their gilding is very durable, and can withstand all Winds and Weather many Years. The City of *Jeddo* is their Metropolis, and its Mag-

Magnitude may be ghest by a Fire that happened in it about the Year 1660. which consumed, in eight Days that it raged, above 120000 Houses, besides above 500 Temples.

THEIR Religion is purely *Pagan*, and *Amida* is their favourite God, but he lives a great Way off, for a Soul is three Years in continual Travel before it can reach *Paradise*, which is only the Suburbs of Heaven; however, when they once get thither, they are pretty sure of getting to Heaven, and they live very quietly in Paradise, because not one Devil dares come there to disturb them.

THE magotty Zealots have a Trick of leaping over high Cliffs into the Sea, in order to give their Souls an easy Passage to Paradise, the Priests giving them Bills of Credit to defray their Charges by the Way, and, no doubt, the mad Man pays the Priest very handsomly for the Bill, and those Bills are so good, that I never heard of one protested and returned.

THEY have several other reputable Gods, and every one of them has their Adorers and Devotees. One has three Faces, and he is Father of the Sun, Moon and Stars: Every God has his own particular Paradise, but none are nearer than three Years Journey. Some of their Zealots cut their own Throats to get an easy Passage, and others hang themselves.

THEY carry their Idols in Procession on Horse-back, with instrumental and vocal Musick to entertain them. They make many

Feaſts and Sacrifices to their Idols, but they are only fed with the Smoke, the Votaries eat up the Meat.

No *Japoneſe* dares leave his Country, and if he does, he never muſt return. They are ſo wedded to their own Cuſtoms and Opinions, and ſo jealous of having new or foreign Cuſtoms introduced, that they will not ſend Embaſſies to other Kings or States, or ſuffer their Merchants to have Commerce out of their own Dominions; only they ſend ſome ſmall *Jonks* or Veſſels in the Summer-time, over to the Land of *Eſo*, about 50 Leagues from the North End of *Japon*, and I have heard ſay, that they bring much Gold from thence; but whether that Country is a Part of their Dominions or no, I never could get Information, but it is reported, that the Natives of *Eſo* are luſty, robuſt, and unciviliz'd, but ſpeak the *Japon* Language.

I alſo heard, that when *De Heer Matſuiker* was General of *Batavia*, he ſent four *Houkers* to make Diſcoveries of the Countries to the Northward, and to the Weſtward of *Japon*, one of which was ſhip-wrackt on the Coaſt of *Corea*, and another on the Northward Coaſt of *Japon*. The other two had been on the Coaſt of *Eſo*, but could not converſe with the Natives. She that was loſt on *Japon*, had moſt of her Men ſaved, and were kindly entertained, and ſent to their Factory: And twelve of the other's Crew that was loſt on *Corea*, got aſhore, and were detained Priſoners. Nine of them died in ſixteen many as ſhe is preſcribed by Law, and the Husbands agree very well, for they cohabit with her in their Turns, according to their Priority of Marriage, ten Days, more or leſs, according as they can fix a Term among themſelves, and he that cohabits with her, maintains her in all Things neceſſary, for his Time, ſo that ſhe is plentifully provided for by a conſtant Circulation.

When the Man that cohabits with her goes into her Houſe, he leaves his Arms at the Door, and none dare remove them, or enter the Houſe, on Pain of Death; but, if there are no Arms to guard the Door, any Acquaintance may freely viſit her. And all the Time of Cohabitation ſhe ſerves her Husband as Purveyor and Cook, and keeps his Clothes and Arms clean.

When ſhe proves with Child, ſhe nominates its Father, who takes Care of its Education, after ſhe has ſuckled it, and brought it to walk or ſpeak; but the Children are never Heirs to their Fathers Eſtates, but the Father's Siſter's Children are, and if there are none, then to the neareſt in Conſanguinity from his Grandmother. And this Cuſtom is alſo practiſed among the *Mahometan Malabars*.

There are many Degrees or Dignities in the Church as well as in the State. The *Nambouries* are the firſt in both Capacities of Church and State, and ſome of them are Popes, being ſovereign Princes in both. The *Brahmans* or *Bramanies* are the ſecond in the

Church only. The *Buts* or Magicians are next to them, and are in great Veneration. The *Nayers* or Gentlemen are next, and are very numerous. The *Teyvees* are the Farmers of Cocoa-nut Trees, and are next to the Gentry Merchants are of all Orders, except *Nambouries*, and are in ſome Eſteem. The *Poulias* produce the Labourers and Mechanicks. They may marry into lower Tribes without Danger of Excommunication, and ſo may the *Muckwas* or Fiſhers, who, I think, are an higher Tribe than the *Poulias*, but the *Poulichees* are the loweſt Order of human Creatures, and are excluded from the Benefit of human and divine Laws.

If a *Poulia* or *Teyvee* meet a *Nayer* on the Road, he muſt go aſide to let his Worſhip paſs by, leſt the Air ſhould be tainted, on Pain of a ſevere Chaſtiſement, if not of Death; but the *Poulichees* are in a much worſe State, for, by the Law, they are not permitted to converſe with any other Tribe, nor can they wear any Sort of Cloth, but only a little Straw made faſt before their Privities, with a Line round their Middle. They are not permitted to build Houſes or Huts on the Ground, nor to inhabit the Plains where there is Corn Ground, but muſt dwell in Woods, and build on the Boughs of Trees, like Birds, with Graſs and Straw. If accidentally they ſee any Body coming towards them, they will howl like Dogs, and run away, leſt thoſe of Quality ſhould take Offence at their breathing in the ſame Air that they do do. They are not permitted to till and ſow the Ground, only in obſcure Places of the Woods they plant Fruits and Roots, whoſe Seeds they ſteal from their neighbouring Gardens in the Plains, in the Night, and if they are caught ſtealing, Death is their Puniſhment, on the Spot where they are taken, without any Form or Proceſs of Law. When they want Food, they come to the Skirts of their Woods, and howl like Foxes, and the charitable *Poulias* and *Teyvees* relieve them with Rice boiled or raw, and ſome Cocoa-nuts and other Fruits, which they lay down in a convenient Place; and when their Benefactors come within twenty Paces of them with their Alms, they walk off, and let the *Poulichees* come to their Food, which they forthwith carry into the Woods. They are very ſwift in running, and cunning in catching wild Beaſts and Fowl; but they have few or no Fiſh among the Mountains.

The inferior Tribes have Liberty of Conſcience in fancying their Deities, and worſhipping them. I have ſeen, at many *Muckwas* Houſes, a ſquare Stake of Wood, with a few Notches cut about it, and that Stake drove into the Ground, about two Foot of it being left above, and that is covered with ſome *Cadjans* or Cocoa-nut Tree Leaves, and is a Temple and a God to that Family. Some worſhip the firſt Animal they ſee in the Morning, let it be Cat, Dog or Serpent, and they pay their Adorations to it the whole Day. Others chooſe a Tree of their Father's or ſome dear Friend's planting, and that he gets conſecrated, and it then becomes his God; but they all believe the Immortality of the Soul and Tranſmigration, and the Adoration of the great God, of whom they have many wild Opinions.

THE great God's Image they can neither fancy nor make, but believe, that he ſent an huge large Fowl from Heaven, that laid a ſwinging Egg in the Sea, and, in Proceſs of Time, it was hatch'd by the Sun, and forth came the World, with all Animals, Vegetables, &c. that inhabit it now, and that poor *Adam* was ſet alone on the Top of an high Mountain in *Zealoan*, which is called, to this Day, *Baba Adam*, from that Tradition, but, being tired of ſo loneſom a Life, he deſcended into the Plain, and there he met with *Hevah*, whom he preſently knew to be his Kinſwoman, and they ſtruck Hands, and were there married.

THE great Men of the Clergy build Temples, but they are neither large nor beautiful. Their Images are all black, and deformed, according as they fancy the infernal Gods to be ſhaped, who, they believe, have ſome Hand in governing the World, particularly about benign or malignant Seaſons that happen in the Productions or Sterility of the Earth, for which Reaſon they pay a lateral Adoration to them. Their Images are all placed in dark Temples, and are never ſeen but by Lamp-light, that burns continually before them.

WHEN

WHEN criminal Cases are brought before the Magistrate, that want the Evidence of Witnesses to support them, the Trial of Truth is by Ordeal. The accused Person is obliged to put his bare Hand into a Pot of boyling Oyl, and if any Blister appears, the Party is found guilty; and I have been credibly informed, both by *English* and *Dutch* Gentlemen, as well as Natives, that had seen the Trial, that the innocent Person has not been in the least affected with the scalding Oyl, and then the Punishment due to the Crime, is inflicted on the Accuser.

THE *Samorin* entred into a War with the *Dutch East-india* Company *in Anno* 1714. and the Chief of the *English* Factory, who was a privy Counseller to the *Samorin*, had a great Hand in promoting it. The Quarrel began about a small Fort that the *Dutch* were building at *Chitwa*. The Ground whereon it stood was a desert Morass by the River's Side, and was claimed both by the King of *Couchin* and the *Samorin*. The King of *Couchin* made over his Claim to the *Dutch*, who made small Account who had the best Title, but carried on their Work with Diligence. The *Samorin*, with, and by the Advice of his Council, got some of his Soldiers to be entred into the *Dutch* Service, under the Disguise of daily Labourers to carry Stones, Morter, *&c.* for building the Fort, and to take their Opportunity to ly in Ambuscade in a Morass overgrown with Reeds near the Fort.

TWO

Two *Dutch* Lieutenants, who had the Overſeeing of the Work, were one Evening diverting themſelves with a Game at Tables in a Guard Room about half a Mile from the Fort. They had let ſome of their *Dutch* Soldiers go ſtraggling abroad, and the Sentinels were careleſs under the Security of Friendſhip, which gave the diſguiſed Workmen an Opportunity to kill the Sentinels, and make their Signal for the Ambuſcade, who, in a few Minutes, took the half-built Fort. The Lieutenants came preſently after, with what Forces they had, to retake it, but one being killed dead in advancing, the other thought it impracticable to attack greater Forces within than he had without, and ſo embarked, with his Men, on board ſmall Boats for *Couchin*, about 10 Leagues from *Chitwa*.

I fortuned to be at *Couchin* when he and his Men arrived, and, by a Court Martial, he was ſentenced to be ſhot to Death, which Sentence I ſaw executed. The *Samorin*'s People next Day erected a Flag-ſtaff, and hoiſted the *Engliſh* Flag, which the *Engliſh* Chief had ſent by the Ambuſcade, and immediately after ſet about demoliſhing the Walls, that were built, of the Fort, and carried off ſome great Guns belonging to the *Dutch*. And this was the Prelude of the War.

I knew pretty well the Strength of the Antagoniſts, what Power the *Samorin* had, and what Powers the Kings of *Couchin*, *Paaru* and *Porcat* could aſſiſt the *Dutch* with, and I wrote

wrote to the Chief the Resolutions of the *Dutch*, and advised him not to embark himself or his Masters in that Affair, because War was a different Province from his. He took my Advice so ill, that he wrote to *Bombay*, that I was in the *Dutch* Interest, opposite to the Right Honourable Company, and also to his Masters in *England*, as if the *Dutch* Company could need my Interest, Advice or Assistance; but, as I had forewarned him, he found the *Samorin* was forced, after three Years War, to conclude a dishonourable and disadvantageous Peace, wherein he was obliged to build up the Fort he had demolished, to pay the *Dutch* Company 7 *per Cent* on all the Pepper exported out of his Dominions for ever, and to pay a large Sum towards the Charges of the War. Some Part of the Money, I believe, he borrowed.

WHETHER our *East-india* Company got or lost by that War, I know not, nor will I pretend to pass Judgment on their Affairs, but this I know, that the Chief lost a good Milk Cow, for the Chiefs of *Calecut*, for many Years, had vended between 500 and 1000 Chests of *Bengal Ophium* yearly up in the inland Countries, where it is very much used. The Water Carriage up the River being cheap and secure, the Price of *Ophium* high, and the Price of Pepper low, so that their Profits were great both Ways; for, if I mistake not, the Company paid the highest Prices for their Pepper, and the *Nayers* in the Company's Pay, were employed about the Chiefs

Chiefs Affairs; and by the unexpected Turn of Affairs caused by the War, that Trade is fallen intirely into the *Dutch* Company's Hands, and it will be a very difficult Task to get it out again.

THE *English* Company were formerly so much respected at *Calecut*, that if any Debitor went into their Factory for Protection, none durst presume to go there to disturb them; but that Indulgence has been sometimes made an ill Use of, to the Detriment of *English* private Traders.

THEY have a good Way of arresting People for Debt, *viz.* There is a proper Person sent with a small Stick from the Judge, who is generally a *Brahman*, and when that Person finds the Debitor, he draws a Circle round him with that Stick, and charges him, in the King and Judge's Name, not to stir out of it till the Creditor is satisfied either by Payment or Surety; and it is no less than Death for the Debitor to break Prison by going out of the Circle.

THEY make use of no Pens, Ink and Paper, but write on Leaves of Flags or Reeds that grow in Morasses by the Sides of Rivers. They are generally about 18 Inches long, and one and an half broad, tapering at both Ends, and a small Hole at one End for a String to pass through. It is thicker than our royal Paper, and very tough. They write with the Point of a Bodkin made for that Purpose, holding the Leaf athwart their left Thumb End over the foremost Finger, and what they have to write is indented, or rather engraven into the Leaf, but it does not pierce the Leaf above half Way through. And on two or three of these Leaves they'll write as much as we can on a Sheet of small Paper. All their Records are written so on Leaves, and they are strung and rolled up in a Scroll, and hung some Time in Smoke, and then lockt up in their Cabinets. And I have seen some such Leaves Smoke-dried, that, they told me, were above 1000 Years old.

In Anno 1703. about the Middle of *February*, I called at *Calecut* in my Way to *Surat*, and standing into the Road, I chanced to strike on some of the Ruins of the sunken Town built by the *Portugueze* in former Times. Whether that Town was swallowed up by an Earthquake, as some affirm, or whether it was undermined by the Sea, I will not determine; but so it was, that in 6 Fathoms at the main Mast, my Ship, which drew 21 Foot Water, sat fast a-fore the Chess-tree. The Sea was smooth, and, in a short Time, we got off without Damage.

THE unfortunate Captain *Green*, who was afterwards hanged in *Scotland*, came on board of my Ship at Sun-set, very much overtaken with Drink, and severals of his Men came in the same Condition. He told me, that he had some small Arms, Powder, Shot and Glass-ware to dispose of, and asked me if I would take them off his Hands at a very reasonable Rate. I told him, that next Morning

ing I would see them, and perhaps be a Merchant for them: He told me, that the Arms and Ammunition were what was left of a large Quantity that he had brought from *England*, but had been at *Don Mascherenas* and *Madagascar*, and had disposed of the rest to good Advantage, among the Pirates, and had carried some Pirates from *Don Mascherenas* to St. *Marys*.

I told him, that, in Prudence, he ought to keep these as Secrets, lest he might be brought in Trouble about them. He made but little Account of my Advice, and so departed.

About ten in the Night his chief Mate Mr. *Mather* came on board of my Ship, and seemed to be very melancholy: He asked me, if I thought one of my Mates would be induced to go with Captain *Green*, that he might be cleared of his Ship, and he would give that Mate that would accept of his Post, a very considerable Gratuity. I told him, that such a good Post as he had on board the *Worcester* was not easily procured in *India*, for we seldom preferred Strangers before we had a Trial of them.

He burst out in Tears, and told me, he was afraid that he was undone. I askt his Reason for his melancholy Conjecture. He answered, that they had acted such Things in their Voyage, that would certainly bring them to Shame and Punishment, if they should come to Light; and he was assured, that such a Company of Drunkards as their Crew

Crew was composed of, could keep no Secret, tho' the Discovery should prove their own Ruin. I told him, I was sorry for his Condition, and that I had heard at *Coiloan*, that they had not acted prudently nor honestly in relation to some *Moors* Ships they had visited and plundred, and in sinking a Sloop, with ten or twelve *Europeans* in her, off *Coiloan*. He askt me if that was known at *Coiloan*. I told him, that the People there made no Secret of it, but as long as you did them no Harm, you are welcom to their Trade. Next Day I went ashore, and met Captain *Green* and his Supercargo Mr. *Callant*, who had sailed a Voyage from *Surat* to *Sindy* with me. Before Dinner-time they were both drunk, and *Callant* told me, that he did not doubt of making the greatest Voyage that ever was made from *England* on so small a Stock as 500 Pounds. I wisht him Joy and Success, but told him, that we *Indians* understood none of those profitable Voyages, but were well content with 30 or 40 *per Cent*.

In the Evening their Surgeon accosted me in my Walk along the Sea Side, and askt if I wanted a Surgeon. I told him I had two, and both very good ingenious Men. He said, he wanted to stay in *India*, for his Life was uneasy on board of his Ship, that tho' the Captain was civil enough, yet Mr. *Mather* was unkind, and had treated him with Blows for asking a pertinent Question at some wounded Men, who were hurt in the Engagement

gagement they had with the aforementioned Sloop. I heard too much to be contented with their Conduct, and so I shunn'd their Conversation for the little Time I staid at *Calecut*. Whether Captain *Green* and Mr. *Mather* had Justice impartially allowed them in their Process and Sentence, I know not. I have heard of as great Innocents condemned to Death as they were.

ABOUT 2 Leagues to the Southward of *Calecut*, is a fine River called *Baypore*, capable to receive Ships of 3 or 400 Tuns. It has a small Island off its Mouth, about half a Mile from the Shore, that keeps it safe from the great Seas brought on that Coast by the South-west Monsoons. Four Leagues more southerly is *Tannore*, a Town of small Trade, inhabited by *Mahometans*. They are a little free State, but pay an Acknowledgment to the *Samorin*. Five Leagues to the Southward of *Tannore*, is *Pennany*, mentioned before. It has the Benefit of a River, and was formerly a Place of Trade. The *French* and *English* had their Factories there, but were removed about the Year 1670. And about four Leagues more to the Southward, is *Chitwa* River, which bounds the *Samorin*'s Dominions to the South.

CHAP.

CHAP. XXVI

Gives an Account of Couchin *its Government and Strength, its ancient and present State, its Product and Commerce, with some Account of the* Jews *inhabiting there.*

THE King of *Couchin*'s Dominions are next in Course along the Sea-coast, and reach from *Chitwa* about 24 Leagues to the Southward. There are so many Rivulets that run off the Mountains of *Gatti*, that they reckon above 1000 Islands made by their Streams. The Mountains come within 8 Leagues of the Sea, and the Rivulets joyn their Stores at *Cranganore*, and make one great Outlet to the Sea, and another great Outlet is at *Couchin* City. *Cranganore* is about 5 Leagues to the South of *Chitwa*. The *Dutch* have here a small Fort, which retains the Name of *Cranganore*. It lies about a League up the River from the Sea. In Times of old it bore the Name of a Kingdom, and was a Republick of *Jews*; who were once so numerous, that they could reckon about 80000 Families, but, at present, are reduced to 4000. They have a Synagogue at *Couchin*, not far from the King's Palace, about 2 Miles from the City, in which are carefully kept their Records, engraven on Copper-plates in *Hebrew* Characters; and when any of the Characters decay, they are new cut, so that they can ſhew their own Hiſtory from the Reign of *Nebuchadnezzar* to this preſent Time.

Myn Heer Van Reede before mentioned, about the Year 1695. had an Abſtract of their Hiſtory tranſlated from the *Hebrew* into low *Dutch*. They declare themſelves to be of the Tribe of *Manaſſeh*, a Part whereof was, by Order of that haughty Conqueror *Nebuchàdnezzar*, carried to the eaſtermoſt Province of his large Empire, which, it ſeems, reacht as far as Cape *Comerin*, which Journey 20000 of them travelled in three Years from their ſetting out of *Babylon*.

WHEN they arrived in the *Malabar* Country, they found the Inhabitants very civil and hoſpitable to Strangers, giving them Liberty of Conſcience in religious Matters, and the free Uſe of Reaſon and Induſtry in Oeconomy. There they increaſed, both in Numbers and Riches, till in Proceſs of Time, either by Policy or Wealth, or both, they came to purchaſe the little Kingdom of *Cranganore*. And there being one Family among them much eſteemed for Wiſdom, Power and Riches, two of the Sons of that Family were choſen by their Elders and Senators, to govern the Common-wealth, and reign joyntly over them. Concord, the ſtrongeſt Bonds of Society, was in a ſhort Time broken, and Ambition took Place, for one of the Brothers inviting his Colleague to a Feaſt, and picking a Quarrel with his Gueſt, baſely killed him, thinking, by that Means, to reign alone; but the Defunct leaving a Son of a bold

bold Spirit behind him, revenged his Father's Death, by killing the Fratricide, and so the State fell again into a Democracy, which still continues among the *Jews* here; but the Lands have, for many Ages, recurred back into the Hands of the *Malabars*, and Poverty and Oppression have made many apostatize.

BETWEEN *Cranganore* and *Couchin*, there is an Island called *Baypin*, that occupies the Sea-coast. It is 4 Leagues long; but no Part of it is 2 Miles broad. The *Dutch* forbid all Vessels or Boats to enter at *Cranganore*: And at *Couchin* the Chanel is about a Quarter of a Mile broad, but very deep, tho' the Bar has not above 14 Foot Water at spring Tides.

THE first *Europeans* that settled in *Couchin* were the *Portugueze*, and there they built a fine City on the River's Side, about 3 Leagues from the Sea; but the Sea gaining on the Land yearly, it is not now above 100 Paces from it. It stands so pleasantly, that the *Portugueze* had a common Saying, *that* China *was a Country to get Money in, and* Couchin *was a Place to spend it in*; for the great Numbers of Canals made by the Rivers and Islands, make Fishing and Fowling very diverting. And the Mountains are well stored with wild Game.

ON the Inside of *Baypin* Island, there is an old Fort built by the *Portugueze*, called *Palliapore*, to inspect all Boats that go between *Cranganore* and *Couchin*: And 5 Leagues up the Rivulets is a *Romish* Church called *Verapoli*, ſerved by *French* and *Italian* Prieſts; and when a Biſhop comes into thoſe Parts, it is the Place of his Reſidence. The *Padre* Superior of *Verapoli*, can raiſe, upon Occaſion, 4000 Men, all *Chriſtians* of the Church of *Rome*; but there are many more St. *Thomas*'s *Chriſtians* that do not communicate with thoſe of *Rome*, and ſome *Portugueze*, called *Topaſes*, that communicate with neither, for they will be ſerved by none but *Portugueze* Prieſts, becauſe they indulge them more in their Villany, and Abſolutions from Crimes are eaſier purchaſed from the *Portugueze* than from the *French* or *Italians*, who are generally much more polite and learned than the *Portugueze*, who are permitted to take the Habit of ſome Order, without being examined whether the Novice has the common Qualifications of School-learning.

About 2 Leagues farther up towards the Mountains, on the Side of a ſmall, but deep River, is a Place called *Firdalgo*, where the Inhabitants of *Couchin* generally aſſemble to refreſh themſelves in the troubleſom hot Months of *April* and *May*. The Banks and Bottom of the River is clean Sand, and the Water ſo clear, that a ſmall Peeble Stone may be ſeen at the Bottom in three Fathoms Water. Every Company makes Choice of a Place by the River's Side, and pitch their Tents, and drive ſome ſmall Stakes before their Tents, in the River, on which they hang up Clothes for Blinds, to hide the Ladies when

when they bath; but most of them swim dextrously, and swim under Water through the Stakes, into the open River, where the Men are diverting themselves, and there they dive, and play many comical mad Tricks, till Breakfast or Supper call them ashore, for it is in Mornings and Evenings that they bath and swim; for in the Heat of the Day the Sun scorches. Very often the Ladies lay Wagers of Treats with the Gentlemen, about their Swiftness and Dexterity in swimming, but generally the Ladies win the Wagers, tho', I believe, if the Men would use their Art and Strength, they might win the Prize. The Heat of the Day they pass with a Game at Cards or Tables for Treats, by which Means they fare sumptuously every Day, sometimes in one Tent, and sometimes in another; and, at Night, every Family sleeps in their own Tent, on the soft clean Sand, Males and Females promiscuously.

THERE is a Place on the Side of that River, called *Hell's Mouth*. It is a subterraneous Cave about four Yards broad, and three high, hewn out of a spungy Iron-coloured Rock. I went into it with a Lantern, and past straight forward about 200 Yards, but saw no End to it. It is an Habitation for Snakes and Bats, who were frightned by the Light of our Candle and Noise. As we were tired with their Company, so we returned back. They have no Tradition why it was made, or by whom.

The Water of this Country, near the Sea-coaſt, from *Cranganore* to St. *Andreas*, which is about 12 Leagues, has a bad Quality of making the conſtant Drinkers of it have ſwell'd Legs. Some it affects in one Leg, and ſome in both. I have ſeen Legs above a Yard about at the Ancle. It cauſes no Pain, but itching; nor does the thick Leg ſeem heavier than the ſmall one to thoſe who have them: But the *Dutch* at *Couchin*, to prevent that Malady, ſend Boats daily to *Verapoli*, to lade with ſmall portable Casks of 10 or 12 *Engliſh* Gallons, to ſerve the City. The Company's Servants have their Water free of Charges, but private Perſons pay Sixpence *per* Cask, if it is brought to their Houſes; and yet, for all that Precaution, I have ſeen both *Dutch* Men and *Women* troubled with that Malady. And no Cure has been yet found to heal or prevent it.

The old *Romiſh* Legendaries impute the Cauſe of thoſe great ſwell'd Legs to a Curſe St. *Thomas* laid upon his Murderers and their Poſterity, and that was the odious Mark they ſhould be diſtinguiſhed by; but St. *Thomas* was killed by the *Tillnigue* Prieſts at *Malliapore* on *Chormandel*, above 400 Miles diſtant from this Coaſt, and the Natives there know none of that Malady.

Couchin is waſht by the greateſt Outlet on this Coaſt, and being ſo near the Sea, makes it ſtrong by Nature; but Art has not been wanting to ſtrengthen it. The City built by the *Portugueze* was about a Mile and an half long,

long, and a Mile broad. The *Dutch* took it from the *Portugueze* about the Year 1660. when *Heitloff Van Ghonz* was General of the *Dutch* Forces by Land, and Commodore of a Fleet by Sea. The Insolence of the *Portugueze* had made several neighbouring Princes become their Enemies, who joyned with the *Dutch* to drive them out of their Neighbourhood, and the King of *Couchin* particularly assisted with 20000 Men. The *Dutch* had not invested the Town long before *Van Ghonz* received Advice of a Peace concluded between *Portugal* and *Holland*; but that he kept a Secret to himself. He therefore made a Breach in the weakest Part of the Wall, and made a furious Assault for three Days and Nights, without Intermission, and relieved his Assailants every three Hours; but the *Portugueze* keeping their Men continually fatigued in Duty all the While, and finding Danger of being taken by Storm, capitulated, and delivered up their City. In the Town there were 400 *Topases*, who had done the *Portugueze* good Service in defending the City, but were not comprehended in the Treaty. Assoon as they knew of that Omission, and the Cruelty and Licentiousness of the *Dutch* Soldiery in *India*, they drew up in a Parade, within the Port that the *Portugueze* were to go out at, and the *Dutch* to enter in, and swore, that if they had not the same Favours and Indulgence that were granted to the *Portugueze*, they would massacre them all, and set Fire to the Town.

Town. The *Dutch* General knew his own Intereſt too well to deny ſo juſt a Demand, ſo he granted what they deſired, and moreover to take thoſe who had a Mind to ſerve in the *Dutch* Service, into Pay, which many of them did.

The very next Day after the *Dutch* had Poſſeſſion, came a Frigat from *Goa*, with the Articles of the Peace made with *Holland*, and the *Portugueze* complained loudly of the General's unfair Dealings, but were anſwered, that the *Portugueze* had acted the ſame Farce on the *Dutch*, at their taking of *Pharnabuke* in *Braſil*, a few Years before. The *Engliſh* had then a Factory in the City of *Couchin*, but the *Dutch* ordered them to remove with their Effects, which accordingly they did to their Factory at *Pennany*.

As soon as the *Dutch* became Maſters of the City, they thought it was too large, and ſo contracted it to what it now is, being hardly one Tenth of what it was in the *Portugueze* Time. It is about 600 Paces long, and 200 broad, fortified with ſeven large Baſtions, and Curtains ſo thick, that two Rows of large Trees are planted on them, for Shades in the hot Times. Some Streets built by the *Portugueze*, are ſtill ſtanding, with a Church for the *Dutch* Service, and a Cathedral for a Ware-houſe. The Commodore or Governor's Houſe, which is a ſtately Structure, is the only Houſe built after the *Dutch* Mode, and the River waſhes ſome Part of its Walls, and a Canal cut from the River up

to

to the Middle of the City, that passes close by the Governor's House.

THEIR Flag-staff is placed on the Steeple of the old Cathedral, on a Mast of 75 Foot high, and a Staff a-top of it about 60 Foot, which is the highest I ever saw; and the Flag may be seen above 7 Leagues off. The Garison generally consists of 300 effective Men: And from Cape *Comerin* upwards they are allowed, in all their Forts and Factories, 500 Soldiers, and 100 Seamen, all *Europeans*, besides some *Topases*, and the Militia. They have their Stores of Rice from *Barsalore*, because the *Malabar* Rice will not keep above three Months out of the Husk, but in the Husk it will keep a Year.

THE Country produces great Quantities of Pepper, but lighter than that which grows more northerly. Their Woods afford good Teak for building, and *Angelique* and *Pawbeet* for making large Chests and Cabinets, which are carried all over the West Coasts of *India*. They have also Iron and Steel in Plenty, and Bees Wax for exporting. Their Seas afford them Abundance of good Fish of several Kinds, which, with those that are caught in their Rivers, make them very cheap.

THE King of *Couchin*, who, at best, is but a Vassal to the *Dutch*, has a Palace built of Stone about half a League from the *Dutch* City; and there is a straggling Village not far from the Palace, that bears the Name of *old Couchin*. It has a *Bazaar* or Market in it, where all Commodities of the Country's Pro-

Product are ſold; but there are no Curioſities to be found in it. The King's ordinary Reſidence is at another Palace 6 Leagues to the Southward of *Couchin*, and 2 from St. *Andrea*; but he keeps but a very ſmall Court.

Mudbay is a Place, that, I believe, few can parallel in the World. It lies on the Shore of St. *Andrea*, about half a League out in the Sea, and is open to the wide Ocean, and has neither Iſland nor Bank to break off the Force of the Billows, which come rolling with great Violence, on all other Parts of the Coaſt, in the South-weſt Monſoons, but, on this Bank of Mud, loſe themſelves in a Moment, and Ships ly on it, as ſecure as in the beſt Harbour, without Motion or Diſturbance. It reaches about a Mile along Shore, and has ſhifted from the Northward, in 30 Years, about three Miles. St. *Andrea* is only a Village, with a Church in it dedicated to St. *Andrew*, and is ſerved by St. *Thomas*'s Prieſts, who generally are both poor and illiterate. About 2 Leagues to the Southward of St. *Andrea* begin the Dominions of *Porcat*, or

Porkah. It is of ſmall Extent, reaching not above 4 Leagues along the Sea-coaſt. The Prince is poor, having but little Trade in his Country, tho' it was a free Port for Pirates when *Evory* and *Kid* robbed on the Coaſt of *India*; but, ſince that Time, the Pirates infeſt the northern Coaſts, finding the richeſt Prizes amongſt the *Mocha* and *Perſia* Traders. The *Dutch* keep a Factory at *Porkah*, but of ſmall Conſequence.

Coil-

Coilcoiloan is another little Principality contiguous to *Porkah*, where the *Dutch* keep alſo a Factory. And next to it is

Coiloan another ſmall Principality. It has the Benefit of a River, which is the ſouthermoſt Outlet of the *Couchin* Iſlands; and the *Dutch* have a ſmall Fort within a Mile of it, on the Sea-ſhore, which they took from the *Portugueze* when they took *Couchin*. It keeps a Gariſon of 30 Men, and its Trade is inconſiderable.

Erwa lies 2 Leagues to the Southward of *Coiloan*, where the *Danes* have a ſmall Factory ſtanding on the Sea Side. It is a thatcht Houſe of a very mean Aſpect, and their Trade anſwers, every Way, to the Figure their Factory makes.

Aujengo lies 2 Leagues to the Southward of *Erwa*, a Fort belonging to the *Engliſh*, built, at the Company's Charge, *in Anno* 1695. It ſtands on a ſandy Foundation, and is naturally fortified by the Sea on one Side, and a little River on the other. It is in the Dominions of the Queen of *Attinga*, to whom it pays Ground Rent. Before it was built, the *Engliſh* had two ſmall Factories in her Country to the South of *Aujengo*. One was called *Brinjan*, the other *Ruttera*; but, being naked Places, were ſubject to the Inſults of Courtiers, whoſe Avarice is ſeldom or never ſatisfied: But I wonder why the *Engliſh* built their Fort in that Place, for there is not a Drop of good Water for drinking within a League of it; and the Road has

has a foul Bottom for anchoring, and continually a great Surf on the Shore, when they might as well have built it near the *Red Cliffs* to the Northward, from whence they have their Water for drinking, and where there is good Anchor-ground, and a tolerable good landing Place for Boats in the North-east Monsoons. The Country produces good Quantities of Pepper and long Cloth, as fine as any made in *India*.

WHEN our Factories were at *Ruttera* and *Brinjan*, they sent a yearly Present to the Queen of *Attinga*, whose Court is about 4 Leagues within Land from *Aujengo*. *In Anno* 1685. when the Present was sent, a young beautiful *English* Gentleman had the Honour to present it to her black Majesty; and assoon as the Queen saw him, she fell in Love with him, and next Day made Proposals of Marriage to him, but he modestly refused so great an Honour: However, to please her Majesty, he staid at Court a Month or two, and, it is reported, treated her with the same Civility as *Solomon* did the Queen of *Ethiopia*, or *Alexander the Great* did the *Amazonian* Queen, and satisfied her so well, that when he left her Court, she made him some Presents.

ABOUT the Year 1720. there were some civil Broils in this Country, and the annual Present being demanded, the *English* Chief refused to pay it to any but to the Queen herself, tho' those that demanded it, assured him, that they came to demand it by the Queen's

Queen's Order, and offered their Receit of it in her Name; but he, being more positive than wise, continued obstinate in his Refusal, upon which the Queen gave him an Invitation to Court; and he, to appear great there, carried two of his Council, and some others of the Factory, with most Part of the Military belonging to the Garison, and, by Stratagem, they were all cut off, except a few black Servants, whose Heels and Language saved them from the Massacre, and they brought the sad News of the Tragedy.

Tegnapatam, where the *Dutch* have a Factory, lies about 12 Leagues to the Southward of *Aujengo*. That Country produces Pepper, and coarse Cloth called *Catchas*: But *Colicha*, which lies between the Middle and West Point of the Cape *Comerin*, affords the best Cloth of that Sort, besides *Tamarinds* in Abundance; but the Road is foul. It also produces Salt; but neither the *English* nor *Dutch* have any Commerce or Traffick there. And close by *Colicha*, at the said middle Point, there is a small Cave or Harbour that can secure small Vessels from all Winds and Weather. It has a clean sandy Bottom, and three Fathoms in it at low Water. Four Leagues off the Cape, in the Sea, there is a small smooth Rock bare at low Water, and shews itself like the Back of a Whale. About 100 Paces from it, on all Sides, there is 28 Fathom Water; and the Sea seldom breaks on it, which makes it the more dangerous. I knew a Ship that rubbed her Side

on

on it, before thoſe on board could diſcover it, tho' they lookt out for it.

Manapaar lies to the North-eaſtward of Cape *Comerin*, about 8 Leagues diſtant, and the *Dutch* have a Factory there, ſtanding on an high Ground about a Mile from the Sea And about 10 Leagues more northerly is *Tutecareen* a *Dutch* Colony, tho' but ſmall

Tutecareen has a good ſafe Harbour, by the Benefit of ſome ſmall Iſlands that ly off it. That Country produces much Cotton-cloth, tho' none fine; but they both ſtain and die it for Exportation. This Colony ſuperintends a Pearl Fiſhery, that lies a little to the Northward of them, which brings the *Dutch* Company 20000 *L.* yearly Tribute. according to common Report. There are ſeveral Villages on the Sea-ſhore between *Tutecareen* and *Coil*, but none in any Account for Traffick. This *Coil* is a Promontory that ſends over a Reef of Rocks to the Iſland of *Zeloan*, called commonly *Adam*'s *Bridge*.

THAT Reef of Rocks has ſo little Water on them, that the ſmalleſt Boats cannot paſs but at an Iſland called *Manaar*, which lies almoſt Mid-way between *Zeloan* and *Coil*, and that Paſſage has not above 6 Foot Water on it, ſo that none but ſmall Veſſels can paſs that Way; and they muſt unlade, and pay Cuſtoms to the *Dutch* who reſide at *Manaar*, and, after the Veſſel is haled over the Bridge, they take in their Cargo again.

THE

THE *Dutch* have fortified *Manaar*, and make uſe of it for a Priſon for *Indian* Princes, whom they can overpower or circumvene, when they are ſuſpected of making Treaties contrary to their Intereſt, or to ſuch as would willingly reaſſume their loſt Freedom, by breaking the unjuſt Yoke of the Company's Tyranny, perhaps drawn on themſelves by too much Faith or Incredulity; for that honeſt Company has always had a Maxim, firſt to foment Quarrels between *Indian* Kings and Princes, and then piouſly pretend to be Mediators, or Arbitrators of their Differences, and always caſt in ſomething into the Scale of Juſtice to thoſe whoſe Countries produce the beſt Commodities for the Company's Uſe, and lend the Aſſiſtance of their Arms to him who is ſo qualified by the Product above mentioned, and, at the Concluſion of the War, make the poor conquered Prince pay their Charges for aſſiſting the Conqueror; and, when all is made up, and Treaties of Peace ready to be ſigned, then the Conqueror, their dear Ally and Friend, muſt ſuffer them to poſſeſs the beſt Sea-ports, and fortify the moſt proper and convenient Places of his Country, and muſt forbid all Nations Traffick but their dear *Dutch* Friends, under Pain of having the Company's Arms turned againſt them, in Conjunction with ſome other potent Enemy to the deluded Conqueror.

THE King of *Charta Scuri*, on the Iſland of *Java*, is a freſh Inſtance of the Truth of what

what I relate. *In Anno* 1704. I saw him at *Samarang* a Sea-port on the said Island, in great Splendor, and in high Esteem with the *Dutch* Commodore; but *in Anno* 1707 he fell under the Displeasure of the General and Council of *Batavia*, and in 1708 falling into their Hands, he was brought their Prisoner to *Manaar*, and cooped up on that small Island, there to spend the Remainder of his Days in Contemplation or Comments on the Deceit of worldly Grandeur, and of the Power and Pleasure of Sovereignty, or in humble Thoughts on Confinement, Exile and Poverty. And here I leave him, and pass over the rest of *Adam*'s *Bridge*, (called by the Natives *Ramena Coil*) and pay a short Visit to *Zeloan*, beginning at the Bridge; and travelling to the Southward, East and Northward, till I reach back again to the North Side of the Bridge.

CHAP. XXVII.

Treats of the Island of Ceylon *or* Zeloan *its Product and Commerce, Religion and Customs, the* Portugueze *Pride and Folly the Cause of its falling into the* Dutch *Company's Hands; with other historical Remarks and Observations, both ancient and modern.*

ZELOAN is an Island famous in many Histories for its Fertility, particularly in producing the Cinnamon Tree, whose Bark is is ſo much eſteemed all over *Aſia* and *Europe*, beſides the precious Stones that grow in it, *viz.* the Emerald, Sapphire and Catſ-eye being all valuable Stones, tho' ſoft.

THE firſt Place, in Courſe, to the Southward of the Bridge, is a long Iſland that lies cloſe to the Shore, and reaches about 12 Leagues ſoutherly, called *Calpetine*. It produces only Timber for building: But *Negombo*, that lies near the South End of it, has a ſmall Fort, and a *Dutch* Gariſon to forbid all Trade to Strangers on that Part of the Coaſt. And 7 Leagues from *Negombo* to the South, ſtands the City of

Colombo, which was at firſt built by the *Portugueze*, about the Year 1638. but, by their Pride and Inſolence, had made the King of *Candia* (who was, at firſt, Sovereign of the whole Iſland) their Enemy. The *Dutch* taking that Opportunity, made a League with the King offenſive and defenſive, and firſt attacked and carried *Galle* or *Ponto de Galle in Anno* 1658 which is a Fort and Harbour on the South-weſt Point of the Iſland, about 20 Leagues from *Colombo*. When they had ſettled Affairs at *Galle*, they embarked, to the Number of 3000 Soldiers, and ſailed to *Pantera*, a ſmall River about 4 Leagues South of *Colombo*, and were joyned by 2 or 3000 of the King of *Candia*'s Men. The *Portugueze* having Information of the *Dutch* landing, and the ſmall Aſſiſtance of the Natives, contemned their Forces, and raiſed an Army of 10000 Men to chaſtiſe their Folly in coming with ſo few Forces. The *Portugueze* Army was commanded by a *Fidalgo*, called *Antonio de Figuera*, a Freſh-water Soldier, but a great *Braggadocio*, and promiſed to bring all the *Dutch* that did not fall by his Sword, into *Colombo* in Chains; and the *Portugueze* Ladies were ſo ſure of his Performances, that they ſent to compliment him, and beg the Favour that he would pick them out ſome luſty *Dutch* Men to carry their *Palenqueens* and *Somereras* or Umbrellas, which he promiſed to do on Honour, and ſo went to meet his Enemies.

THE *Dutch* advancing towards the City, met the *Portugueze* unexpectedly, and there being a little ſhallow River between them, the *Portugueze* pretended to ſtop the *Dutch* there, and began to fire very briskly, tho' at too great a Diſtance, but did not advance towards their Enemy. Upon which the *Dutch* paſt the River, and advanced till they came within Piſtol-ſhot, and then fired on the *Portugueze* with ſo good Succeſs, that they preſently broke, and betook them to their Heels, and the *Dutch* kept a running March after them, and being nimbler than the *Portugueze*, entred the City with them, and made themſelves Maſters of it, wherein they found immenſe Treaſures: But the poor *Portugueze* Ladies were ſtrangely diſappointed to find the *Dutch* were become their Bed-fellows inſtead of their Slaves.

THE *Dutch* had one Game more to play before they had done with that Expedition. They

They knew that Reinforcements were ſent from *Goa*, who came in Sight two or three Days after the City was taken, and the *Dutch* Fleet, which then lay in the Road, pretended Fear, weighed their Anchors on Sight of the *Portugueze* Fleet, and feigned a Flight, while the *Dutch*, in the City, hoyſted *Portugueze* Colours, and fired ſome Guns towards the Sea, to make thoſe in the *Portugueze* Fleet believe, that the Firing was at the *Dutch* Fleet. The Stratagem took, and the *Portugueze* came and anchored in the Road about a Mile from the City, and ſent their Boats aſhore, where they were detained; and the *Dutch* Fleet being in the Offing, came in with the Sea Winds, and fell on the *Portugueze* Fleet, which ſoon yielded to them, for which Piece of Civility they had good Quarter.

Upon the Conqueſt of *Colombo*, followed all the other Forts on the Iſland, *viz. Calkiſſie* and *Barbarin*, between *Colombo* and *Galle*; and, on the South End, *Valta* and *Matura*; on the Eaſt Side *Batacola* and *Trankamalaya*; and, on the North End, *Jafnapatam*, with a Fort 4 Leagues from *Galle*, within Land, called *Biblegam*; and *Tutecareen* and *Nagapatam* on the main Continent, yielded.

The *Dutch* were no ſooner Maſters of the Sea-coaſts of *Ceyloan*, but they began to give Laws to their Ally the King of *Candia*, forbidding him to trade with any foreign Nation but theirs, which Uſage the King could not well digeſt, whereupon a War broke out, that continued many Years, but, in the End, the *Dutch* made a Peace upon very advantagious Conditions. And *Colombo* being too large to be defended with a few Forces, they have contracted it into one Quarter of its ancient Bounds, and have fortified it ſtrongly with a Wall and Baſtions. It is now about a Mile in Length, and three Quarters of a Mile in Breadth; and the *Chriſtians* and other Natives inhabit a Part of the old Town, without the Walls of the new. The Streets of the new Town are wide and ſpacious, and the Buildings after the new Mode. The Governor's Houſe is a noble Fabrick, and ſeveral other Houſes are beautiful. It wants the Benefit of a River, but has a ſmall deep Bay capable to receive ſmall Ships, and ſhelter them in the South-weſt Monſoons.

Ponto de Galle, I have mentioned before, is a Bay with a dangerous Entrance for Shipping, but is capable to receive Ships of the greateſt Burden. About the Year 1670, *Lewis* XIV. of *France* had a great Mind for a Settlement on *Zeloan*, and equipt ſeven or eight Sail of Ships for that Enterprize; and when they came to Sea, and opened their Orders, they found *Galle* was the Place they were to take and fortify, and the Management of that Affair intruſted to one Mr. *de l'Haye*, which one Mr. *Jean Martin*, who had ſerved the *Dutch* many Years in good Poſts in *India*, and who had laid down that Project, was ſo chagrin'd with the Diſappoint-

ment

ment of another having the first Post in that Affair, that when they came to *Galle* they had but bad Success. They expected the *Portugueze* there before them to assist, but none came; but soon after *Hitlof Van Gouze* was with them, whom the *French* not caring to engage with, being equal in Number of Ships, and superior in Force, the *French* fled, and left their Project on *Galle* unattempted.

THEY went then to *Trankamalaya*, and anchored in that Bay, designing to force that small Garison to a Surrender; but that vigilant *Dutch* Man was soon after them with his Fleet, and forced them to fight disadvantgeously in *Trankamalaya* Bay, wherein the *French* lost one half of their Fleet, being either sunk or burnt. With the rest they fled to St. *Thomas*, on the Coast of *Cormandel*, designing to settle there; but *Van Gouze* was soon there also, and seized their Ships, many of their Guns being dismounted and carried ashore: But they finding they could do no Good against so powerful and vigilant an Enemy, treated and capitulated with the *Dutch*, to leave *India*, if they might be allowed Shipping to carry them away, which the *Dutch* agreed to, and allowed them their Admiral's Ship, called the *Grand Briton*, and two more, to transport themselves whither they pleased; but Mr. *Martin* was carried to *Batavia*, and there confined for his Lifetime, with a Pension of a *Rix* Dollar *per* Day.

Zeloan is fruitful in Rice, Pulse, Fruits, Herbage and Roots. And *Jafnapatam* exports great Quantities of Tobacco, and ſome Elephants. Thoſe of this Iſland's Brood are reckoned the moſt docil of any in the World, but they are not large, few of them exceeding three Yards in Height. They catch them wild by Stratagem, and ſoon make them tame after they are caught.

THE Way they catch them, as they told me, is, they drive large Stakes into the Ground for 2 or 300 Paces, in a Plain, and, about 100 Paces diſtant, they begin another Row of Stakes, that almoſt meets one of the Ends of the firſt Row, only leaving 7 or 8 Foot open between them, for a Door, and farther out from the Door-place, are ſome Stakes driven thicker than in the Rows, like a ſquare Chamber. In the Door-place is a wooden Portcullice or Trap-door, fitted to pull up or let down at Pleaſure, When all is ready, they bring a female Elephant trained up for a Decoy, and ſhe is put into the Chamber, and the Trap-door kept open. There are Men placed in a little cloſe Place built on the Top of the Stakes at the Trap-door, and the female Elephant makes a loud doleful Mone. If a male Elephant is near, he preſently approaches the Chamber, on the Outſide; but finding no Entrance there, he walks along the Outſide, till he finds the End, then walking back on the Inſide of the Stakes, he finds the Door, and enters. Aſſoon as he is in, the Watchmen let fall the Trap-door, and go and bring two tame Elephants to accompany him that is decoyed to their

their Stables. When they come near the Trap-door, it is pulled up, and they enter, and place themselves one on each Side. If he proves surly, they bang him heartily with their Trunks, and the Female bestows some Blows on him too. When he is tired with their Treatment, and finds no other Remedy but Patience, he even grows tame, and walks very orderly between his two Guards, whithersoever they please to conduct him, and continues very sociable ever after, except when Rutting Time comes, and then, if he be young, he becomes very rude and troublesom. That Time is known by a great Sweating in his Head, so they have strong Fetters ready to put on his Legs, and fastned to a great Tree for eight or ten Days that his Madness continues.

THERE are several Dangers, and Rocks above Water, on all the Coasts of *Zeloan*. The great *Baxias* are above Water on its East Side, not far from the South End of the Island; and the small *Baxias* are under Water about 3 Leagues to the North of the other, and dangerous Banks of Sand within them. To the Northward of *Trankamalaya* there are some Rocks high above Water, and some also under Water; and several Spits of Sand jetting a pretty Way into the Sea from Points of Lands. I knew a Gentleman that run his Ship on one Spit near Point *Pedro*, by too much Confidence of his own Knowledge of that Coast, for his Mate told him, that, in his Opinion, they kept too near the Shore.

Shore. His Captain anſwered, that his Knowledge of that Coaſt was ſo good, that if a ſingle Shovel-ful of Sand was carried off the Sea-ſhore, he would infallibly miſs it; but a few Minutes after, his Ship was faſt on a Bank, and he and his Crew deſerted her, and went aſhore, and the Ship found the Way off again of her own Accord, which when the Captain heard of, he, with ſome of the Crew, returned, and took Poſſeſſion of her again.

POINT *Pedro* has the moſt dangerous Banks off it, for they ly above four Leagues from the Shore, and the Land being very low, makes thoſe Banks the more dangerous. I have known ſeveral Ships loſt there; and *in Anno* 1723. one *Williams* loſt his Ship there, and he and all his Crew were ſeized by the Natives, and carried to the King at *Candia*, and, I am afraid, will be forced to end their Days there.

THE Religion of *Zeloan* is *Paganiſm*, and, for want of a better Image or Relict to adore, they worſhip a Monkey's Tooth. When the *Portugueze* were ſettled there, the Prieſts loſt their adorable Tooth, and a ſly Fellow, who had accompanied a *Portugueze* Ambaſſador there from *Colombo*, pretended he had found it three Years after it was miſſing. He had, it ſeems, ſeen it, and got one as like it as was poſſible. The Prieſts were ſo overjoyed that it was found again, that they purchaſed it of the Fellow for a round Sum, reported to be above 10000 Pounds *Sterl.*

ALL

All the Natives of this Island believe, that *Adam* was created on this Spot, and there is the Shape of a Man's Foot cut out of a Rock on the Top of the high Hill (called *Adam*'s *Peak* by the *English*) about 5 or 6 ordinary Foot long. This Opinion is also spread over many Provinces on the Continent, which brings many Pilgrims to visit the Footstep. And they also believe, that, on *Adam*'s Transgression, the Bridge, before spoken of, was made by Angels to carry him over to the main Land, whither I am obliged to follow him, having no more of *Zeloan* to treat you with, but some of the best Arecka in the World that grows there.

CHAP. XXVIII.

Treats of the Countries on the Sea-coast, from Adam's *Bridge at* Zeloan, *to Fort St.* George; *with an Account of St.* Thomas's *Martyrdom, according to the* Portugueze *Legend.*

THE first Place of Note, to the Northward of *Adam*'s Bridge, on the Continent, is *Nagapatam* a *Dutch* Colony and Fortress taken from the *Portugueze*. It has the Benefit of a River, which formerly bounded the Dominions of *Malabar*, tho' their Language was, and is used farther Northward. The River washes the Fort Walls, and its Waters are reckoned very unhealthful; but about

about the Year 1693. by the Ingenuity and Care of *Myn Heer Van Reede*, whom I have formely mentioned, that Cauſe of a mortal Malady was removed, for he built ſome Water Boats, and ſent them 4 Leagues off to another River, whoſe Waters were reckoned very healthful, and, by theſe Boats, furniſhed the Gariſon with good Water. In a ſhort Time there was a viſible Alteration for the better in the State of the Inhabitants Health, and making an Eſtimate of the Charges of thoſe Water Boats, and the uſual Charges of the Hoſpital, the Company found that they gained by the Water Boats. This Colony produces very little beſides Tobacco and long Cloth. The Natives are *Heathens*.

HAVING thus run along the Sea-coaſt of *Malabar*, from *Decully* to *Nagapatam*, I muſt viſit the *Maldiva* Iſlands, which ly off this Coaſt and that of *Zeloan*, about 60 Leagues diſtant from the neareſt Part of them.

THIS Cluſter of Iſlands, which reaches from 7 Degrees 20 Minutes North Latitude into 1 Degree South, are all low, ſandy and ſteril, bearing no Sort of Corn, and their only Product is Cocoa-nut. Their Trees are not ſo high nor groſs bodied as thoſe which grow on the Continent, or on *Zeloan*, but their Fruit is pleaſanter. Of that Tree they build Veſſels of 20 or 30 Tuns. Their Hulls, Maſts, Sails, Rigging, Anchors, Cables, Proviſions and Firing are all from this uſeful Tree. It alſo affords them Oyl for their Kitchin and Lamps, Sugar and candied Sweet-meats, and

and pretty strong Cloth. Their Seas produce Abundance of Fish, but their Trade is chiefly from a small Shell-fish called *Courie* and the *Bonetta*.

THE *Couries* are caught by putting Branches of Cocoa-nut Trees with their Leaves on, into the Sea, and, in five or six Months the little Shell-fish sticks to those Leaves in Clusters, which they take off, and digging Pits in the Sand, put them in, and cover them up, and leave them two or three Years in the Pit, that the Fish may putrify, and then they take them out of the Pit, and barter them for Rice, Butter and Cloth, which Shipping bring from *Ballasore* in *Orixa* near *Bengal*, in which Countries *Couries* pass for Money from 2500 to 3000 for a Rupee, or half a Crown *English*.

THE *Bonetta* is caught with Hook and Line, or with Nets. They come among those Islands in the Months of *April* and *May*, in Sholes, as our Herrings do. They cut the Fish from the Back-bone on each Side, and lay them in a Shade to dry, sprinkling them sometimes with Sea Water. When they are dry enough to put in the Sand, they wrap them up in Leaves of Cocoa-nut Trees, and put them a Foot or two under the Surface of the Sand, and, with the Heat of the Sun, they become baked as hard as Stock-fish, and Ships come from *Atcheen* on the Island of *Sumatra*, and purchase them with Gold Dust. I have seen *Comelamash* (for that is their Name

after

after they are dried) ſell at *Atcheen*, for 8 *L. Sterl. per* 1000.

THEIR Religions are *Paganiſm* and *Mahometiſm*, and their Language *Chingulay*, or the *Zeloan* Language. The King reſides on an Iſland in the Latitude of 4 Degrees North, and his Iſland, which bears the Name of the *King's Iſland*, is fortified with a Stone Wall, without Lime or Morter, and has a great many ſmall Cannon for his Defence. And his Reign is arbitrary.

THE Iſlands are ſo many, and, in moſt Places, ſo near to one another, that they could never yet be numbred. They are moſt Part inhabited; but the Inhabitants very poor. None of them dare wear any Clothing above their Girdle, but a Turband on their Head, without a ſpecial Warrant from the King. He ſets Governors of Provinces over ſuch a Number of Iſlands, and they lord it over the poor Subjects as much as a Dragoon does over an *Hugonot* in *France*. They give Burial to their Dead, and not Burning. And, at the Iſland of *Hammandow*, which lies in 7 Degrees, I ſaw Carving on ſome Tomb-ſtones, as ingeniouſly cut with Variety of Figures as ever I ſaw in *Europe* or *Aſia*.

THEIR Wells furniſh them with all the Freſh-water they uſe, and they dig them near the Depth of high Water Mark, which is about 5 or 6 Foot; and if they go deeper, it becomes brakiſh, becauſe there being no Subſtance of ſolid Earth under the Surface of the Sand, the Sea-water percolates thro' the

the Sand, and mixes with the Rain-water that ſupplies the Springs. So having given the beſt Account I can of a Parcel of Iſlands that cannot be counted, I return back to *Nagapatam*, from whence I took my Departure, and ſtretch along the Coaſt of *Chormondel*.

I begin at the River of *Nagapatam*, becauſe it is the ſouthermoſt Bounds of *Golcondah*, and coaſt along Shore to *Trincumbar* a Fortreſs and Colony belonging to the *Danes*. The Fort is ſtrong, the Sea waſhing one half of its Walls; but the Colony is miſerably poor. *In Anno* 1684. they were ſo diſtreſt with Poverty, that they pawn'd three Baſtions of their Fort to the *Dutch*, for Money to buy Proviſions, which then was very ſcarce and dear in that Country; but next Year they redeemed all again, paying their Debts by an unknown Fund, which ſtill remains a Secret: But that the *Engliſh* had a Ship called the *Formoſa*, which, in her Paſſage Home to *Surat*, called at *Calecut* for Water, Wood and other Stores. The *Danes*, at that Time, had two Ships cruizing between *Surat* and Cape *Comerin*, upon what Account none could tell but themſelves. The *Formoſa* left *Calecut* at Mid-night, and ſtood to Sea, in order to proceed on her Voyage, and being out of Sight of Land, about 11 in the Forenoon, thoſe aſhore heard a great firing of Cannon from the Sea, and the *Formoſa*, nor none of her Crew were ever heard of ſince that Time. They ſtill keep their Fort, but drive an inconſiderable Trade either to and from

Eu-

Europe, or in *India*, for what they have to live by, is the Hire that they freight their Ships for to *Atcheen*, *Malacca* and *Johore*, and ſometimes, but rarely, to *Perſia*, by which they keep up the Name of a Company, but reſemble one no more than that of the *Miſſiſſipi* does in *France*.

THEY have a Set of Clergy there lately come as Miſſioners from *Denmark*, to teach the Natives *Chriſtianity*, which deſerves both Commendation and Encouragement, but what Proſelytes they make, I cannot tell, tho' I ſaw ſome of the poorer Sort become Diſciples. The Product of the Country is Cloth, white and dyed.

THE next Place of Commerce is *Porto Novo*, ſo called by the *Portugueze*, when the Sea-coaſts of *India* belonged to them; but when *Aurengzeb* ſubdued *Golcondah*, and the *Portugueze* Affairs declined, the *Mogul* ſet a *Fouzdaar* in it, and gave it the Name of *Mahomet Bander*. The *Europeans* generally call it by its firſt Name, and the Natives by the laſt. The Country is fertil, healthful and pleaſant, and produceth good Cotton Cloth of ſeveral Qualities and Denominations, which they ſell at Home, or export to *Pegu*, *Tanaſereen*, *Quedah*, *Johore*, and *Atcheen* on *Sumatra*. The Bulk of the People are *Pagans*.

FORT St. *David* is next, a Colony and Fortreſs belonging to the *Engliſh*. About the Year 1686. a *Moratta* Prince ſold it to Mr. *Elihu Yale*, for 90000 *Pagodoes*, for the Uſe

Use and Behoof of the *English East-india* Company. The Fort is pretty strong, and stands close to a River; and the Territories annext to the Fort by Agreement, were as far as any Gun the *English* had, could sling a Shot, every Way round the Fort; but whether the Buyer or Gunner were Conjurers or no, I cannot tell, but I am sure that the *English* Bounds reach above 8 Miles along the Sea-shore, and 4 Miles within Land. The Country is pleasant, healthful and fruitful, watered with several Rivers, that are as good as so many Walls to fortify the *English* Colony. And ever since the Time that *Aurengzeb* conquered *Visapore* and *Golcondah*, there are great Numbers of Malcontents and Freebooters that keep on the Mountains, and often fall down into the open Country, and commit Depredations, by ravaging and plundring the Villages; and all the *Mogul's* Forces cannot suppress them.

When the *English* bought Fort St. *David*, the *Dutch* had a little Factory there, about a Mile from the Fort, and the good-natured *English* suffer them still to continue a few Servants in it. Our Company did not find so much Grace from the *Dutch* at *Couchin*, nor the Gentlemen of *Bantam* and *Indrapoura*, when the *Dutch* seized those Places. It is true, the *Dutch* can drive no open Trade there, but what they must pay the *English* Company Customs for.

About the Year 1698. the Freebooters aforementioned had almost made themselves

Ma-

Maſters of the Fort by Stratagem and Surprize. They pretended, that they had been ſent from the *Mogul's* Vice-roy at *Viſapore*, to take Charge of the Revenue collected at *Porto Novo*, and to carry it to the Treaſury at *Viſapore*, and deſired Leave to put their feigned Treaſure into the Fort for a few Days, to ſecure it from the *Moratta* Freebooters aforementioned, who, they ſaid, were plundring the open Country, which Favour Mr. *Frazer*, Governor at that Time, granted, ſo they brought into the Fort ten or twelve Oxen loaded with Stones, and each Ox had two or three Attendants, and about 200 more of that Gang, who came along with the Carriage Beaſts as a Guard, lodged themſelves in a Grove near the Fort Gate, to be ready, on a Signal given, to enter the Fort. The Freebooters within took an Opportunity the very next Morning, and killed the Sentinel and a few more that were aſleep in the Gate-way next to the Grove; but, before they could break the Gate open, the Gariſon was alarmed, and killed all their treacherous Gueſts, and the Ambuſh without being come into the Parade before the Gate, met with ſo warm a Reception, that they retreated in Confuſion, and the *Engliſh* purſuing them, killed ſeverals, but loſt ſome of their own Men.

Mr. *Frazer* ordered directly the Grove to be cut down, for fear of future Danger from it, but Fort St. *David* being ſubordinate to Fort St. *George*, the Governor and Council

Council there called Mr. *Frazer* to their Court, and fined him for Presumption, in cutting down so fine a Grove for Enemies to sculk in, without Leave askt and given in due Form; but their Right Honourable Masters adjusted all that Matter, and ordered the Fine to be refounded, with the Interest; but Governors of different Views and Humours seldom agree.

THIS Colony produces good long Cloths in large Quantities, either brown, white, or blue dyed, also *Sallampores*, *Morees*, *Demities*, *Ginghams*, *Succatoons*, and Steel. And, without the Assistance of this Colony, that of Fort St. *George* would make but a small Figure in Trade to what it now does.

THE River is but small, tho' very convenient for the Import and Export of Merchandize. And *Cuddelore*, that lies about a Mile to the Southward, is capable to receive Ships of 200 Tuns in the Months of *September* and *October*: The Rivers have both of them Bars, but are very smooth, whereas Fort St. *George* is always dangerous in going ashore and coming off.

THE Company has a pretty good Garden and Summer-house, where generally the Governor resides; and the Town extending itself pretty wide, has Gardens to most of their Houses. Their black Cattle are very small, but plentiful and cheap. And their Seas and Rivers abound in good Fishes.

Punticherry is the next Place of Note on this Coast, a Colony settled by the *French*.

It lies about 5 Leagues to the Northward of Fort St. *David*. The Fortifications are fine, regular and ſtrong, but its Trade is very ſmall, tho' the Country produces the ſame Commodities that cauſe the Trade circulate in Fort St. *David*. About the Year 1690. the *Dutch* brought Forces from *Batavia*, and beſieged it, and being then very ſcarce in Men, Magazines and Money, the *French* were forced to capitulate, and ſurrender on pretty honourable Terms, but, in the Concluſion of King *William*'s War, the *Dutch* were obliged to return it by the Articles of Peace, which verified the Fable of the Cuckow in ſeizing of other Birds Neſts weaker than herſelf, in the Spring, and quitting them again in Autumn.

Connymere or *Conjemeer* is the next Place, where the *Engliſh* had a Factory many Years, but, on their purchaſing Fort St. *David*, it was broken up, and transferred thither. At preſent its Name is hardly ſeen in the Map of Trade.

NEAR *Connymere* are the ſeven Pagods, one of which, whoſe Name I have now forgot, is celebrated among the *Pagans* for Sanctity, and is famous for the yearly Pilgrimages made there. The God was very obſcene, if his Image rightly repreſents him, and his Nymphs as lewd as any in *Drury-lane*, if their Poſtures were really figured and carved as they are to be ſeen on the Outſide of the Temple. Here it was that St. *Thomas*'s Perſecution firſt began, becauſe he could draw

a

a ſhort Tree to a great Length, as Wire-drawers do Metals, and the *Pagan* Prieſts being ignorant of ſuch Pieces of Art, made them cry out, that St. *Thomas* was an arrant Conjurer; for, as the *Romiſh* Story goes, the Freſhes coming down in Rivulets, had made ſome of them pretty deep to what they uſed to be, and a Lady going to Church, could not get over one of them, becauſe a Tree, that was laid for a common Bridge, was too ſhort at that Time, and St. *Thomas*, who preached in the Country Villages, a Doctrine oppoſite to the eſtabliſhed Church, accidentally being there, drew the Tree to ſuch a Length, that the Lady could paſs without wetting her Foot, upon which ſhe became a Convert, to the great Diſſatisfaction of the eſtabliſhed Clergy, who loſt a devout and charitable Benefactreſs by that Trick of St. *Thomas*'s.

THE Prieſts, as is uſual in ſuch Caſes, cried out, that the Church was in Danger, and ſo inflamed the Minds of the Populace, that St. *Thomas*, finding himſelf in greater Danger than the Church, thought it beſt to get out of Harm's Way, and ſo marched to the Northward, whither I muſt follow him to

Saderaſs, or *Saderaſs Patam*, a ſmall Factory belonging to the *Dutch* to buy up long Cloth. The Country is healthful, and the Ground fertil, which make them capable of aſſiſting their Neighbours at Fort St. *George* with Sallading and Pot Herbs, the Ground there being very ſteril.

Cabelon is next, where the *Oſtenders* have ſettled a Factory. There is nothing remarkable there, but a Point of Rocks that runs about half a Mile into the Sea, and thoſe make a ſmooth Landing-place in the Southweſt Monſoons.

St. *Thomas* is next, which lies about three Miles to the Southward of Fort St. *George*. The City was built by the *Portugueze*, and they made the Apoſtle its Godfather; but, before that, it was called *Malliapore*. There is a little dry Rock on the Land, within it, called the *Little Mount*, where the Apoſtle deſigned to have hid himſelf, till the Fury of the *Pagan* Prieſts his Perſecutors had blown over. There was a convenient Cave in that Rock for his Purpoſe, but not one Drop of Water to drink, ſo St. *Thomas* cleft the Rock with his Hand, and commanded Water to come into the Clift, which Command it readily obeyed; and, ever ſince, there is Water in that Clift, both ſweet and clear. When I ſaw it, there were not above 3 Gallons in it. He ſtaid there a few Days, but his Enemies had an Account of his Place of Refuge, and were reſolved to ſacrifice him, and, in great Numbers, were approaching the Mount. When he ſaw them coming, he left his Cave, and came down in order to ſeek Shelter ſome where elſe; and, at the Foot of the Mount, as a Teſtimony that he had been there, he ſtampt with his bare Foot, on a very hard Stone, and left the Print of it, which remains there, to this Day, a Witneſs againſt thoſe per-

persecuting Priests. The Print of his Foot is about 16 Inches long, and, in Proportion, narrower at the Heel and broader at the Toes than the Feet now in Use among us. He fleeing for his Life, to another larger Mount, about two Miles from the little one, was overtaken on the Top of it, before he was sheltred, and there they run him through with a Lance; and, in the same Place where he was killed, he lies buried.

When the *Portugueze* first settled there, they built a Church over the Cave and Well on the little Mount, and also one over his Grave on the great one, where the Lance that killed the Apostle, is still kept there as a Relict; but how the *Portugueze* came by that Lance is a Question not yet well resolved. In that Church there is a Stone tinctured with the Apostle's Blood, that cannot be washt out. I have often been at both Mounts, and have seen those wonderful Pieces of Antiquity.

At the Foot of the great Mount, the Company has a Garden, and so have the Gentlemen of Figure at Fort St. *George*, with some Summer-houses where Ladies and Gentlemen retire to in the Summer, to recreate themselves, when the Business of the Town is over, and to be out of the Noise of Spungers and impertinent Visitants, whom this City is often molested with.

The City of St. *Thomas* was formerly the best Mart Town on the *Chormondel* Coast, but, at present has very little Trade, and the

the Inhabitants, who are but few, are reduced to great Poverty. The *English* settling at Fort St. *George* were the Cause of its Ruin, and there is little Prospect of its Recovery.

CHAP. XXIX.

Gives a short Description of Fort St. George *its first Settlement and Rise, its Situation and Sterility, and some Remarks on its Government, and the Actions of some of its Governors.*

FORT St. *George* or *Maderass*, or, as the Natives call it, *China Patam*, is a Colony and City belonging to the *English East-india* Company, situated in one of the most incommodious Places I ever saw. It fronts the Sea, which continually rolls impetuously on its Shore, more here than in any other Place on the Coast of *Chormondel*. The Foundation is in Sand, with a Salt-water River on its back Side, which obstructs all Springs of Fresh-water from coming near the Town, so that they have no drinkable Water within a Mile of them, the Sea often threatning Destruction on one Side, and the River in the rainy Season Inundations on the other, the Sun from *April* to *September* scorching hot; and if the Sea-breeses did not moisten and cool the Air when they blow, the Place could not possibly be inhabited. The Reason why a Fort was built in that Place is not

not well accounted for; but Tradition ſays, that the Gentleman, who received his Orders to build a Fort on that Coaſt, about the Beginning of King *Charles* II's. Reign after his Reſtauration, for protecting the Company's Trade, choſe that Place to ruine the *Portugueze* Trade at St. *Thomas*. Others again alledge, and with more Probability, that the Gentleman aforeſaid, which I take to be Sir *William Langhorn*, had a Miſtris at St. *Thomas* he was ſo enamoured of, that made him build there, that their Interviews might be the more frequent and uninterrupted; but whatever his Reaſons were, it is very ill ſituated. The Soil about the City is ſo dry and ſandy, that it bears no Corn, and what Fruits, Roots and Herbage they have, are brought to Maturity by great Pains and much Trouble. If it be true, that the Company gave him Power to ſettle a Colony in any Part of that Coaſt that pleaſed him beſt, I wonder that he chooſed not *Cabelon*, about 6 Leagues to the Southward, where the Ground is fertil, and the Water good, with the Conveniency of a Point of Rocks to facilitate Boats landing, or why he did not go nine Leagues farther northerly, and ſettle at *Policat* on the Banks of a good River, as the *Dutch* have done ſince, where the Road for Shipping is made eaſy by ſome Sand Banks, that reach 3 Leagues off Shore, and make the high turbulent Billows that come rolling from the Sea, ſpend their Force on thoſe Banks before they can reach the Shore. The

Soil is good, and the River commodious, and convenient in all Seasons. Now whether one of those Places had not been more eligible, I leave to the Ingenious and those concerned to comment on.

However, the War carried on at *Bengal* and *Bombay*, by the *English* against the *Mogul's* Subjects, from 1685 to 1689. made Fort St. *George* put on a better Dress than he wore before; for the peaceable *Indian* Merchants, who hate Contention and War, came flocking thither, because it lay far from those Incumberers of Trade, and near the Diamond Mines of *Golcondah*, where there are, many Times, good Bargains to be made, and Money got by our Governors. The black Merchants resorting to our Colony, to secure their Fortunes, and bring their Goods to a safe Market, made it populous and rich, notwithstanding its natural Inconveniencies. The Town is divided into two Parts. One where the *Europeans* dwell is called the *white Town*. It is walled quite round, and has several Bastions and Bulwarks to defend its Walls, which can only be attacked at its Ends, the Sea and River fortifying its Sides. It is about 400 Paces long, and 150 Paces broad, divided into Streets pretty regular, and Fort St. *George* stood near its Center. There are two Churches in it, one for the *English*, and another for the *Romish* Service. The Governor superintends both, and, in filling up Vacancies in the *Romish* Church, he is the Pope's *Legate a latere* in Spiritualities

ties. There is a very good Hospital in the Town, and the Company's Horse-stables are neat; but the old College, where a great many Gentlemen Factors are obliged to lodge, is ill kept in Repair.

THEY have a Town-hall, and underneath it are Prisons for Debtors. They are, or were a Corporation, and had a Mayor and Aldermen to be chosen by the free Burgers of the Town; but that scurvy Way is grown obsolete, and the Governor and his Council or Party fix the Choice. The City had Laws and Ordinances for its own Preservation, and a Court kept in Form, the Mayor and Aldermen in their Gowns, with Maces on the Table, a Clerk to keep a Register of Transactions and Cases, and Attornies and Solicitors to plead in Form, before the Mayor and Aldermen; but, after all, it is but a Farce, for, by Experience, I found, that a few *Pagodoes* rightly placed, could turn the Scales of Justice to which Side the Governor pleased, without Respect to Equity or Reputation.

IN smaller Matters, where the Case, on both Sides, is but weakly supported by Money, then the Court acts judiciously, according to their Consciences and Knowledge; but often against Law and Reason, for the Court is but a Court of Conscience, and its Decisions are very irregular; and the Governor's dispensing Power of nulling all that the Court transacts, puzzles the most celebrated Lawiers there to find Rules in the statute Laws.

THEY

THEY have no martial Law, so they cannot inflict the Pains of Death any other Ways than by whipping or starving, only for Piracy they can hang; and some of them have been so fond of that Privilege, that Mr. *Yale* hanged his Groom (*Cross*) for riding two or three Days Journey off to take the Air; but, in *England*, he paid pretty well for his arbitrary Sentence. And one of a later Date, *viz.* the orthodox Mr. *Collet* hang'd a Youth who was an Apprentice to an Officer on board of a Ship, and his Master going a pirating, carried his Servant along with him; but the Youth ran from them the first Opportunity he met with, on the Island of *Jonkceyloan*, and informed the Master of a Sloop, which lay in a River there, that the Pirates had a Design on his Sloop and Cargo, and went armed, in Company with the Master, to hinder the Approach of the Pirates, and was the first that fired on them, yet that merciful Man was inexorable, and the Youth was hang'd.

THAT Power of executing Pirates is so strangely stretched, that if any private Trader is injured by the Tricks of a Governor, and can find no Redress, if the injured Person is so bold as to talk of *Lex talionis*, he is infallibly declared a Pirate.

In Anno 1719. I went on a trading Voyage to *Siam*, on the Foundation of a Treaty of Commerce established *in Anno* 1684. between King *Charles* and the King of *Siam*'s Ambassador at *London*; but, *in Anno* 1718. Mr. *Collet*

let ſent one *Powney* his Ambaſſador to *Siam*, with full Power to annul the old Treaty, and to make a new one detrimental to all *Britiſh* Subjects, except thoſe employed by *Collet* himſelf. It was ſtipulated, that all *Britiſh* Subjects that had not *Collet*'s Letter, ſhould be obliged to pay 8 *per Cent*. new Cuſtoms, and Meaſurage for their Ship, which come to about 500 *L*. for a Ship of 300 Tuns, to ſell their Cargoes to whom they pleaſed, but the Money to be paid into the King's Caſh, that he might deliver Goods for it at his own Prices, whether proper for their homeward Markets, or no. I coming to *Siam*, ſent my ſecond Supercargo up to the City, with Orders to try the Market, and hire an Houſe for the Uſe of the Cargo and ourſelves. He could not get a Boat to bring him back, before the Ship arrived at *Bencock*, a Caſtle about half-way up, where it is cuſtomary for all Ships to put their Guns aſhore, ſo then being obliged to proceed with the Ship to the City, I underſtood the Conditions of the new Treaty of Commerce, which I would, by no Means, adhere to, but deſired Leave to be gone again. They uſed many Perſwaſions to make me ſtay, but to no Purpoſe, unleſs I might trade on the old and lawful Treaty. They kept me from the Beginning of *Auguſt* to the latter End of *December*, before they would let me go, and then I was obliged to pay Meaſurage before they parted with me.

I

I wrote my Grievance to Mr. *Collet*, complaining of *Powney*'s villanous Tranſactions, not ſeeming to know that they were done by *Collet*'s Order, and let ſome Hints fall of *Lex talionis*, if I met with *Powney* conveniently, which ſo vext Mr. *Collet*, that he formally went to the Town-hall, and declared me a rank Pirate, tho' I and my Friends came off with above 3000 *L.* Loſs.

I ſhould not have been ſo particular, but that I ſaw ſome printed Papers at *London*, *in Anno* 1725. that extolled his Piety, Charity and Juſtice in very high Encomiums; but it muſt have been done by ſome mercenary Scribler that did not know him; but now he is dead, I'll ſay no more of him.

The black Town is inhabited by *Gentows*, *Mahometans* and *Indian Chriſtians*, viz. *Armenians*, and *Portugueze*, where there are Temples and Churches for each Religion, every one being tolerated; and every one follows his proper Employment. It was walled in towards the Land, when Governor *Pit* ruled it. He had ſome Apprehenſion, that the *Mogul*'s Generals in *Golcondah* might, ſome Time or other, plunder it, ſo laying the Hazard and Danger before the Inhabitants, they were either perſwaded or obliged to raiſe Subſidies to wall their Town, except towards the Sea and the white Town.

The two Towns are abſolutely governed by the Governor *Sola*, in whoſe Hands the Command of the Military is lodged; but all other Affairs belonging to the Company, are manag-

managed by him and his Council, most Part of whom are generally his Creatures. And I have been and am acquainted with some Gentlemen, who have been in that Post, as well as some private Gentlemen, who resided at Fort St. *George*, Men of great Candor and Honour, but they seldom continued long Favourites at Court.

ONE of the Gates of the white Town looks towards the Sea, and it is, for that Reason, called the Sea-gate. The Gate-way being pretty spacious, was formerly the common Exchange, where Merchants of all Nations resorted about 11 a Clock, to treat of Business in Merchandize; but that Custom is out of Fashion, and the Consultation Chamber, or the Governor's Apartment serves for that Use now, which made one Captain *Hart*, a very merry Man, say, *that he could never have believed that the Sea-gate could have been carried into the Consultation Room, if he had not seen it.*

THE Company has their Mint here for coining Bullion that comes from *Europe* and other Countries, into Rupees, which brings them in good Revenues. The Rupee is stampt with *Persian* Characters, declaring the *Mogul*'s Name, Year of his Reign, and some of his Epithets. They also coin Gold into *Pagodoes* of several Denominations and Value. There are also Schools for the Education of Children, the *English* for Reading and Writing *English*, the *Portugueze* for their Language and *Latin*, and the *Mahometans*, *Gen-*

tows,

tows, and *Armenians* for their particular Languages. And the *English* Church is well endowed, and maintains poor Gentlewomen in good Housewifery, good Clothes and *Palankines*.

THE Diamond Mines being but a Week's Journey from Fort St. *George*, make them pretty plentiful there; but few great Stones are now brought to Market there, since that great Diamond which Governor *Pit* sent to *England*. How he purchased it Mr. *Glover*, by whose Means it was brought to the Governor, could give the best Account, for he declared to me, that he lost 3000 *Pagodoes* by introducing the Seller to Mr. *Pit*, having left so much Money in *Arcat* as Security, that if the Stone was not fairly bought at Fort St. *George*, the Owner should have free Liberty to carry it where he pleased for a Market; but neither the Owner nor Mr. *Glover* were pleased with the Governor's Transactions in that Affair.

SOME Customs and Laws at the Mines are, when a Person goes thither on that Affair, he chooses a Piece of Ground, and acquaints one of the King's Officers, who stay there for that Service, that he wants so many Covets of Ground to dig in; but whether they agree for so much, or if the Price be certain, I know not: However, when the Money is paid, the Space of Ground is inclosed, and some Sentinels placed round it. The King challenges all Stones that are found above a certain Weight, I think it is about 60 Grains; and if any Stones be carried clandestinely a-

way

way above the ſtipulated Weight, the Perſon guilty of the Theft, is puniſhed with Death. Some are fortunate, and get Eſtates by digging, while others loſe both their Money and Labour.

THE current Trade of Fort St. *George* runs gradually ſlower, the Trader meeting with Diſappointments, and ſometimes with Oppreſſions, and ſometimes the Liberty of buying and ſelling is denied them; and I have ſeen, when the Governor's Servants have bid for Goods at a publick Sale, ſome who had a Mind to bid more, durſt not, others who had more Courage and durſt bid, were browbeaten and threatned. And I was Witneſs to a Bargain of *Surat* Wheat taken out of a Gentleman's Hands, after he had fairly bought it by Auction, ſo that many trading People are removed to other Parts, where there is greater Liberty and leſs Oppreſſion.

THE Colony produces very little of its own Growth or Manufacture for foreign Markets. They had formerly a Trade to *Pegu*, where many private Traders got pretty good Bread by their Traffick and Induſtry; but the Trade is now removed into the *Armenians*, *Moors* and *Gentows* Hands, and the *Engliſh* are employed in building and repairing of Shipping. The Trade they have to *China*, is divided between them and *Surat*, for the Gold, and ſome Copper, are for their own Markets, and the Groſs of their Cargo, which conſiſts in Sugar, Sugar-candy, Allom, *China* Ware and ſome Drugs, as *China* Root, *Galling-*

Galling-gal, &c. are all for the *Surat* Market.

THEIR Trade to *Persia* must first come down the famous *Ganges*, before it can come into Fort St. *George*'s Chanels to be conveyed to *Persia*. They never had any Trade to *Mocha* in the Product and Manufactories of *Chormondel* before the Year 1713. and Fort St. *David* supplies the Goods for that Port, so that Fort St. *George* is an Emblem of *Holland* in supplying foreign Markets with foreign Goods.

THE Colony is well peopled, for there is computed to be 80000 Inhabitants in the Towns and Villages; and there are generally about 4 or 500 *Europeans* residing there, reckoning the Gentlemen, Merchants, Seamen and Soldiery. Their Rice is brought, by Sea, from *Ganjam* and *Orixa*, their Wheat from *Surat* and *Bengal*, and their Fire-wood from the Islands of *Diu*, a low Point of Land that lies near *Matchulipatam*, so that any Enemy that is superior to them in Sea Forces, may easily distress them.

CHAP.

CHAP. XXX.

Gives an Account of the Coast of Chormondel *from Fort St.* George *to* Ganjam, *the eastermost Town in the ancient Kingdom of* Golcondah; *with Observations on their* Pagan *Worship, and some Occurrences that happened to the* English *Factory at* Vizagapatam *while I was there.*

POLICAT is the next Place of Note to the City and Colony of Fort St. *George*, and, as I observed before, is a Town belonging to the *Dutch*. It is strengthned with two Forts, one contains a few *Dutch* Soldiers for a Garison, the other is commanded by an Officer belonging to the *Mogul*. The Country affords the same Commodities that Fort St. *George* doth; and the People are employed mostly in knitting Cotton Stockings, which they export for the Use of all the *European* Factories in *India*.

THERE are several Places along the Coast to the Northward, which, in former Times, had Commerce abroad, but now are neglected and unfrequented. *Armagun* is one, and *Kisnipatam* is another, that brought good Store of Cloth, of several Sorts, to the *English* Factories. *Kisnipatam* has the Benefit of a good large River, that has a Bar of 15 Foot Water on it. *Carrera* has the Benefit of a large River, that reaches a great Way into the Country. *Pettipoly* had once *English* and *Dutch* Factories settled in it, but were withdrawn many Years ago, becauſe the inland *Rajahs* diſturbed Commerce by their Impoſitions and Exactions.

Matchulipatam, being the next Place of Figure, lies in the Way along the Sea-coaſt. It ſtands on the North-eaſt Side of *Diu* Point, about 5 Leagues diſtant from it. In the latter Part of the laſt Century this Town was one of the moſt flouriſhing in all *India*, and the *Engliſh* Company found it to be the moſt profitable Factory that they had. They had a large Factory built of Teak Timber; but now there are no *Engliſh* there, tho' the *Dutch* continue their Factory ſtill, and keep about a Dozen of *Hollanders* there to carry on the Chint Trade, for that Commodity is not, as yet, forbid to appear in *Holland*.

THE Town is but ſmall, built on a little Iſland, and is much ſtronger by Nature than Art. Towards the Continent Side, there is a deep Moraſs, over which is a wooden Bridge about half a League long, and on breaking a Part of that Bridge, the Town is ſecured from Enemies on the Land Side.

THE *Mogul* has his Cuſtom-houſe here, and the Commiſſioner of the Cuſtom-houſe is Governor of the Town. The Country and adjacent Iſlands are fruitful in Grain, Timber for building, and Tobacco the beſt in *India*. The Iſlands of *Diu* produce the famous Dye called *Shaii*. It is a Shrub growing in Grounds that are overflown with the Spring-tides. It ſtains their Calicoes in the moſt beautiful and lively Colours in the World;

and

and I have ſeen Butter from thence of as good a Colour and Taſte as ever I ſaw in *Europe.*

A few Years ago, the *Nabob* or Vice-roy of *Chormondel,* who reſides at *Chickacul,* and who ſuperintends that Country for the *Mogul,* for ſome Diſguſt he had received from the Inhabitants of *Diu* Iſlands, would have made a Preſent of them to the Colony of Fort St. *George,* and the Inhabitants were very willing to change their Maſters; but certain Reaſons, that I am unacquainted with, made the Governor and his Council reject the Preſent, and the Vice-roy and the Iſlanders became Friends again; but, after a Year or two, the *Engliſh* having conſidered better of the Matter, would accept of the Vice-roy's Profer, and ſent ſome Ships, with Men and Ammunition, to fortify a Factory, but the Inhabitants took Arms, and forbad them to land, ſo they returned as they went abroad.

Next to *Matchulipatam* is *Narſipore,* where the *Engliſh* had a Factory for long Cloth, for the Uſe of their Factory of *Matchulipatam,* when they manufactured *Chints* there. It alſo affords good Teak Timber for building, and has a fine deep River, but a dangerous Bar, which makes it little frequented. And paſſing round *Corrango* Point, a little Way up in *Corrango* Bay, is *Angerang,* that has the Benefit of a large deep River, that penetrates far up into the Continent. It has a Bar ſoft at the Bottom, and three and an half-Fathoms on it at high Water. Here the best and finest long Cloth is made that *India* affords, and is sold cheap; but the inland Countries lying near the River, are in the Hands of different *Rajahs*, and each being Sovereign in his own small Dominions, makes such Impositions and Exactions on the Cloth that comes down the River, that they ruine that beneficial Trade of *Angerang*, and make it little frequented.

In Anno 1708. the *English*, from *Vizagapatam* settled there; but whether the Factory was starved for Want of Money, or whether the Constituent and constituted Chiefs of the Factories disagreed about dividing the Bear's Skin, I know not, but the Factory was soon withdrawn, and the Project lost.

COASTING along Shore, there are several little Ports between *Matchulipatam* and *Vizagapatam*, besides *Narsipore* and *Angerang*, but *Watraw* is the most noted, for it produces Rice for Exportation, besides some long Cloth, but it is not frequented by *Europeans*, and therefore I proceed to

Vizagapatam, a fortified Factory belonging to the *English*. It is regularly fortified with four little Bastions, and has about 18 Guns mounted in it. It has the Advantage of a River, but a dangerous Bar to pass over before we get into it. The Country about affords Cotton Cloths, both coarse and fine, and the best *Dureas*, or stript Muslins, in *India*; but the Factory is generally heart-sick for want of Money to refresh it.

In

In Anno 1709. the Factory drew a War on themselves from the *Nabob* of *Chickacul*, for one Mr. *Simeon Holcomb*, who had been Chief at *Vizagapatam*, had borrowed considerable Sums of the *Nabob*, and affixt the Company's Seal to the Bonds he gave for them. Mr. *Holcomb* dying, the *Nabob* demanded his Money from the succeeding Chief, who would not pay him, alledging, that *Holcomb* had borrowed it for his own private Use, and not for the Company's, and that he must get Payment out of *Holcomb*'s private Estate, if there was enough found to pay the Debt, otherwise he might get his Money from some inland *Rajahs*, who stood indebted to *Holcomb*, by his Books of Accounts, in a greater Sum than would pay his Principal and Interest; and that he being the *Mogul*'s General, could compel those *Rajahs* to pay their just Debts, which they would make over to him: But the *Nabob*, not caring to enter into a War with his Country-men on such a Foundation, sent Agents to acquaint the Governor and Council of Fort St. *George*, with his Affairs at *Vizagapatam*. They proved deaf to all the Agent's Propositions and Arguments, and hardly treated him civilly, so he went back to his Master, with the Account of his ill Success. Upon which the *Nabob* came to a Garden about half a League from *Vizagapatam*, accompanied with 500 Horse, and 3500 Foot, to demand his Money. I being accidentally there in a small *Dutch*-built Ship, that I had bought from the *French*, on my Credit, at Fort St. *George*, and the Factory being but ill mann'd, Mr. *Hastings*, who was then Chief, and my Friend, desired the Assistance of my Arms and Counsel in that Juncture of Affairs, which I very freely gave him; and my Opinion being askt in Council, what I thought about the Affair, I advised him and his Council to compound the Matter as well as they could, and spin out Time, that we might better fortify the Avenues to the Factory. My Advice of compounding the Matter was rejected, but the other Part we followed, so, with seven *Europeans* that belonged to the Factory, and twelve that were with me, and twenty *Topases*, and 280 Natives, most of them Fishers, that lived under the Company's Protection, we fortified some Rocks that the Enemy was obliged to pass within Pistol-shot of, if they had a Mind to attack us. We threw up Breast-works between the Rocks, and moored my Ship within Pistol-shot of the Shore, and had eight minion Guns to scour the Sands, if they had attempted to come that Way, and, for six Weeks we continued on our Guard, and were often alarmed in the Night, but finding us always ready to receive them, they did not think it proper to force an Entry into the Town.

I had the Honour to command all the Outguards, and the Chief, with eight *Europeans* and twenty Blacks, kept the Fort. Thus we continued in perpetual Watchings and Alarms, till Reinforcements arrived from Fort St. *George*,

George, and then I left them, and proceeded on a Voyage to *Pegu*. Both Parties being very busy, one striving to get his Money by Compulsion, and the other, to save the Company's Money on any Terms, right or wrong. The War being drawn to a greater Length than was imagined at first, and Charges rising higher than was expected, inclined them to make all up amicably, which was at last effected by the Company's paying near the Sum that was at first demanded.

THE *Nabob*, whose Name was *Fakirly Cawn*, would hear of no Peace, without the Company's Merchant, who was a *Gentow* called *Agapa*, and a Subject of the *Mogul's*, who was very active in the War, in encouraging the Town's People to defend themselves and the Company's Interest, and who also had wrote to some neighbouring *Rajahs*, to embroil the *Nabob*'s Affairs in his Absence, in order to divert him from pursuing his Demands on *Vizagapatam*, should be delivered up to him, which, at last, he was, and was put to a very cruel Death. He was set in the hot scorching Sun three Days, with his Hands fastned to a Stake over his Head, and one of his Legs tied up till his Heel touched his Buttock, and, in the Night, put into a Dungeon, with some venomous Snakes to bear him Company, and this was repeted till the third Night he ended his miserable Life; but the Company's Merchants, for the future, will be cautious how they espouse the Company's Interest again.

There was one *Baily*, a Recruit from Fort St. *George*, on some Discontent, deserted the Company's Service, and entred into the *Nabob*'s; but falling into an Ambush, was taken Prisoner by our Men, and was sent to Fort St. *George*, where, for his Desertion he was deservedly whipt out of this World into the next, and there I leave him.

After the War was ended, and all quiet, the *Nabob* returned to *Chickacul*, but could neither forget nor forgive his Treatment at Fort St. *George* and *Vizagapatam*, but finding by Force he could not get the Factory into his Hands, without great Loss of Men and Money, he had Recourse to Stratagem, by surprising it. He came into the Town one Day with 100 Horse, and some Foot, without advertising of his coming, as was usual, at the Town-gate, and before the Chief could have Notice, he was got into the Factory, with twenty or thirty of his Attendants. The Alarm being given, a resolute bold young Gentleman, a Factor in the Company's Service, called Mr. *Richard Horden*, came running down Stairs, with his Fuzee in his Hand, and his Bayonet screwed on its Muzzle, and, presenting it to the *Nabob*'s Breast, told him in the *Gentow* Language, (which he was Master of) that the *Nabob* was welcom, but if any of his Attendants offered the least Incivility, his Life should answer for it. The *Nabob* was surprisingly astonished at the Resolution and Bravery of the young Gentleman, and sat down to con-

sider

ſider a little, Mr. *Horden* keeping the Muzzle of his Piece ſtill at his Breaſt, and one of the *Nabob*'s Servants ſtanding all the While behind Mr. *Horden*, with a Dagger's Point cloſe to his Back, ſo they had a Conference of half an Hour long, in thoſe above mentioned Poſtures, and then the *Nabob* thought fit to be gone again, full of Wonder and Admiration of ſo daring a Courage.

THERE are many ancient Pagods or Temples in this Country, but there is one very particular that ſtands upon a little Mountain near *Vizagapatam*, where they worſhip living Monkies; and, by Report, many Hundreds breed there, which are nouriſhed by the zealous Prieſts, whoſe Devotion conſiſts moſtly in boyling Rice and other Food for their comical little Gods, which, at Meal-times, aſſemble at the Pagod, and eat what is prepared for them, and retire again in good Order; but it is leſs dangerous to kill a Man near that Temple than a Monkey. I won't venture to be a Judge, to determine whether the Prieſt or the God is the moſt ridiculous Brute, and yet I think the Prieſt has ſome Advantage of thoſe on *Zeloan*, who worſhip a Monkey's Tooth only.

Bimlipatam lies about 4 Leagues to the North-eaſt of *Vizagapatam*. The *Dutch* keep a ſmall Factory there, conſiſting of four *Europeans*. The Country People manufacture Cloth, both coarſe and fine, which the *Dutch* buy up for *Batavia*. About 4 Miles off Shore, at *Bimlipatam*, there are ſome Rocks that appear

appear above Water, called *Sancta Pilla*. A Ship may paſs between them and the Shore without Danger. And that is all worth Obſervation there.

THERE are no *European* Factories to the Eaſtward on the Coaſt of *Chormondel*, but *Ganjam*. It is kept for the Chief of *Vizagapatam*'s Uſe, tho' a Company might find their Account there better than in many Places that they keep Factories in. It lies about 55 Leagues to the North-eaſtward of *Vizagapatam*; but there are ſeveral other Places between them on the Coaſt, that drive a ſmall Trade in Corn. *Pondee*, *Callingapatam* and *Sunapore* are the moſt noted, but are not frequented by *Europeans*.

THE Country about *Ganjam* is fruitful in Rice and Sugar-cane, and they make pretty good Sugars, both white and brown. It has the Benefit of a River, but not navigable, nor the Bar paſſable for Ships, till the Month of *September*, that the Freſhes from the Mountains open it, and then there is three Fathoms on it, but it ſhuts again about the Beginning of *November*, and, in the other Months, there are not above 7 or 8 Foot at High-water.

THE Town ſtands about a Mile within the Bar, on a riſing Ground, and is governed by a *Chowdrie*, an Officer deputed by the *Nabob*. And there is a Pagod in it, dedicated to an obſcene God, called *Gopalſami*: He is carried ſometimes in Proceſſion thro' the Streets, and ſometimes into the Fields

near

near the Town. They allow him a Coach becauſe he cannot walk, and he has always above a Dozen of Clergymen to accompany him in his Coach. Around his Temple, and on the Coach, are carved Figures of Gods and Goddeſſes, in ſuch obſcene Poſtures, that it would puzzle the *Covent Garden* Nymphs to imitate. One of his Company in the Coach has a Stick about two Foot in Length, and one End is carved in Shape of a *Priapus*. The Stick is placed between his Legs, and the End ſticking out before him, and all Virgins and married Women that never had Children, come and worſhip the Stick, and the Prieſts beſtow Bleſſings on them to make them fruitful. The Woods produce Timber for building. It is very heavy, but the ſtrongeſt Wood I ever ſaw, tho' not laſting. They alſo produce Bees-wax and *Sticklack*, and pretty good Iron. And the inland Countries manufacture Cotton into ſeveral Sorts of Cloths, both fine and coarſe, all fit for Exportation. The Seas produce many Sorts of excellent Fiſhes, and the Rivers the beſt Mullets ever I ſaw. In *November* and *December* they have great Plenty of Seer-fiſh, which is as ſavoury as any Salmon or Trout in *Europe*. I have ſeen them bought for three half Pence *per* Piece, each above 20 *lb.* Weight. Wild Geeſe and Duck are plentiful and good here, and Antilopes are ſold for fifteen Pence *per* Piece.

CHAP.

CHAP. XXXI.

Treats of the Sea-coast and some inland Countries in the ancient Kingdom of Orixa, *by the Natives called* Oria; *with an Account of the famous Temple of* Jagarynat.

IN the Year 1708. I had Occasion to travel from *Ganjam* to *Ballasore*, by Land, which gave me an Opportunity to see more of the Countries thro' which I travelled, than most others could have who travelled by Sea. About three Miles to the Eastward of *Ganjam* is *Illure*, at the End of a Ridge of Mountains, that divide the ancient Kingdom of *Golcondah* from *Orixa*. Its End runs within Pistol-shot of the Sea, and there were three or four Sentinels to demand a Tax on every Head that past out of, or into *Orixa*. I had seventeen Servants to carry my *Palanqueen* and Baggage, and all the Tax amounted to about three Shillings *Sterl.* Proceeding farther, I came to *Manikapatam*, where there is a great Inlet from the Sea; but, about a Mile from its Mouth, it divided itself into many Chanels, which made many small Islands. The *Mogul* had an Officer there, who examined from whence we came, and whither we were bound. Our Answers were satisfactory, and he presented us with some Poultry, Rice and Butter, and gave us a Place to lodge in. And, altho' we saw Plenty of Fish in the Rivers, yet Money could not purchase one of them, because there is a Pagod

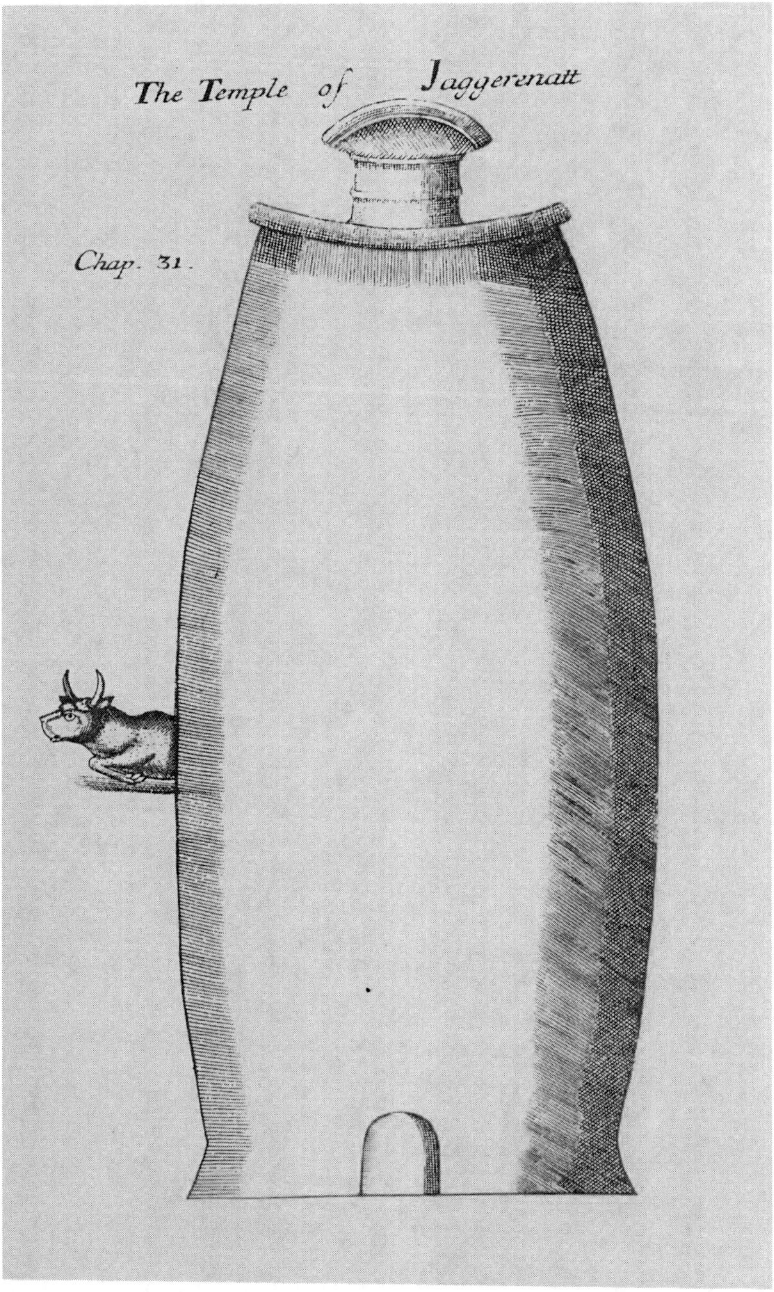
The Temple of Jaggerenatt
Chap. 31.

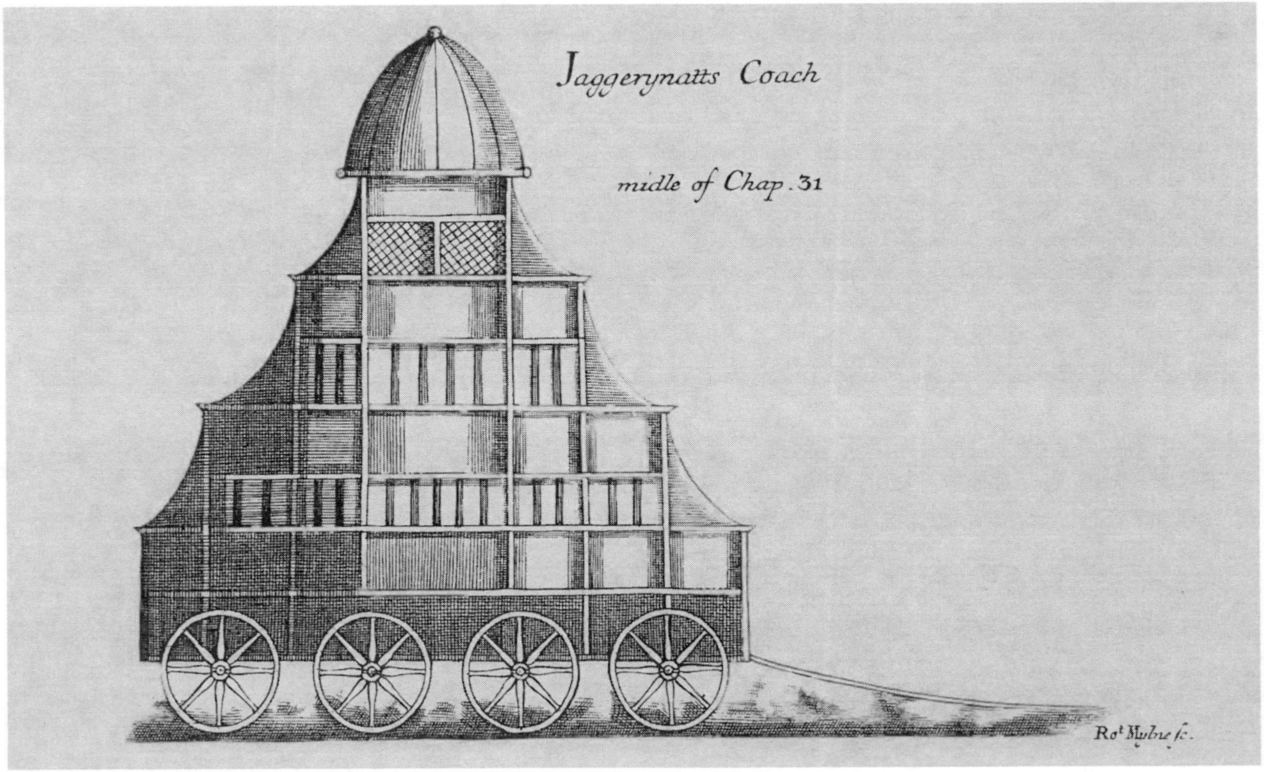
Jaggerynatts Coach
midle of Chap. 31
Rot Mylne fc.

god on a little Hill built of Iron-coloured Stone, where all the Animals of the watery Element are worshipped. And Water-fowls are so sacred, that they must not be killed. Our next Stage was at the famous Temple of *Jagarynat*, which, in clear Weather, may be seen from *Manikapatam*. In our Way we saw great Numbers of Deer and Antilopes, so tame, that they would not move out of our Way, till we approacht within five or six Yards of them. Water wild Fowl were also numerous and fearless, for none dares kill them under Pain of Excommunication, which cannot be removed but by round Sums to the Church. Poultry there is plentiful, but cannot be killed by the *Pagans*, because they worship them; nor can Strangers purchase them, only the *Mahometans*, who make no Account of their canon Laws, make bold to sacrifice them, and Fish too, as we do in *Great Britain*.

IN all this Tract between *Ganjam* and *Jagarynat*, the visible God in most Esteem is *Gopalsami*, whose Temples, as I said before, are decorated with obscene Representations of Men and Women in indecent Postures, also of Demons and Caco-demons, whose Genitals are of a prodigious Size in Proportion to their Bodies. The filthy Image is worshipped by all the *Heathens* of both Sexes, but barren Women are his greatest Devotees, and bring him the best Oblations.

Jagarynat has vast Crowds of Pilgrims to visit him from all Parts of *India*. His Temple stands

ſtands in a Plain about a Mile from the Sea, and no Mountains nor Outlets of Rivers near it. It is built of a free hard Stone, the Pedeſtal of large ſquare Stone, and cloſe by it is a Ciſtern built about with large oblong ſquare Stones of different Colours, *viz.* Brick-colour, light blue, gray and white. The Ciſtern has Steps that run the whole Length of the Ciſtern, which is about 40 or 50 Yards, and, at the End oppoſite to the Pagod, Steps of the whole Breadth of it, which is about 25 or 30 Yards, each Step about a Foot deep, deſcending, by Gradation, under the Surface of the Water, which did not ſeem to be clear, but, they ſay, is three Fathoms deep in the Middle. This Ciſtern or *Tank* is walled round with a Stone Wall about 5 Foot high, with two Iron Gates to let in Pilgrims, and keep out unſanctified Perſons, as *Chriſtians*, *Mahometans*, &c. for all Pilgrims are obliged to waſh in that *Tank* before they go into the Temple to worſhip. The Temple is built in the Shape of a *Canary* Pipe ſet on End, about 40 or 50 Yards high, about the Middle is the Image of an Ox cut in one intire Stone, bigger than a live one. He looks towards the South-eaſt, and his hinder Parts are fixt in the Wall. The Fabrick is crowned with a Top about the ſame Diameter that it is in the Middle, and the Temple being exactly round, makes no contemptible Figure in Architecture. On the Weſt Side of the Pagod, there is a large Chapel that joyns it, wherein Sermons are daily preach-

preached; and there are ſome Convents at a little Diſtance for the Prieſts to lodge in, who daily officiate. There are, in all, about 500 of them that belong to the Pagod, who daily boyl Rice and Pulſe for the Uſe of the God. They report, that there are five Candies daily dreſt, each Candy containing 1600 *lb.* Weight. When ſome Part has been carried before the Idol, and the Smoke had ſaluted his Mouth and Noſe, then the Remainder is ſold out, in ſmall Parcels, to thoſe who will buy it, at very reaſonable Rates, and the Surplus is ſerved out to the Poor, who are ever attending the Pagod out of a pretended Devotion: And this Food, that is dreſt for the Pagod, has a particular Privilege above other Eatables, that the purified *Heathen* is not contaminated by eating out of the ſame Diſh with polluted *Chriſtians* or *Mahometans*, tho' in another Place, it would be reckoned a mortal Sin.

I ſtaid there one Day and two Nights, and my Lodgings were in an Houſe very near the Pagod. The Nights were ſpent in beating on Tabors and Braſs Cymbals, with Songs of Praiſes on *Jagarynat*, who is only a Stone God, not carved into a Figure, but an irregular pyramidal black Stone of about 4 or 500 *lb.* Weight, with two rich Diamonds placed near the Top, to repreſent Eyes, and a Noſe and Mouth painted with Vermilion, to ſhew his Devotees that he can both ſmell and taſte. There are no Windows in the Temple to give Light, ſo that he has Uſe

for

for about 100 Lamps continually burning before him. He is railed about, that none may approach near him but his Priests; and only those of the first Quality dare enter into the *Sanctum sanctorum*.

I would fain have gone into the Temple, but could not be admitted, tho' I profered the Value of three Guineas for Admittance, but I sent one of my Servants, who was a *Gentow*, to observe what he could, and he brought me the foregoing Account.

HE is never removed out of the Temple, but his Effigie is often carried abroad in Procession, mounted on a Coach four Stories high. It runs on eight or ten Wheels, and is capable to contain near 200 Persons. It is drawn thro' a large Street about 50 Yards wide, and half a League long, by a Cable of 14 Inches Circumference, and, at convenient Distances, they fasten small Ropes to the Cable, two or three Fathoms long, so that upwards of 2000 People have Room enough to draw the Coach, and some old Zealots, as it passes thro' the Street, fall flat on the Ground, to have the Honour to be crusht to Pieces by the Coach Wheels, and, if they meet with that good Fortune to be killed outright, the Priests make the Mob believe, that the Defunct's Soul is much in favour with the Idol, but if only a Leg, a Thigh or an Arm are crusht, then the Devotee is not sanctified enough to be taken Notice of, however, if they die of their Bruises, their Bodies are burned as well as the others, and their

their Souls go into Paradiſe, or a Place very near it, without ſtopping at the half-way Houſe to be purged from their Sins, as others leſs pure are obliged to do.

THEY have a Tradition, that this famous Idol was not originally of the Country he now ſtays in, but, 3 or 4000 Years ago, he ſwimm'd over the Sea, and ſome Fiſhers ſeeing him ly at High-water Mark, went near him, and, to their great Aſtoniſhment, heard him ſay in their own vernacular Language, *that he came out of pure Charity to reſide among them, and deſired that he might have a good Lodging built for him, on that ſame Spot of Ground that he now dwells on.* The Fiſhers told this Story to their ghoſtly Fathers, who came in Troops to ſee the Stone that could talk ſo prettily, and would have excuſed themſelves of the Trouble of building an Houſe fit to entertain his Godſhip, but he would not be denied; and, tho' there are no Stone-quarries nor Mountains to be ſeen within Reach of the Eye, he promiſed to furniſh them with good Stone and Lime to build his Houſe, if they would but take the Trouble, and ſo, every Night, Materials were brought as there was Need, and, in a ſhort Time, his Houſe was built, as it now is. And there are reckoned, in the ſame Town, no leſs than 400 Temples built in Honour to *Jagarynat* and his Relations.

HAD *Jagarynat* ſtaid but twenty or thirty Centuries, and ſwimm'd to the Shore of ſome *Chriſtian Catholick* Country, he would have found an hearty Welcome, and would not have been obliged to confine himſelf to one Houſe without Windows, but would have had an hundred Palaces built for him, with ſwinging great Windows for to give him Daylight, and Hundreds of good Wax-candles burning before him Night and Day, inſtead of Lamps, whoſe Charge is much leſs than Virgin Wax, and their Light much dimmer.

WHETHER this Story of *Jagarynat*, or thoſe of the miraculous Adventures of *Xavier*, and the Ship that run from Cape *Bona Eſperanza* to *Goa* in one Night, are moſt to be credited, I leave to the Determination of the unprejudiced Judges of Controverſy in Points polemical.

THE Prince of this Country is an *Heathen*, and pays a Tribute to the *Mogul* of a Lack of Rupees yearly, or 12500 *L. Sterl.* which is paid into the Exchequer at *Cattack*. And the Prince exacts a Tax of half a Crown *per* Head on every Pilgrim that comes to the Pagod to worſhip, which generally amounts to 75000 *L. per Annum.*

THIS Country abounds in Corn, Cloth, Cattle, Deer and Antelopes. Bears and Monkies are very numerous and fearleſs. There is alſo Plenty of Water-fowl, Partridge and Pheaſant, all tame, becauſe none dares kill them but the Prince, except thoſe whom he gives written Licences to, and they are but ſeldom obtained. The Country is watered with many ſmall Rivers, whoſe Outlets to the Sea are at *Manikapatam* and *Arſipore*

ſipore, and there are many Bridges of Stone over thoſe little Rivers, and great Numbers of Beggars near thoſe Bridges, asking Alms in the Name of *Jagarynat*.

THE Prince who reigned *in Anno* 1708. had a peculiar Eſteem for *Europeans* in general, for, one Day as he was a hunting, his Horſe fell, and the Prince broke his Thigh-bone, and accidentally an *European* Surgeon being in the Town, ſet the Bone, and made a perfect Cure, and was rewarded with 45 *L. Sterl.* for it.

WHEN I was there, he was abroad a hunting, and he ſent me a Compliment, that he deſired to ſee me; but I excuſed myſelf on account of my having a Fit of the Gout, and he was ſatisfied with the Excuſe, and ſent me a good fat Buck for my Supper; and ſeveral of the beſt Gentlemen in Town, came, with their Compliments, next Morning, to invite me to ſtay a few Days till his Highneſs returned from hunting; but my Buſineſs being preſſing, I returned their Civilities in the propereſt Terms I could, and took Leave to proceed on my Journey.

WHEN I had travelled three or four Leagues from *Jagarynat*, I left the Sea-ſhore, and took my Way towards *Cattack*, on a very fine Road, where I ſaw many Droves of Cattle and wild Game, and ſeveral Monuments of zealous Pilgrims, who had ſignalized themſelves by ſevere Penances, and one particularly, that, about three Months before I was there, had, out of Zeal, built a Tomb for himſelf, and, when it was finiſhed, took his Leave of his Friends in Form, and entred into his new Cell, and ſtaid till he died for Want of Suſtenance. I challenge any *Chriſtian* Penitents to do more, in Acts of Supererogation, than this blind *Heathen* did.

CHAP. XXXII.

Is an Account of the maritim Towns on the Coaſt of Orixa, *which terminates at* Ballaſore; *alſo of ſome inland Places through which I travelled.*

FROM the Dominions of *Jagarynat*, I came into thoſe of *Arſipore*. The Town, where the *Rajah* reſided, is named after the Province, and there is a fine River that invites Strangers to frequent it for Cotton Cloth and Rice, that this Country affords in great Plenty. And, in ſixſcore Miles that I travelled between *Jagarynat* and *Cattack*, I found little elſe worth noticing but Numbers of Villages interſperſt in the plain Countries, and, at every ten or twelve Miles End, a Fellow to demand *Junkaun* or Poll-money for me and my Servants, which generally came to a Peny or three half Pence a Piece, ſo that, in the whole, it coſt me about 1 *L. Sterl.* for Paſſage-gilt.

THE next Place to *Arſipore*, on the Sea-coaſt, is *Raypore*, that ſtands on the Banks of the River of *Cattack*, where it diſembogues

into

into the Sea, about mid-way between Point *Falso* and Point *Palmeira*. It has a fine Bar affording ſeven Fathoms Water on it in Spring-tides. It is not frequented by *Europeans*, tho', no Doubt, it was before *Aurengzeb* conquered the Country, for it produceth Corn, Cloth very fine, Butter and Oyl in great Abundance. The City of *Cattack* ſtands on an Iſland of this River, about 25 Leagues from the Sea.

WHEN I came to the River of *Cattack*, I eſpied a ſmall Pagod, built in Form of a Cupola. The Out-ſide had Holes in it, like the Holes of a Pigeon-houſe, placed in Order, and in each Hole was a Man's Skull. Enquiring the Reaſon why ſuch a Number of Skulls were put there, I was informed, that when *Aurengzeb*s Army came to beſiege *Cattack*, there was a Conſpiracy in the Town to betray it, but being detected, above five Hundred that were concerned in it, were, by Order of the King of *Orixa*, who was then in the City, condemned to be beheaded, and their Heads to be placed in thoſe Holes, and there they have continued ever ſince. Cloſe by that Temple, we took Boat to carry us to the City, the River, on that Side, being about a Mile broad, and ſounding it in the Middle, I found ſix Fathoms. The River Water is very clear, and wholſom to drink, and deſcends with a ſlow Stream.

THE Springs of the River are from the Mountains of *Gatti*, within 40 Leagues of *Goa*, and, in its Paſſage, waſhes Part of the

Kingdoms of *Talinga*, *Visapore*, *Golcondah*, and *Orixa*, blessing all the Countries that it passes through, with Fertility of Corn, even to the Place where it loses it self, and there it is also beneficent, in affording a convenient Harbour for Shipping, tho' it is not much frequented by Strangers, and not at all by *Europeans*. I believe the Reason is, that many *Rajahs*, of different Interests, have their Countries on the Sides of the River, and they load the Trade with so many Taxes and Impositions, that the industrious Merchant cannot get any Profit by his Labour; and the Reins of the *Mogul*'s Government being so slack in those Parts, the *Nabob* of *Orixa* is not capable to keep the contentious *Rajahs* in better Order.

Cattack is still a large City, walled round, and a good many Cannon planted on its Walls, but neither the Wall nor Artillery are kept in good Order. The Town is not one Quarter Part inhabited; but the Ruins of many large Buildings shew sufficiently its ancient Grandeur, when Kings kept their Courts there Its Figure is an Oblong for a League long, and a Mile broad. It is garisoned with 5000 Foot, and 500 Horse.

THE *English* Company had once a fine Factory in *Cattack*. Most of its Walls were standing *in Anno* 1708. and a Garden that belonged to the Factory, was then in good Repair, kept by a Person of Quality in the Town. The Country about abounds in Corn and Cattle; and tame and wild Fowl are very plenti-

plentiful and good. Their Manufactory is in Cotton Cloths, coarse and fine of all Sorts, and very cheap, and so are Butter and Oyl. I bought a few *Seerbands* and *Sannoes* there, to know the Difference of the Prices between *Cattack* and *Ballasore* Markets, and I found *Cattack* sold them about 60 *per Cent*. cheaper than *Ballasore*; but, on the Road, which is about 35 Leagues long, we paid seven or eight Times Toll for our Heads and Goods, which made them come out about 28 *per Cent* better than *Ballasore* Market.

THAT Part of the River, on the North Side of *Cattack*, is very shallow. When I past it, there were not above three Foot Water in it. They have a Custom in this Town, that, when any Stranger travels thro' it, he must find Surety, that he'll carry none of the Inhabitants off with him, without the *Nabob*'s Permission, and if the Stranger can find no Security, the *Nabob*'s Secretary becomes bound for paying him ten Rupees for the Danger he runs. Two *Dutch Renagodoes*, who were in the *Nabob*'s Service as Gunners, came to wait on me, with a Present of Mutton, Fowl and Fish, and profered to be my Sureties. I rewarded them with the usual Perquisite due to the Secretary, and gave them a Bottle of *French* Brandy, which they set a great Value on.

WHEN I left *Cattack*, I travelled about 50 Miles in two Days, and came to *Badruck*, which stands on the Side of a River, that runs into the Sea at *Cunnaca*, about 20 Miles below

Badruck. There are about 1000 Houſes in it, and a ſmall Mud-wall Fort, but never a Gun in it. The Inhabitants are moſtly employed in Husbandry, Spinning, Weaving and Churning, and Butter here is pretty cheap, being accounted dear at a Peny *per* Pound Weight. In two Days I travelled from *Badruck* to *Ballaſore*, and ſaw nothing in the Way, but Things common and indifferent, the Product of the Country being Corn and Cloth, Iron, Anniſe and Cummin-ſeeds, Oyl and Bees wax. Iron is ſo plentiful, that they caſt Anchors for Ships in Moulds, but they are not ſo good as thoſe made in *Europe*.

I muſt now return back to *Raypore*, and travel along the Sea-coaſt. Four Leagues from *Raypore* is the Iſland of *Palmeira*, which lies about a Mile from the Shore, and has a Chanel of two Fathoms deep between them. The Country is here very low, but the Iſland lower, and it ſends off a very dangerous Sand Bank ſo far into the Sea, that the Iſland can ſcarcely be ſeen till a Ship is aground. Within 50 Paces of the Bank are ſixteen Fathoms Water, which ſudden Shallowings make it the more dangerous.

THREE Leagues to the Northward of the Point *Palmeira*, is *Cunnaca*, which River is capable to receive a Ship of 200 Tuns. It has a Bar, but not dangerous, becauſe the Sea is ſmooth, and the Bottom ſoft. The *Nabob* of *Cattack* commands the North Side of the River, and a *Rajah* the other, which makes them both court the Merchant that comes

comes to trade there, for he pays Custom only to the Sovereign, whose Side of the River his Ship lies on. The Produce and Manufactories of the Country, I mentioned already.

About 12 Leagues to the Northward of *Cunnaca*, is the River's Mouth of *Ballasore*, where there is a very dangerous Bar, sufficiently well known by the many Wracks and Losses made by it. Between *Cunnaca* and *Ballasore* Rivers there is one continued sandy Bay, where prodigious Numbers of Sea Tortoises resort to lay their Eggs; and a very delicious Fish called the *Pamplee*, comes in Sholes, and are sold for two Pence *per* Hundred. Two of them are sufficient to dine a moderate Man.

The Town is but four Miles from the Sea by Land, but, by the River, twenty. The Country is fruitful to Admiration, producing Rice, Wheat, *Gram*, *Doll Callavances*, several Sorts of Pulse, Annise, Cummin, Coriander and Caraway Seeds, Tobacco, Butter, Oyl and Bees-wax. Their Manufactories are of Cotton in *Sannis*, *Cassas*, *Demeties*, *Mulmuls*, Silk, and Silk and Cotton *Romals*, *Gurrahs* and *Lungies*; and of *Herba* (a Sort of tough Grass) they make *Ginghams*, *Pinascos*, and several other Goods for Exportation.

The *English*, *French* and *Dutch* have their respective Factories here, but, at present, are of little Consideration, tho' in former Times, before the Navigation of *Hugh-*

ly River was cultivated, they were the head Factories in the Bay or Gulf of *Bengal.*

THE Town of *Ballasore* drives a pretty good Trade to the Islands of *Maldiva.* Those Islands, as I observed before, have no Rice or other Grain of their own Product, so that *Ballasore* supplies them with what Necessaries they want, and, in Return, bring *Cowries* and *Cayar* for the Service of Shipping. The Sea-shore of *Ballasore* being very low, and the Depths of Water very gradual from the Strand, make Ships, in *Ballasore* Road, keep at a good Distance from the Shore, for, in four or five Fathoms, they ride three Leagues off.

FROM *April* to *October* is the Season for Shipping to come into the Bay of *Bengal.* Pilots ly ready at *Ballasore* to carry them up the River *Hughly*, which is a small Branch of the famous *Ganges*. The *European* Companies, before mentioned, keep theirs always in Pay; but, when none of their own Shipping is there, their Pilots have the Liberty to serve other Ships, which is no small Advantage to them.

THE People about *Ballasore* have one particular Custom that I never heard of in any other Country, *viz.* they take a Piece of soft Clay, and make it in the Form of a large Suppository, and they harden it in the Sun, till it comes to the Consistence of soft Wax, and, when they think it fit for Use, they put it into the right Intestine, immediately after Exoneration. This, they alledge, keeps them

them cool, tho', after it has been in Use a Day and a Night, it becomes hard, but every Morning they have a new one ready for Use.

THERE is a Report current among the *English* in *India*, that the old *East-india* Company desired one Captain *Goodlad*, who was going in their Service Commander of a Ship to *Bengal*, that he would bring them Home some *Indian* Rarity that had never been seen in *England* before. And being lodged in the Factory at *Ballasore*, looking out of his Window one Morning, he saw some People making Use of their Suppositories, and leaving the old hard bak'd ones behind them. He immediately bethought himself of the Commission he had from his Masters, and judged that they might be Rarities never seen in *Europe* before, and ordered a small Keg to be filled with them. When he brought them to *England*, they proved to be such as they had never seen. Some Gentlemen, more curious than the rest, scrapt some of them to try the Taste, but they still continued in the Dark, till the comical Captain gave them an Account of their Use and Virtue.

THE Sides of the River are overgrown with Bushes, which give Shelter to many fierce and troublesom Tigers, who do much Mischief. I knew an *English* Man that was in a Ship's Boat laden with fresh Water, lying in the River, waiting the Tide to carry her over the Bar, and this Man had the Curiosity to step ashore, and being a little Way from

from the Boat, had a Call to exonerate, and had no ſooner put himſelf in a Poſture near the Buſhes, but out leaps a Tiger, and caught both his Buttocks in his Mouth, and was for carrying him away, but one of the Seamen in the Boat ſeeing the Tragedy, took up a Musket, and placed a Bullet in the Tiger's Head, while the Man was in his Mouth helpleſs. The Tiger immediately let him fall, and ſculkt in among the Buſhes, and the wounded Man was carried on board of his Ship, and the Surgeon made a perfect Cure of the Wounds. I ſaw the Marks of the Wounds three or four Years after the Accident happened to him.

AND now having led you as far Eaſtward as *Alexander* the *Great* led his Army, even to the famous River *Ganges*, which put a Stop to his Travels, I'll venture farther, and viſit both the Banks of that River, upwards and downwards, and then march as far Eaſt as our *European* Navigation has as yet diſcovered. The ſecond Volume will diſcover whether I keep my Promiſe or not, and ſo I proceed.

The End of the firſt Volume.